The World Economy

© 2006 by Blackwell Publishing Ltd
First published as Volume 28, Issue 9 of *The World Economy*

BLACKWELL PUBLISHING
350 Main Street, Malden, MA 02148-5020, USA
9600 Garsington Road, Oxford 2DQ, UK
550 Swanston Street, Carlton, Victoria 3053, Australia

First published 2006 by Blackwell Publishing Ltd

Library of Congress Cataloging-in-Publication Data has been applied for

ISBN 1-4051-4515-3
ISBN -13: 9-781-4051-4515-3

A catalogue record for this title is available from the British Library.

Set in 11/13pt Times
by Graphicraft Limited, Hong Kong

The publisher's policy is to use permanent paper from mills that operate
a sustainable forestry policy, and which has been manufactured from pulp
processed using acid-free and elementary chlorine-free practices. Furthermore,
the publisher ensures that the text paper and cover board used have met
acceptable environmental accreditation standards.

For further information on
Blackwell Publishing, visit our website:
www.blackwellpublishing.com

The World Economy

Global Trade Policy 2005

Edited by

David Greenaway
Leverhulme Centre for Research on
Globalisation and Economic Policy
University of Nottingham

Blackwell
Publishing

Contents

INSTITUTIONAL FOCUS

Foreword

Each year *The World Economy* publishes an issue dedicated to developments in global trade policy. That issue always includes a number of ingredients: evaluations of a range of WTO Trade Policy Reviews; a regional feature; and a 'special feature' devoted to a current issue. Because of the interest in this particular issue of the journal, it is always published also as a stand alone book.

Global Trade Policy 2005 includes Trade Policy Reviews of The Gambia, Singapore, Turkey and the United States. The 'special feature' is on Agriculture and the Doha Round; and the 'institutional focus' is on the International Monetary Fund. I am grateful to contributors for the timely delivery of manuscripts and to Blackwell for the expeditious publication of this volume.

David Greenaway,
Director, Leverhulme Centre for
Research on Globalisation
and Economic Policy,
University of Nottingham.

Contributors

Kym Anderson	–	The World Bank
Graham Bird	–	University of Surrey
Antoine Bouët	–	Université de Pau et des Pays de l'Adour
Jean-Christophe Bureau	–	Trinity College, Dublin
Yvan Decreux	–	CEPII, Paris
Sébastien Jean	–	CEPII, Paris
Andrew McKay	–	University of Bath
Will Martin	–	The World Bank
Arvind Panagariya	–	New York University
Thomas Prusa	–	Rutgers University
Shandre Thangavelu	–	National University of Singapore
Subidey Togan	–	Bilkent University
Mun-Heng Toh	–	National University of Singapore

Trade Policy Issues in a Small African Economy: The Trade Policy Review of The Gambia 2004

Andrew McKay

1. INTRODUCTION

SMALL developing economies face distinctive issues in relation to trade policy, both in theory and in practice. They will almost invariably be unable to influence the terms on which they can supply and demand commodities in world trade, given that in virtually all cases they are small players in a large market. In addition, countries with small populations and low per capita incomes have very limited opportunities for economic diversification, with the risks that implies. Consequently such countries need to import a wide range of commodities, but their exports will typically be dominated by a limited number of commodities, often primary commodities (Kennes, 2000). Of necessity small countries will tend to be more open to trade in terms of their ratios of exports and imports to GDP; but their reliance on a limited number of export commodities makes countries very exposed to the impacts of price and quantity shocks, with consequent implications for foreign exchange and government revenue. In addition, small low income countries face unique disadvantages in terms of the provision of key public goods (e.g. infrastructure or transport), and are also likely to face higher costs of governance (Kennes, 2000), affecting in this context participation in international trade discussions, as well as the effectiveness of policy formation in general.

The Gambia, a low income economy of 1.3 million people in West Africa, illustrates many of these issues very well. The country covers an area of around 11,300 square kilometres situated around the river Gambia, and surrounded by Senegal, with access to around 80 km of coastline. In 2002 The Gambia had a per capita GDP of $320 in 2002 and lay 160th out of 173 countries in terms of its

Human Development Index. The economy is relatively open, with tourism and groundnuts as its leading exports, and has in recent years pursued what appears to be a relatively liberal trade policy.

It is clear that international trade is a very important influence on the perform-ance of The Gambian economy. The publication of the WTO's *Trade Policy Review: The Gambia 2004* (henceforth referred to as the *Review*) provides a comprehensive assessment of recent trade policies and practices in relation to the country's overall performance, and provides a good basis for assessing how trade and trade policy can best contribute to development and poverty reduction in this small open economy.

2. ECONOMIC BACKGROUND AND TRADE PATTERNS

Growth performance in The Gambia has been generally weak over the past 25 years. This improved in some recent years (1997–2001), although the growth rate slowed again after this (due primarily to a decline in tourist numbers). The improvement in growth performance in these years coincided with the consolida-tion and strengthening of economic reforms, and increased aid inflows which accompanied this. Trade liberalisation measures were an important component of this reform programme, as was the development of plans for privatisation of state-owned enterprises (the latter only very partially implemented).

The Gambian economy is very open in trade terms, with exports of good and non-factor services representing between 45 and 50 per cent of GDP over the period 1997–2000, and imports between 55 and 60 per cent of GDP over the same period. The composition of trade in The Gambia has a distinctive composi-tion, in that for a long time a very high proportion of merchandise trade has been accounted for by re-exports, including of manufactured commodities, to other countries in the region (partly enabled by the porous nature of borders) and to East Africa, as well as diamonds to Europe. However, it appears that The Gambia's advantage as a channel for re-exports is now being eroded due to a loss of competitiveness of Banjul port, reflecting increased efficiency in neighbouring countries as well as the appreciation of the euro.

The porous nature of borders in the region and the importance of re-exports raises an important issue not discussed in the *Review*: the accuracy of the trade data. The Gambia does seem to suffer from poor quality trade data, and it is important to consider the implications of this for the issues under discussion.[1]

---

[1] In addition there are questions about the consistency of some of the data used in the *Review*. For example, the total export figures including re-exports in Appendix Table A1.2, are quite similar to those excluding re-exports in Table A1.1, yet we are told that re-exports of some of these commodities are substantial.

Aside from re-exports, The Gambia's predominant exports are of agricultural commodities, especially groundnuts, and tourism, with the European Union as a major market accounting for around half of exports (most of the rest being to other African countries). However, exports of both these major commodities have been erratic over time reflecting both domestic factors (e.g. groundnut marketing arrangements) and external factors (e.g. the post-11 September contraction in international travel). This implies not only significant export volatility but also large fluctuations in growth performance. The Gambia is a net importer of food, with rice, a key staple, being a major imported commodity; other important import commodities include machinery and transport equipment, and fuels. Again the EU accounts for around half of imports. The importance of fuels in The Gambia's imports is another important source of vulnerability to the economy, given its importance for transport and because it is the sole means of electricity generation.

In recent years, The Gambia has received significantly higher volumes of foreign direct investment (FDI) compared to earlier years. This has partly been a response to greater macroeconomic stability, but also due to privatisation. The *Review* reports that in 1999 and 2000 FDI inflows accounted for 60 per cent of gross fixed capital formation. In general FDI has been concentrated chiefly in financial institutions, tourism and manufacturing. Imports appear to have increased and decreased in line with FDI flows, reflecting investment in re-exporting activities as well as the importance of imported inputs associated with tourism investment.

As is common in many developing countries (Greenaway and Milner, 1991; and Winters et al., 2004), trade is also a very important source of revenue for the Government with around 50 per cent of government revenue being derived from trade taxes in 2001. This is therefore a very important factor to consider in assessing trade policy and its reform in The Gambia.

3. TRADE POLICY IN THE GAMBIA: THE INSTITUTIONAL CONTEXT

Overall responsibility for trade policy, as well as investment, industrial and competition policies, lies with the Department of State for Trade, Industry and Employment, which therefore takes the leading role in trade negotiations. In practice, though, many other government departments are also involved in trade policy formulation and practice, with, for example, import tariffs (the key trade policy instrument) being set by the Department of State for Finance and Economic Affairs and collected by the Department of State for Customs and Excise. Many other Departments and institutions are involved in other aspects, for instance in setting and monitoring sanitary and phytosanitary requirements. While there have been various initiatives at coordination between these actors in different areas relating to trade policy, the *Review* identifies lack of coordination as a significant problem (WTO, 2004, p. 13). This has also affected The Gambia's ability to meet the WTO commitments it has made.

In addition, the *Review* finds that trade policy is not well integrated into the country's key development strategies and policy initiatives. For example, while trade and industrial policy issues are discussed in general terms in the Government's long-term *Vision 2020* document (Government of The Gambia, 1996), there are few specific proposals for this. And in its later Poverty Reduction Strategy (Government of The Gambia, 2002), the links between trade policy and the overall strategies aiming to reduce poverty are not made sufficiently,[2] yet trade policy can have a significant positive or negative impact on poverty (Winters et al., 2004). In other words, the potentially central role of trade policy in relation to growth and poverty reduction, especially in a highly open economy like The Gambia, does not seem to be sufficiently stressed in discussions of trade policy.

The *Review* repeatedly highlights capacity constraints and the need for technical assistance in key areas relating to trade policy, for example, in the application of WTO-consistent valuation procedures for imports which The Gambia has committed to but not proceeded to implement. As discussed in Section 1, in this respect smallness constitutes a significant disadvantage – for example, in The Gambia not being able to have a permanent representative at the WTO in Geneva. Consequently, the per capita need for technical assistance will be greater in a small country such as The Gambia. The importance of technical assistance is widely recognised in the *Review* and by the Minister, the discussant and all participants in the Trade Policy Review meeting in February 2004. But there still needs to be a clearer identification of what these technical needs are, a point stressed by the discussant, but apparently not resolved in the meeting. In a small country technical assistance needs to be more clearly directed to the key priority areas.

Internationally, The Gambia has been a member of the WTO from its inception, and its Least Developed Country (LDC) status means that it can benefit from special and differential treatment (SDT). It also participates in a number of preferential trading arrangements with both developed and developing countries. It benefits from non-reciprocal preferential treatment under the Generalised System of Preferences (GSP) from many industrialised countries. With the European Union, its largest trading partner for both exports and imports, it has access to the preferential terms available to ACP countries under the Cotonou (and formerly Lomé) Agreement, as well as the benefits available to all LDCs under the Everything but Arms (EBA) Initiative. It has shown a willingness to participate in discussions about forming a Regional Economic Partnership Agreement (requiring reciprocal preferential access) with the EU, as required by the WTO

---

[2] However, to be fair, this criticism applies to the majority of recent PRSPs.

TABLE 1

Utilisation in 2001 by The Gambia of Trade Preferences Granted by Major Industrialised Countries

Preference Scheme/Year	Exports from The Gambia (US$'000)	Exports MFN Dutifiable (US$'000)	Exports GSP Covered (US$'000) (1)	Exports GSP Received (US$'000) (2)	Utilisation Rate (Per cent) (2)/(1)
EU-ACP, 2001	18,274	8,449	9,981	6,620	66.3
EU, EBA, 2001	18,387	8,526	8,499	35	0.4
Canada, 2001	2,122	10	10	0	0.0
Japan, 2001	597	565	565	241	42.6
USA, 2001	229	115	51	1	1.6

Note:

The year selected is typical; similar figures apply for preferences in earlier years.

Source: Summarised from Table II.4 (WTO, 2004).

if ACP preferences can be continued beyond 2007. In addition The Gambia will be eligible to take advantage of the Africa Growth and Opportunity Act (AGOA) with the US. Within Africa, it is also a member of the Economic Community of West African States (ECOWAS) as well as the African Union.

In practice, though, The Gambia has been able to derive limited benefits from its participation in many of these arrangements (Table 1). It has only made limited use of preferential trading arrangements with key industrialised countries; thus with the EU it has taken reasonable advantage of preferential opportunities provided by the Cotonou Agreement (receiving GSP terms on 66 per cent of exports potentially covered), but very little advantage of other schemes (some of which, like EBA, are potentially wider in coverage). According to the *Review*, this lack of take up of preferences reflects a number of factors, including lack of familiarity with specific schemes by potential exporters, and potentially demanding rules of origin and documentation requirements. Again, capacity constraints may be relevant. In relation to the region there has been very little progress in liberalisation of intra-regional trade within ECOWAS, and so The Gambia neither receives, nor offers, preferential treatment on intra-ECOWAS trade. Thus, while it is sometimes argued that small countries may benefit particularly from participation in regional trading arrangements, this has not effectively operated to date in the case of West Africa.

Even in relation to the WTO, while The Gambia has shown strong commitment to multilateral liberalisation in many areas (for example, making commitments in 12 service subsectors under GATS), it has not been able to implement a number of its basic WTO obligations, as for instance in relation to customs valuation procedures (see below). Moreover, it has played only a very limited role in multilateral trade negotiations, undoubtedly partly due to not having a representative in Geneva.

4. TRADE POLICY IN PRACTICE

On paper The Gambia pursues a relatively liberal trade policy. It has been a member of the WTO since its inception, as well as a participant in regional trading arrangements, in preferential trading arrangements with industrialised countries and various bilateral trade agreements. In addition, as noted above, it pursued a policy of significant trade reform in 1998–2000. During this period The Gambia changed its MFN tariff structure from 30 bands ranging from 0 per cent to 90 per cent to six bands ranging from 0 per cent to 18 per cent. However, the analysis in the *Review* shows that the trade reform measures were much less liberalising than they appear at first sight and trade protection remains widespread, sometimes in counterproductive and unintended directions.

a. Import and Export Taxes

Trade policy measures in The Gambia predominantly take the form of customs duties and export taxes. While the structure of customs duties was simplified considerably in the recent reform, and the highest rates were reduced significantly, at the same time the number of duty-free items was reduced; consequently the simple average tariff only fell from 13.6 per cent prior to the reform to 12.7 per cent afterwards (WTO, 2004, p. 33). Protection is highest in the agricultural sector (see Table 2), with 71 per cent of lines subject to the highest tariff rate of 18 per cent (including cereals and fish and fish products) and only 9.5 per cent being duty free (including rice, a key staple). While a limited number of tariff rates were bound during Uruguay Round discussions, these were generally at such high levels (110% for agriculture) as to have no practical effect. Thus the reform of customs duties was much less liberalising than it appears at first sight. This tariff structure in agriculture reflects a government desire to stimulate domestic production, although, as will be discussed below, there are also many

TABLE 2
Selected Summary Information on The Gambia's MFN Tariff Rates, 2003

	2003	UR Bound Rate
Simple average tariff rate	12.7	102.0
Agricultural products (HS01-24)	16.0	110.0
Non-agricultural products (HS25-97)	12.2	52.4
Agricultural products (WTO definition)	15.3	103.6
Non-agricultural products (WTO definition)	12.3	58.3
Duty-free tariff lines (per cent of all tariff lines)	15.5	0.0
Bound tariff lines (per cent of all tariff lines)	13.7	–

Source: Taken from WTO (2004, Table III.1).

internal factors accounting for poor agricultural sector performance. The tariffs of course are also an important revenue source.

All tariffs are applied on an *ad valorem* basis, apart from specific duties applied to petroleum. Duties on petroleum potentially have an important impact on the economy given that, as seen below, weaknesses in the transport sector and the unreliability of the electricity supply are regarded as important constraints to the development of a manufacturing sector.

At the same time a range of exemptions for taxes and duties is given, with apparently considerable discretion in doing so. Exemptions are to be justified for purposes of encouraging export promotion, import substitution, or the use of local raw material inputs; but this is quite wide ranging and in practice the *Review* makes it clear that there is a lack of clarity on how exemptions are made. In addition, it is difficult even to track the value of exemptions approved, so that the *Review* could not consider applied tariff rates. This lack of transparency and predictability is likely to have an adverse impact on investment incentives.

Moreover, the structure of duties is such as to give negative tariff escalation in several sectors; in other words, lower tariff rates on semi-processed or processed commodities in a sector compared to raw materials. This indicates a clear bias against investment in producing processed and semi-processed products in many sectors, including several manufacturing sectors, and so constitutes an anti-export bias. This clearly conflicts with government objectives in its investment strategy, which is to promote the use of local primary products and to promote processed exports. It therefore discourages rather than encourages the promotion and diversification of exports, including the development of a domestic manufacturing sector.

Another important issue relating to import duties is the basis used for valuation of imports. The Gambia currently does not use the procedures required by the WTO Customs Valuation Agreement (CVA) for this, but rather an older Brussels hybrid method which uses the maximum of declared values and reference prices. This is a source of inefficiency and delay in implementing customs procedures, as well as potentially being less transparent or more subject to challenge. The *Review*, as well as the report's discussant and other commentators, considers it a key priority that The Gambia implements a CVA-compatible valuation method as soon as possible, and stress this as being one of the key areas for which technical assistance is required.

As well as the explicit tariffs on imports, some imported commodities, especially food and beverages, are subject to a discriminatory sales tax which does not apply to domestically produced commodities. A similar principle applies for some excise duties. Consequently these constitute additional levels of protection, generally for the domestic agricultural sector.

Turning to exports, taxes are levied, generally at ten per cent, on all commodities except for exports of groundnuts, fish and fish products, which are exempt, as

also are exports to the EU. No export subsidies are applied, but as will be seen
shortly, some exemptions are provided from export taxes through investment
promotion initiatives, notably, but not only, through a free zone presently being
developed providing tax exemptions for firms with a high export potential.

b. Other Trade Policy Measures

The Gambia currently has very few trade policy measures in place other than
taxes on imports and exports. It does not apply quantitative restrictions in trade,
apart from some prohibitions on sanitary, phytosanitary, security or moral grounds.
In any case, the sanitary and phytosanitary requirements are difficult to enforce,
given that different areas fall under the responsibility of different institutions.
Aside from this there are no domestic standards applied in trade in relation to,
say, consumer protection.

The Gambia does not have any contingent trade legislation, such as anti-
dumping measures. It does, though, have legislation in relation to government
procurement, having passed an Act to this end in 2001 establishing a Government Procurement Agency. Government procurement above a given minimum
value is open to international tendering, and the Act does not allow for any
preference for local suppliers.

c. Other Relevant Measures

Industrial policy measures (or the absence of such) can have significant implications for trade. One important area already mentioned above is measures to
promote investment. Under an Investment Promotion Act in 2001, investors in
'priority' sectors and activities, that satisfy various one or more conditions in
relation to local economic impact (e.g. use of raw materials, creation of employment or generation of foreign exchange savings through exporting or import
substitution), can apply for special investment status, which among other things
provides exemption from some domestic taxes and customs duties on production
inputs. However, this does not appear to be a particularly targeted measure, in
that the number of sectors and activities covered is broad, and there are no
specific objective criteria to assess the extent to which a given investment can
help achieve the objectives. Similarly, at the same time the Government adopted
the Free Zones Act, whereby export-oriented firms can operate in a free zone
close to Banjul Airport and benefit from favourable incentives, notably customs
duty exemptions. By the end of 2003 three investors who had been granted
licences were in the process of commencing activities.

Privatisation of state-owned enterprises has been a repeated commitment in
reform programmes dating back to 1986, but has been only partially realised. Where
it has happened it has often been a source of increased foreign investment, as for

example in tourism, and this in turn can bring important trade benefits in terms of increased tourism exports. Further privatisations are planned in a number of sectors. However, one issue has been the lack of a regulatory authority for newly privatised enterprises; this lack of regulatory powers has meant that some privatisations in the past simply resulted in state monopolies being substituted by private monopolies without any welfare gain (e.g. in the groundnuts sector in the first phase of privatisation before the 1994 coup). The ability to develop effective regulation for newly privatised industries and an effective authority to monitor compliance is likely to be an important factor affecting the realisation and economic impact of the many planned future privatisations.

Similarly, The Gambia had no legislation on competition policy until 2003, which is potentially important given the small size of the domestic market, though the likely implications of this for foreign trade and investment are not explored in the *Report*. In addition, The Gambia has very little legislation in relation to intellectual property, and most of what it does have is very outdated.

d. Some Future Trade Policy Issues

Looking ahead, The Gambia's participation in regional integration arrangements in Africa and in preferential trading arrangements with industrialised countries is likely to have clear implications for future trade policy. Within Africa, if or when internal liberalisation occurs within ECOWAS, The Gambia will need to give preferential or duty-free access to imports from other member countries. This can potentially have a major impact given the importance of re-exports, many within the region, in its trade. Further, if ECOWAS at some point achieves its objective of forming a customs union, this would imply the need for a common external tariff, which may be set at a higher level than the current maximum rate of 18 per cent. With industrialised countries, the requirement for reciprocity in the formation of an Economic Partnership Agreement with the EU to enable Cotonou preferences to continue beyond 2007 will mean liberalising trade policy with respect to EU imports on a duty-free basis – admittedly probably over a long time horizon given The Gambia's LDC status. But this could potentially have substantial economic impacts, not least in its revenue impact. And AGOA will require extended duty-free access to selected apparel products, among other conditions.

The implications of these future changes in the trade policy environment are discussed in the *Review*, but would merit further emphasis than they are given.

5. THE IMPACT OF TRADE POLICY ON SECTORAL PERFORMANCE

The *Review* provides a useful discussion of the impact of trade policy and other factors on the performance of different productive sectors in The Gambia.

As expected, many other factors besides trade policy explain the economic performance of different sectors and subsectors; and equally these other factors affect trade volumes through their impact on domestic production levels and patterns.

a. Agriculture, Forestry and Fishing

The agricultural sector employs around 70 per cent of the labour force in The Gambia and generates around 30 per cent of GDP; it also generates around 30 per cent of foreign exchange, chiefly through groundnuts. Recent domestic agricultural policy reforms have liberalised the commercialisation of the main food crops, and current policy initiatives now focus on new techniques and varieties, extension and credit. The sector, though, continues to be dominated by rain-fed cultivation on small-scale plots, with little mechanisation – implying low productivity. In addition to this, a major constraint that remains to be addressed is land policy. Only around 40 per cent of potential arable land is in fact cultivated, for a variety of reasons identified in the *Review*, including the complexity of land tenure arrangements. This is obviously a major constraint on production and potential agricultural exports.

Groundnuts, the traditional export crop, account for over 40 per cent of cultivated area in The Gambia. Production fluctuated erratically in the 1990s due to the effects of the privatisation and then renationalisation of The Gambia Groundnut Corporation, but has remained at a steady level since. Producers benefit from an 18 per cent import tariff, as well as a guaranteed minimum price, but this has the impact that marginal producers remain in the sector instead of switching to another activity; it also does not create incentives to cultivate higher quality varieties. Productivity levels are quite high for the region, but quite low globally. The Gambia enjoys preferential treatment in terms of tariffs in major export markets, but faces problems due to the fact that many Gambian groundnuts have a high aflatoxin content. This is the major reason why the quality issue raised above is very important. Groundnuts are generally exported in unprocessed form. The tariff structure, combined with the limited industrial capability in the country, also does not create incentives to invest in processing activities which would generate higher value added. Thus, only one private company produces groundnut oil.

Fish and fish products, also protected by high tariffs, constitute the other main export earner in this sector. However, concerns about sustainability (especially of key export species) limit further expansion. Furthermore, infrastructural weaknesses such as limited storage and transport facilities have meant The Gambia losing out to foreign operators. River fishing may offer new opportunities, but the potential for this activity remains to be investigated. The main potential for developing non-traditional exports is in the area of horticulture.

Overall, The Gambia is a net food importer, with massive imports of rice being a major contributor to this. Rice is a key staple food commodity, but The Gambia can only satisfy around 12 per cent of its requirements from domestic production – and that despite some favourable recent developments (WTO, 2004, p. 64). The limited area for irrigated agriculture remains a major constraint. Besides seeking to expand this, current policy initiatives focus on improved seed varieties and on extension services.

b. Industrial Sector

The Gambia has relatively few mineral deposits, although there is the prospect of offshore hydrocarbon deposits; the Government grants licences for petroleum exploration and production, which would provide royalty income if exploitation occurs. At present all petroleum and gas is currently imported, and this is a major source of government revenue, with import duties on oil providing 50 per cent of total import duties collected since 1997. The majority state-owned National Water and Electricity Company, which produces electricity using petroleum, receives an 80 per cent discount on its petroleum imports. Nevertheless, it is a highly inefficient producer, and the power supply is erratic and unreliable, which itself is an important supply-side constraint on other industrial activities.

The Gambia's manufacturing sector is very small, accounting for only around five per cent of GDP and employing less than 20,000 people. It is concentrated in a few activities, including groundnut decortication, brewing and soft drinks, and soap. It has benefited from some foreign direct investment, including as a result of divesture; the sector accounted for 22 per cent of The Gambia's FDI in 2000. But it is very uncompetitive, as evidenced by a comparison with the extent to which The Gambia is able re-export manufacturing commodities to its neighbours. It also has few linkages with the tourism sector, which potentially could be an important market. This lack of competitiveness is partly a consequence of serious supply-side problems, including the cost of credit, the erratic electricity supply and transport costs. But trade policy also plays a very import-ant role here, including the serious anti-export biases associated with negative tariff escalation in some industries. The high tariffs in themselves also constitute anti-export biases in some industries such as soap that received tariff protection initially on infant industry grounds but where the domestic price exceeds the world price.

The Government has identified sectors that have the potential to be competitive exporters, such as in food processing and textiles and clothing. While the recently established free zones can help to create manufacturing exports, the *Review* is almost certainly correct in its unstinting advocacy for across-the-board tariff reform in this sector to remove anti-export biases, accompanied by measures to address the supply-side constraints. This is likely to be a major challenge.

c. Services

The services sector accounts for around 65 per cent of GDP, with the most important subsector being in distribution services, which is strongly connected to re-exporting and the informal sector. In trade policy terms, The Gambia has made commitments in 12 service subsectors as part of GATS, covering most of the main subsectors, including major sectors such as transport, telecommunications and tourism.

Tourism is particularly important as an export earner, with this sector earning around 60 per cent of gross foreign exchange receipts, excluding re-exports, in 2000. The sector accounted for 12 per cent of GDP in 2001 and is considered to be the second largest employer in the country. However, it is also a volatile export earner, with numbers of arrivals strongly linked to global economic conditions and conditions in the main source countries. Thus weak economic conditions in Germany contributed to a significant slump from 2000 onwards, and the 11 September attacks obviously had a long-lasting impact on international travel. Tourism is also a highly competitive sector which may be subject to fashions, especially in relation to the package holiday market.

These fluctuations can best be insured against by diversifying the tourist base, and investing in quality. The Gambia Tourist Authority has thus been investing in human resource development, in helping to set and monitor standards and in compiling information. The Gambia has also developed new markets in other countries, and has been seeking to exploit its potential for a wider range of holidays, including ecotourism, while maintaining environmental sustainability. The overall aim is to invest in raising quality and to try to reduce fluctuations in the demand. The Investment Promotion Act provides incentives for activities consistent with these ends.

However, the links between tourism and the rest of the economy remain weak, though as discussed above this partly reflects the weaknesses of the industrial sector itself.

6. CONCLUSIONS

As with Trade Policy Reviews, The Gambia *Trade Policy Review* provides a very useful compilation of information on trade and trade policy issues and of the country's recent economic performance, which seemed to form the basis for a useful and constructive discussion at the Trade Policy Review meeting. But there remain some major challenges in taking this agenda forward.

As is evident from this discussion, The Gambia does indeed demonstrate many of the characteristics in relation to trade and trade policy as discussed in the introduction in relation to a small open economy. Its economy is indeed very open to trade, with specialised exports (in this case in groundnuts and tourism) but with a wide range of import requirements, including in this case of key food commodities as well as petroleum. Further, there is quite strong evidence of the difficulty in providing key public goods, here in particular energy and infrastructure, and for high costs of governance, as evidenced by the capacity constraints repeatedly discussed in the *Review*.

These high costs of governance impose restrictions on the type and range of trade policy measures that can be implemented, as does the requirement to raise government revenue. Consequently, it is unsurprising that trade policy relies very strongly on import and export taxes that are both relatively easy to implement and raise significant revenue. It is also not surprising that The Gambia makes much less use of potentially more complex trade policy measures. In addition, it does not take advantage of many preferential trading arrangements in which it participates, with again the complexity of many such arrangements being an important factor.

The *Review* argues strongly that current trade policy in The Gambia shows a strong anti-export bias, both by protecting inefficient production practices in many sectors, including groundnuts, and because the pattern of tariff escalation is frequently such as to create disincentives for investment in processing activities that could generate significantly higher value added.

Further, the emphasis in much trade policy discussion seems to have been in terms of protecting key sectors (here especially agriculture) and in terms of its revenue-raising potential. Such a strategy is not necessarily conducive to growth. In any case this connection of trade policy to wider issues in The Gambia such as growth or poverty reduction is not strongly reflected in key government documents, where it is often discussed as a separate issue. Trade policy is of course only one factor, but it can be very important, especially in a small open economy such as The Gambia. The small movements towards trade reform and to encourage foreign direct investment did contribute to a period of faster growth in the 1990s. But the reforms were minor; and the current trade policy stance is still not conducive to sustained growth and poverty reduction.

REFERENCES

Government of The Gambia (1996), *The Gambia Incorporated: Vision 2020* (Banjul, The Gambia).
Government of The Gambia (2002), *Strategy for Poverty Alleviation (SPAII)/Poverty Reduction Strategy Paper* (Banjul, The Gambia).
Greenaway, D. and C. Milner (1991), 'Fiscal Dependence on Trade Taxes and Trade Policy Reform', *Journal of Development Studies*, **27** (April), 95–132.
Kennes, W. (2000), *Small Developing Countries and Global Markets: Competing in the Big League* (Palgrave-Macmillan).
Winters, L. A., N. McCulloch and A. McKay (2004), 'Trade Liberalization and Poverty: The Evidence So Far', *Journal of Economic Literature*, **XLII** (March), 72–115.
World Trade Organisation (WTO) (2004), *Trade Policy Review: The Gambia, 2004* (Geneva).

2

Bilateral 'WTO-Plus' Free Trade Agreements: The WTO Trade Policy Review of Singapore 2004

S. M. Thangavelu and Mun-Heng Toh

1. INTRODUCTION

THE World Trade Organisation's 2004 Trade Policy Review of Singapore (WTO-TPR Singapore 2004) depicts the small and outward-oriented economy as one of the most open countries to international trade and investment. The review highlights the benefits of the outward-oriented strategy that has enabled the Singapore economy to weather recent external shocks such as the Asian financial crisis to the SARS and to the recent unfavourable conditions in the Middle East. In particular, the report commended Singapore's efforts on its liberalisation of the services sector and its economic benefits to consumers and global trade. However, the WTO-TPR Singapore 2004 highlights several key areas of concerns: (a) the commitment to multilateral agreements with the rising number of bilateral free trade agreements signed by Singapore and (b) the lack of growth of total factor productivity, a key indicator for long-run efficiency of the economy. The paper addresses the above key concerns raised in the WTO's TPR of Singapore in terms of its commitment to global trade in terms of WTO-plus bilateral FTAs, which intends to support a multilateral trading system, and its overall industrial strategies to raise its competitiveness.

Section 2 discusses the overall development trends of the Singapore economy. Section 3 reviews the bilateral free trade agreements in terms of its implications for multilateral trading systems. The long-run growth strategies and the importance of productive performance of the economy are reviewed in Section 4. Section 5 provides the conclusion.

2. ECONOMIC PERFORMANCE OF SINGAPORE IN 1999–2003:
EMERGING SERVICES SECTOR

Since the Asian crisis in 1997, the growth of the Singapore economy has been lacklustre and volatile due to such events as the Asian financial crisis, the slowdown in the US and global economies, SARS, and the ongoing war on terrorism. Over 1999–2003, Singapore's real output growth was at an average rate of 3.6 per cent p.a. as compared to nearly an average of 9 per cent in 1991–1997 (see Table 1). The volatility in output is also reflected in rising unemployment, as the unemployment rate had risen from 3.5 per cent in 1999 to nearly 4.7 per cent in 2003. However, the economy has shown some strong output growth in 2004, growing at a rate of 8.4 per cent with the unemployment rate falling to 4 per cent (MIT, 2005). It has been forecasted that the economy will grow at the average potential output level of 3–5 per cent for the coming years with an average unemployment rate of 3.5 per cent.

In addition to the volatility in output, the structural adjustment of the economy to higher value-added activities also contributed to the slower growth in employment. Throughout this period, the services sector has led much of the growth, both in terms of GDP and employment growth. The share of the service industries account for a total of nearly 64 per cent of Singapore's gross value-added and

TABLE 1
Key Macroeconomic Indicators: 1999–2003

	1999	2000	2001	2002	2003
Real GDP (1995 market price and per cent change)	6.9	9.7	−1.9	2.2	1.1
Manufacturing	13.0	15.1	−11.6	7.8	2.8
Services	6.3	8.0	2.4	1.4	1.0
Construction	−9.0	−0.7	−2.6	−10.8	−10.7
Share of Gross Value Added (per cent)					
Manufacturing	23.1	26.8	23.7	25.8	26.3
Services	63.6	61.9	64.5	63.5	63.4
Construction	7.9	6.3	6.1	5.4	5.0
Others	5.1	5.0	5.7	5.3	5.3
Employment Share (per cent)					
Manufacturing	21.0	20.8	18.8	18.2	17.9
Services	71.1	65.5	74.2	75.0	75.6
Construction	6.9	13.1	6.1	5.9	5.6
Others	1.0	0.6	0.9	0.9	0.9
Unemployment rate (per cent change)	3.5	3.1	3.3	4.4	4.7

Note:
Services sector includes: Wholesale and Retail Trade, Hotels and Restaurants, Transport and Communication, Financial Services, Business Services, Other Services.

Source: WTO TPW Singapore 2004.

72 per cent of employment growth respectively, over the period of 1999–2002. With the emergence of low-cost competitors in the region and in China, there is a strong pressure for the Singapore economy to move to higher value-added activities to sustain its competitiveness. However, the Government believes that both manufacturing and services will form the 'twin engines' of growth, where manufacturing is expected to contribute around 20 per cent of GDP (Economic Review Committee, 2002).

Despite the volatile global economy, Singapore's exports rose at an average rate of 4.8 per cent in 1999–2002 and strengthened further by 12 per cent in 2003. Manufactured exports in electronics goods still forms a significant component of its exports, where exports in office machines & telecommunication equipments and chemical products form nearly 42 and 17 per cent of total domestic exports respectively (WTO-TPE Singapore 2004). In 1999, exports to China only accounted for 3.4 per cent of total domestic exports, but it rose to nearly 10 per cent in 2003. ASEAN is the key trading partner for Singapore as it absorbs nearly 25 per cent of total domestic exports from Singapore. The major sources of imports for Singapore are from Malaysia (16.8 per cent), the United States (13.9 per cent), the European Union (12.5 per cent) and Japan (12 per cent). Trade in services grew at the rate of 7.7 per cent on an average in 1999–2003 and the exports in financial and transportation services have been the most vibrant.

The emergence of the services sector is also observable in other Asian countries. The share of the services sector is rising for all the selected countries in Table 2. Hong Kong and Japan tend to have the highest share of services sector of over 70 per cent of GDP and Taiwan's share is rising to nearly 67 per cent in 2004. The importance of services sector for GDP and its growth is also reflected in the two key countries in ASEAN, Malaysia and Thailand have nearly 60 and 46 per cent share of services sector to GDP respectively, for the period of 1999–2004.

3. MULTILATERAL, REGIONALISM AND FREE TRADE AGREEMENTS

a. Bilateral 'WTO-Plus' Free Trade Agreements: The Way Forward

Singapore is a staunch advocate of free trade. Singapore's export-oriented strategy has carried the economy from Third-World status after independence to arguably First-World status in just over thirty years. The total annual value of trade has been about three times the country's GDP for the last 15 years. Besides being an avid supporter of a multilateral trading system, and abiding by the practice of granting most-favoured-nation (MFN) treatment to all members of the WTO, Singapore is also actively involved in regionalisation. This is reflected

TABLE 2
The Share of Services Sector to GDP in Selected Asian Countries: 1999–2004 (Per cent)

Country	Share of Gross Value Added	1999	2000	2001	2002	2003	2004
Hong Kong	Manufacturing	14.6	14.4	13.7	13.0	12.1	11.3
	Services	85.2	85.4	86.2	86.8	87.9	88.6
	Other	0.2	0.2	0.1	0.2	0.0	0.1
Japan	Manufacturing	28.3	28.6	27.2	26.0	25.8	25.3
	Services	70.1	69.9	71.3	72.6	72.9	73.4
	Other	1.6	1.5	1.5	1.4	1.3	1.3
Korea	Manufacturing	40.2	40.6	39.1	38.4	39.2	40.8
	Services	54.5	54.3	56.1	57.6	57.1	55.9
	Other	5.3	5.1	4.8	4.0	3.6	3.3
Malaysia	Manufacturing	33.4	34.9	32.9	32.9	33.5	33.4
	Services	58.5	57.1	59.4	59.5	58.9	59.2
	Other	8.1	8.0	7.7	7.6	7.6	7.4
Taiwan	Manufacturing	33.1	32.3	30.7	30.9	30.1	31.0
	Services	64.2	65.5	67.3	67.2	68.0	67.3
	Other	2.7	2.2	2.0	1.9	1.9	1.7
Thailand	Manufacturing	40.9	41.9	42.1	42.3	43.4	44.2
	Services	49.6	48.9	48.7	48.1	46.3	46.4
	Other	9.5	9.2	9.2	9.6	10.3	9.4

Source: Economists Intelligence Unit, *The Economist*.

by its membership in the Association of Southeast Asian Nations (ASEAN), the Asia-Pacific Economic Cooperation (APEC), and the Asia Europe Meetings (ASEM), which have further highlighted the fact that Singapore is an active proponent of international trade to enhance welfare. ASEAN has always been the important nexus for multilateral negotiations for APEC and WTO. However, one major and most notable change in Singapore's trade policy since the late 1990s is the decision to pursue bilateral free-trade agreements with its trading partners. As of July 2005, Singapore has signed FTAs with New Zealand, Japan, the European Free Trade Area (EFTA) States, Australia, the United States, Jordan, Trans-Pacific SEP and India; and currently is negotiating with Canada, Bahrain, Kuwait, United Arab Emirates, Egypt, Mexico, Peru, Sri Lanka and Korea. Under ASEAN, negotiations are also under way with China, India, Korea and Japan. The bilateral arrangements were preceded with equal and multi-track emphasis on regionalism and multilateral trading activities.

The recent rise in the number of bilateral agreements was due to two important events. The post-Asian crisis revealed significant divergence in the economic and financial restructuring among ASEAN countries, with Singapore taking a more proactive role in opening up with its economic liberalisation policy especially in the services sector and, on the other hand, ASEAN countries like Malaysia were adopting a semi-protected economic policy. This differential policy adoption by the ASEAN countries reflects large gaps in institutional quality, stages of growth and economic policies, and thus there was policy divergence and lack of response in the recent WTO meetings (Sally, 2004). Further, there is a growing perception that the WTO is a weak forum for an open multilateral trading system since the early 1990s and it was accentuated by the collapse of the Doha agenda at the World Trade Organisation (WTO) Ministerial meetings in Cancún in September 2003. The above problems were further accentuated by the decline in the flow of FDI into the Southeast Asian region. The FDI flow into ASEAN dropped from US$21.5 billion in 1997 to US$13.1 billion in 1999 as compared to rising FDI into North-East Asia and especially China (Low, 2003).

The immediate benefit of Singapore's Free Trade Agreements (FTAs) is that they increased the focus and diverted attention back to the ASEAN and South-East Asian region, with the backdrop of the strong global focus on North-East Asia and China. Second, they energised and raised the urgency for the other ASEAN countries to become more proactive in open trading activities. The response from ASEAN, especially Malaysia and Thailand, was to seek their own FTAs to match the record number of FTAs signed by Singapore. Third, they highlight the importance of the services sector for continual growth of the Singapore economy and the ASEAN countries.

However, given Singapore's strong integration and production network in ASEAN, the multilateral trading system and regionalism is still superior and the key for sustainable growth for the economy (Low, 2003). The importance of the multilateral trading system is emphasised by the representative from Singapore in the WTO-TPR Singapore 2004:

> Many in the WTO, as well as at APEC and ASEAN, believed that FTAs could be complementary, and serve as building blocks, to the multilateral process. Singapore believed that FTAs could be building blocks if they were WTO-plus (going beyond WTO commitments), WTO-consistent (covering substantially all trade) and open to others prepared to make the same commitments. . . . Both could learn in the process, and as they got used to a higher level of liberalization, this could serve in multilateral negotiations.

The FTAs by Singapore are mostly based on services and go beyond the GATS commitments that include financial services, business and professional services, telecommunications, education, and environmental services (WTO-TPR Singapore 2004). Trade in services is the main component of the US-Singapore FTA, where there is substantial market access to the services sectors subject to a 'negative list' that deals with sensitive government institutions and policy (Soesastro, 2003). Singapore's commitment to go beyond the WTO commitments are reflected by the FTAs with Australia and the US, where there is commitment to enact the competition law, to develop intellectual property rights and customs provisions and to make provisions for trade and environmental issues (see Appendix Table A.1).

Worthy of mention is the Integrated Sourcing Initiative (ISI) incorporated in the US-Singapore FTA, which is an ingenious innovation to adopt rules of origin (ROO) taking into account the globalisation of manufacturing in a knowledge-based world economy. The ISI is a 'new age' ROO guideline that applies to non-sensitive, globalised sectors, such as IT or electronics manufacturing. The ISI list includes 266 products that are already entering the US at zero tariffs, of which 236 of the products are covered under the WTO ITA[1] list. Under the ISI, these products are conferred Singapore origin, regardless of where they are made. Hence, as finished products, goods that are covered under the ISI list would enjoy the waiver of 0.21 per cent Merchandise Processing Fee imposed by the US if they are shipped to the US through Singapore. However, if these goods are used as components in the manufacturing of final products in Singapore, it would help to boost the Singapore content of the final products, thus making them more likely to meet the ROO requirement and qualify for the preferential tariff treatment. As such, given that there is no geographical limit in the application of the ISI, it may encourage investors to source these components from Singapore's neighbouring countries, given their close geographical proximity and strong industrial linkages to Singapore's manufacturing sector.

Commitment to promote competition by addressing anti-competitive practices through legislature is one of the key provisions in the US-Singapore and Singapore-Australia FTAs. This law is expected to apply to all activities including the private sector and Government Linked Corporations (GLCs) in all sectors, unless there are exclusions and exemptions for reasons of public policy and interest. Singapore has also engaged in efforts to improve corporate governance through a voluntary Code of Corporate Governance for all listed companies. Specifically, a Council on Corporate Disclosure and Governance was established in 2002 to prescribe and strengthen existing accounting standards, disclosure practices and reporting standards in Singapore.

Due to the FTAs with Australia, the European Union, New Zealand and the United States, there are significant changes in the framework of intellectual property rights. For example, Singapore extends copyright protection to the life of the author plus 70 years; as measures against the circumvention of technologies that protect copyright works; imposes protection of well-known marks; and there is an extension of the patent term for pharmaceuticals because of the delays in marketing approval (WTO-plus TPE Singapore 2004). Further, Singapore has acceded

---

[1] The main gist of the ITA focuses on the key role that trade in IT products plays in the expansion of the world economy. It seeks to encourage the continued technological development of the IT industry on a world-wide basis, by binding and eliminating customs duties on covered products. All products covered under this agreement will be subjected to zero tariffs with the implementation through basic staging in 2000 and extended staging in 2005. Another major aspect of the agreement covers the need to consult on non-tariff measures, the need to develop international standards for IT products and the need for an MRA of conformity assessment.

to some international agreements regarding copyrights and marks (e.g. the Madrid Protocol on 31 October, 2000, Patent Cooperation Treaty, Trademark Law Treaty, UPOV convention in 1991, WIPO Copyright in 1991 and 1996, and Phonograms Treaty in 1996) that are due to be effective by the beginning of 2005.

The 'new age' partnership agreement between the Japan-Singapore FTA (JSEPA) goes beyond the WTO commitments (Soesastro, 2003). The ultimate goal of the FTA is to focus on the services sector liberalisation and in the promotion of foreign direct investment between the two countries. In addition to reducing tariffs and non-tariff barriers (NTBs), JSEPA also covers issues such as regulatory reforms; facilitation of customs procedures; cooperation in science and technology, media and broadcasting, electronic commerce, advancing information and communication technology; movement of natural persons; and human resource developments. By including issues such as smoother trans-border flow of capital and labour, significant reductions in customs costs, and collaboration on education and training, the Japan-Singapore FTA can complement multilateral trade liberalisation. The economic benefit of the Japan-Singapore FTA to Singapore is projected to be around S$69 million per year and may lead to nearly S$330 million within the next five years (Soesastro, 2003). The estimated global returns from JSEPA are expected to exceed US$9 billion annually and most of this is expected to accrue to Japan due to its proactive approach to open up and reform its economy (Hertel et al., 2001).

b. Are the Bilateral 'WTO-plus' Free Trade Agreements a Sufficient Building Block for Multilateral Liberalisation?

Singapore strongly believes that the bilateral 'WTO-plus' FTAs are part of 'competitive liberalisation' and are a building block for multilateral liberalisation through the WTO (WTO-TPR Singapore 2004; and Sally, 2004). In fact, the key component of the building block for multilateral trading arrangements is the role ASEAN plays in APEC and the WTO. However, given that most of the WTO-plus FTAs by Singapore are mostly in the services sector, WTO-TPR Singapore 2004 highlights that it is not directly clear if the FTAs provide sufficient building blocks for strengthening ASEAN and thereby supporting multilateral liberalisation.

Given the prominent FTAs with Australia, Japan, New Zealand and the US, Singapore is very keen to open up its services sector for greater competition and thus enhance its global competitiveness in this sector. Singapore has progressively liberalised its financial sector and the Monetary Authority of Singapore (MAS) has lowered its barriers in banking and insurance and also deregulated the securities market.

In the banking sector, Singapore has been implementing its liberalisation policy since 1999 to open up the relatively closed domestic retail banking sector. In 1999, the 40 per cent foreign shareholding restriction on local banks was lifted and the 70 per cent limit on foreign ownership was removed for Stock Exchange Singapore (SES) members. In addition to lowering the barriers for foreign owner-ships, additional steps have been taken to strengthen supervision and corporate governance in banks. In the insurance sector, restrictions were removed on foreign investment and entry into the sector by insurance companies. The pace of liberalisation is also reflected in the telecommunications sector, where it was liberalised two years earlier than originally planned in 2000 (see www.ida.gov.sg under competition policy for further details). All direct and indirect equity limits in the telecommunications services have been lifted. This has resulted in a con-siderable increase in the number of service providers and telecommunication charges have been reduced.

Given the unilateral liberalisation of its services sector, Singapore is more willing and keen to see progress in the GATS negotiations. However, the gap in liberalisation of the services sector among the ASEAN countries tends to be quite diverse and incoherent. ASEAN countries comprising Malaysia, Indonesia, Thailand and the Philippines tend to take a more protected view in the post-Asian crisis liberalisation of the services sector and thereby adopt a defensive and cautious approach to the GATS negotiation (Sally, 2004). Given its different policy stance on the services sector and with the large economic development gap, it is not very clear if there are any substantial gains for ASEAN. For instance, it is considered by some ASEAN countries that Singapore's FTA might be a back-door entry for its FTA partners to gain entry into the ASEAN Free Trade Area (AFTA) (Tongzon, 2003). Further, the US-Singapore FTA is consid-ered by some as creating little direct benefit for the ASEAN countries, except for some provisions such as the Integrated Sourcing Initiative agreement (ISI) which allows components such as medical and ICT products produced by neighbouring ASEAN countries as being of Singapore origin when they are used for produc-tion in Singapore (Soesastro, 2003; and Tongzon, 2003). The rising number of FTAs signed by Singapore also raises important concerns on the 'spaghetti bowl' effects in terms of overlapping FTAs with complicated provisions and rules of origins (Low, 2003; and Sally, 2004).

However, the key reasons for WTO-plus bilateral agreements are political as well as economic. Participating countries must be willing to negotiate on key sensitive sectors and reduce barriers in these sectors as opposed to excluding their 'sensitive sectors' from the negotiation agenda. The 'competitive liberalisa-tion' argument for FTAs is based on sensitive trade and cross-border issues that could not be dealt with under the multilateral settings such as the WTO, but it could be effectively negotiated in bilateral agreements. As Singapore demonstrated that it is willing to negotiate on key 'sensitive sectors', other ASEAN countries must be prepared to negotiate on their 'sensitive sectors' and realise the potential gains from more open trading systems (Elek, 2003). This will be a crucial build-ing block for WTO-plus FTAs to support a multilateral trading system.

Multilateral and broader regionalism is still the first-best equilibrium as compared to bilateral and cross-regional trading arrangements given the potential gains from larger and diverse markets. Singapore is integrated in the South-East Asian region, and its production networks are entrenched and linked to the neighbouring ASEAN countries. The success of Singapore's trade and industrialisation policy depends not only on its successful undertakings but also on the economic success of the neighbouring ASEAN countries. Therefore, the success of a WTO-plus FTA as a building block for a multilateral trading system depends on the unified and coordinated framework for ASEAN to pursue a cohesive and credible trade policy. Given the rise of North-East Asia with China as the next growth pole in the world, ASEAN is realising the potential gains from a unified and coordinated framework for trade negotiations. ASEAN as a group must consider its strategy to deal with trade proposals for ASEAN-China, ASEAN-US, ASEAN-India, ASEAN-Korea and ASEAN-Japan trade agreements.

The importance of the services sector for sustained growth of the ASEAN and East Asia could not be under-emphasised. It is in the services sector that Singapore's FTA framework could play an important role in the South-East Asian region. Firstly, it has been observed that the demand for services is highly income elastic and that the demand for services increases concurrently as the income for Asian countries rises. Thus the demand for services such as education, health care, telecommunication services and travel services are expected to expand faster than the demand for manufactured and agricultural goods as Asian countries experience continued growth in income and standard of living. Secondly, services activities are becoming an important source of export growth for the Asian countries. Services activities are becoming the fastest growing cross-border and FDI activities in East and South-East Asia for the past decade. For instance, travel and tourism have traditionally been considered as the important source of external income for developing countries. However, with infrastructures in telecommunication and information technology, a growing number of Asian countries are becoming large exporters of services such as back-office processing, transaction processing, and developing information and software products. Thus the potential gains for the future growth of the ASEAN and Asian economies are enormous from the growth in services sector and also from the liberalisation of the services. This is particularly evident in Malaysia and Thailand as the share of services sector to GDP is expected to rise higher than 60 per cent in the next few years.

Given the potential gains in the liberalisation of the services industries, there are also significant gains from international cooperation in key services activities across countries. For instance, regional networking and hubs activities in financial, transport and telecommunication activities might be of significant importance for ASEAN economies. However, the bilateral and multilateral cooperation in these areas is yet to be fully exploited among the Asian countries (Chin, 2001).

Services activities also affect production activities within and across regions. In particular, the producer services activities as intermediate inputs in production are growing in importance. Both telecommunication and information technologies have increased and allow for greater access of producer services in cross-border trading activities. Thus the quality and cost competitiveness of the services is key for the growth in the services industries in the region. Hence, regulatory reform and liberalisation of services activities could be expected to reap substantial economic gains for the domestic economy.

4. TRADE POLICY AND INDUSTRIAL STRATEGY OF SINGAPORE:
THE IMPORTANCE OF TOTAL FACTOR PRODUCTIVITY (TFP)

Although Singapore has weathered the recent external shocks such as the Asian financial crisis, SARS and the Middle-East crisis, WTO-TPE Singapore 2004 highlights the declining total factor productivity (TFP) as an important indicator of an economic efficiency since the mid-1990s. It suggests that the

> longer term outlook may well be influenced by measures now being taken to deal with the developments in TFP growth as well as the structural changes taking place in the economy as a result of increased pressure from other low-cost regional producers (WTO-TPE Singapore 2004).

From Singapore's perspective, FTAs encourage greater efficiency and productivity in domestic sectors, thereby enhancing its competitiveness in the world market. A recent study by Lee (2000) on the Japan-Singapore FTA suggests that TFP and spillovers play an important role in reaping large gains from bilateral trading activities. Based on his simulation, increase in competition from open trading activities tends to raise efficiency and TFP leading to reductions in export prices and expansion of exports in both Japan and Singapore and the rest of the world. At the same time, greater intermediate and final demand of the two countries will expand their demand for imports from most of the trading partners. In this scenario, real GDP of Japan and Singapore in 2020 is expected to be 1.4 and 1.8 per cent higher than their baseline values respectively.

As opposed to the aggregated TFP measure, a more disaggregated TFP will provide a better sense of the productive improvements of the small-open economy. The disaggregated TFP by selected manufacturing and services industries is given in Table 3. The key industries of electrical & electronics and chemical (includes pharmaceutical and biochemical) products tends to indicate declining TFP growth after the post-Asian crisis. This must be a key concern for Singapore as these two industries tend to account for a large share of output and exports for the manufacturing sector. One key factor for the declining TFP growth in these two sectors might be due to the structural adjustments to more technological-intensive activities. The large capital investments in the chemical, biochemical

TABLE 3

Total Factor Productivity Growth of Selected Manufacturing and Services Industries in Singapore

	1990–1996	1997–2002
Manufacturing		
Electrical and Electronics Products	7.6	−5.7
Chemical Products	6.2	−16.2
Machinery Products	10.3	3.8
Petroleum and Petroleum Products	3.3	−7.1
Precision Instrumentation	12.9	12.2
Transport	4.7	10.9
Fabricated Metals	2.5	−0.6
Printing	6.1	−5.6
Wearing Apparels	1.2	0.5
Food and Beverage	9.5	−6.9
Wood	4.9	5.1
Rubber and Plastic	3.4	2.8
Basic Metal	−3.2	−2.0
Other Manufactures	2.0	3.9
Services		
Land Transport Services	2.8	−3.7
Water Transport Services (Ports, etc.)	−1.4	4.0
Air Transport Services	−2.1	8.7
Logistics Services (Storage and Warehousing)	1.2	12.1
Postal and Telecommunications	2.9	−8.8
Financial Services	2.9	−0.3
Insurance Services	1.3	−0.8
Business Services	−2.2	−1.4

Notes:

The data for the manufacturing industry is derived from the *Report on Census of Industrial Production*, EDB, Singapore (various issues). The data for services industry is derived from the *Report on Services*, Department of Statistics, Singapore (various issues). All the variables are based on 1985 prices. The standard growth accounting framework is used to derive the TFP measure. The capital stock is derived by Perpetual Inventory Method.

and pharmaceutical industries in the late 1990s might account for falling TFP growth in these industries. There are strong positive signs from precision instruments and transport equipments industries that indicate strong TFP growth in 1997–2002.

Notwithstanding the importance of TFP growth for medium- to long-term growth, the average TFP growth for the small-open economy tends to move in the opposite direction to the structural adjustments in the Singapore economy (Thangavelu, 2004). The negative relationship between capital accumulation and TFP growth suggests that there must be sufficient 'gestation' or 'learning-by-doing' effects in the economy before there are signs of positive TFP growth. In this case, the economy needs the lag periods to sufficiently learn new technologies and acquire technology-specific skills, as the economy structurally adjusts through large capital investments (Toh and Ng, 2002). In the period 1999–2003, Singapore was structurally adjusting to higher value-added activities in chemicals, biomedical, electronics and telecommunication clusters with large investments in industrial and science parks. Given the vast improvements in quality of labour through education and skills, we could see significant improvements in productivity growth as human capital complements new technological changes through capital investments in the next few years.

The key services industries tend to produce higher TFP growth as compared to the key industries in the manufacturing sector. The key services industry of air transport, water transport and logistics services tend to achieve a higher productivity growth in 1997–2002. However, the other key sector such as the financial services sectors tend to show a falling TFP growth in the post-Asian crisis, again raising important concerns for productivity improvements in this sector. The transportation sector (including communication) accounts for nearly 11.1 per cent of Singapore's GDP and provides employment to nearly 10.6 per cent of Singapore's labour force. This is an important sector that is given high priority for potential growth area and a key component of Singapore's industrial strategy (WTO-TPE Singapore 2004). The strong productive performance of these services industries in 1997–2002 is encouraging and an indication of the competitiveness of the services sector.

As the economy matures and moves into higher value-added activities, productive performance of the economy will be crucial for the Singapore economy to sustain its long-term growth in the global economy. Several key factors are already in place for improving the efficiency and productive performance of the economy. Firstly, if the competition policy is sufficiently implemented, there could be strong improvements in efficiency from greater competition from more open economic activities. The adoption and recognition of global standards on intellectual property rights will have a significant impact on innovation and greater spillovers from foreign direct investments in the Singapore economy.

Although the Singapore government is well known to have played a pervasive and active role in economic development, its impact on the productivity of the economy is unlikely to be as negative as that asserted by Fernald and Neiman (2003). Singapore's government-linked companies (GLCs) and statutory boards (SBs) are well known to be competitively run and are generally surplus-generating enterprises. As the economy becomes more complex and the competition intensifies across more industries and countries, the requirement of new management skills and mindset is recognised. Nonetheless, any shortcoming is not casually ignored. There are significant efforts made to privatise state monopolies and GLCs (e.g. telecommunication, power generation, Port Authority of Singapore) and engaging private sector managers to run state-owned companies. In fact, Competition Policy Legislation is targeted to be implemented by 2005 to ensure a competitive landscape that will be favoured by both the public and private sectors.

However, there are two key areas of importance for sustainable productive improvements for Singapore: development of strong small and medium-sized enterprises (SMEs) and human capital development. With the disinvestment of GLCs and the introduction of competition policy, there should be greater scope for SMEs to compete in critical markets that were mainly dominated by GLCs. The industrial strategy for moving to higher value-added activities mostly focuses on multinational activities and GLCs to move the economy into key industries. In this process, SMEs are critically marginalised and 'crowded-out' of the industrial development. The development of SMEs will be crucial for the next phase of growth for the Singapore economy and to reap the full-potential benefits of the FTAs through linkages and spillovers from open industrial activities.

The other important area of development is in human capital. Given that Singapore still has nearly 34 per cent of its labour force with below secondary education, it is imperative that the workforce should be retrained and upgraded for the new growth areas in both the manufacturing and services sectors. The aim of the Workers Development Agency (WDA) is to enhance the productivity and employability of the workers through training, retraining and retaining workers in the labour market.

5. CONCLUDING REMARKS

A strong domestic economy and the cohesive external economy of ASEAN are the key components for Singapore's long-term sustainable growth. In the domestic arena, the government has adopted pragmatic macroeconomic policy and industrial strategies to liberalise the services sector and move the manufacturing sector to higher value-added activities. The disinvestment of GLCs with the introduction of competition policy, and also liberalising the services sector such as financial and telecommunication sectors, are policies that will improve the efficiency and competitiveness of the domestic economy.

The adoption of WTO-plus bilateral FTAs by Singapore is in the right direction for the changing regional and global conditions. Although it is expected to provide potential gains, bilateral agreements are still the second-best solutions as compared to regionalism and multilateral agreements. Given that Singapore has taken a strong position in the WTO-plus bilateral FTAs, the full benefits of such an undertaking could only be attained if ASEAN sees the potential benefits of the WTO-plus bilateral FTAs in the services sector. Given that the services sector will be crucial for the next phase of growth, there might be a framework for cohesive and coordinated ASEAN to engage bilateral agreements with major trading partners.

APPENDIX

TABLE A.1

Elements of Singapore's Bilateral Free-trade Agreements

Agreement/Sector	ANZSCEP	JSEPA	ESFTA	SAFTA	USSFTA
	Agreement between Singapore and New Zealand on a Closer Economic Partnership, in force since January 2001. To be reviewed biannually.	Agreement between Singapore and Japan for a New-Age Economic Partnership in force since November 2002. To be reviewed annually.	Agreement between Singapore and EFTA states in force since January 2003. To be reviewed biannually.	Agreement between Singapore and Australia in force since July 2003. To be reviewed annually.	Agreement between Singapore and the United States in force since January 2004. To be reviewed annually.
Goods	Elimination of customs duties on date of entry into force.	Singapore eliminated all remaining customs duties on imports from Japan on entry into force. Based on a positive list. For most exports to Japan, tariff elimination is immediate. For the rest, tariff elimination is phased over a $3^1/_2$ to 8-year period.	Elimination of duties on industrial goods on entry into force. Liberalisation of duties on agricultural goods based on positive list and on agreements with each EFTA state; duties on processed agricultural and fish products to be liberalised based on positive lists with each EFTA state.	Elimination of customs duties on entry into force.	Based on a positive list. Singapore eliminated all remaining customs duties on imports from the United States on entry into force. For most exports to the United States, immediate tariff elimination, and a transition period of 3 to 10 years for others.

Services	Based on a positive list and to be reviewed with the goal of free trade in services by 2010. Preferential treatment extended to non-parties engaged in 'substantive business operations' in either of the parties. Singapore's commitments beyond GATS include professional, telecommunications, financial, business, and transport services.	Based on a positive list; preferential treatment also extended to non-parties engaged in 'substantive business operations' in either of the parties. Singapore's commitments beyond GATS include professional, telecommunication, financial, business, and transport services.	Based on a positive list and to be reviewed with the goal of eliminating substantially all remaining restrictions in services covered at the end of ten years. Singapore's commitments beyond GATS include professional, telecommunication, financial, business, and transport services.	Based on a negative list; exceptions to market access and national treatment listed in annexes. Preferential treatment extended to non-parties engaged in 'substantive business operations' in either of the parties. Singapore's commitments beyond GATS include professional, telecommunication, financial, business, and transport services.	Based on a negative list, with exceptions to market access and national treatment listed in annexes. Singapore's commitments beyond the GATS include professional, telecommunications, financial, business, and transport services.
Contingency measures	No right to take safeguard measures against each others' imports; anti-dumping provisions are stricter than those applied under GATT Article VI.	May take emergency measures against each others' imports only during the ten-year transition period; anti-dumping measures to be in accordance with GATT Article VI.	May take emergency measures against each others' imports but not anti-dumping measures.	No right to take safeguard measures against each others' imports; anti-dumping rules are stricter than those applied under GATT Article VI.	Safeguard measures may be taken during the ten-year transition period; anti-dumping measures may be taken in accordance with GATT Article VI.
Intellectual property rights	WTO TRIPS Agreement provisions to apply.	WTO TRIPS Agreement provisions to apply. Cooperation on IPR matters, including through a Joint Committee.	WTO TRIPS Agreement provisions to apply.	WTO TRIPS Agreement provisions to apply. Cooperation *inter alia* on enforcement and education.	Singapore to accede to international conventions including WIPO Copyright Treaty, WIPO Performances and Phonographs Treaty, and UPOV. TRIPS-plus provisions include extending copyright

TABLE A.1 Continued

Agreement/Sector	ANZSCEP	JSEPA	ESFTA	SAFTA	USSFTA
					protection to life of author plus 70 years, measures against the circumvention of technologies that protect copyright works, protection of well-known marks, extension for unreasonable curtailment of patent term for pharmaceutical products due to delays in marketing approval process.
Competition	Commitment to creating and maintaining open and competitive markets; endeavouring to implement the APEC Principles to Enhance Competition and Regulatory reform. Parties also agreed to consult with each other in the development of any new competition measures.	Cooperation on controlling anti-competitive practices including the exchange of information on such practices.	Cooperation through consultations on eliminating anti-competitive business practices.	Commitment to promote competition by addressing anti-competitive practices including through consultation and review. Within six months of a generic competition law being enacted by Singapore, a review of the competition provisions of the FTA to be conducted.	Commits Singapore to enacting generic competition legislation by 2005 and ensuring that GLCs do not engage in agreements that restrain competition or in exclusionary practices that substantially lessen competition.

Investment	Provisions apply to all goods and those services listed in the parties' schedules.	Provisions apply to all goods and those services listed in the parties' schedules. Performance requirements are prohibited.	Provisions on investment do not apply to measures affecting trade in services and to investors investing in services (subject to a review after ten years).	Provisions apply to all goods and services (except where reservations have been listed by the parties).	Negative list for goods and services except those scheduled, and detailed investor-state dispute settlement provisions. Performance requirements are prohibited.
Government procurement	Single market between the two parties for procurement valued at over SDR 50,000.	Provisions of the WTO GPA apply. Procurement threshold of SDR 100,000.	Provisions of the WTO GPA apply.	Single market between the two parties.	Preferences up to S$102,710 for goods and services for Ministries (S$910,000 for statutory boards), and S$11,376,000 for construction services.
Others					Provisions on labour and environment.

Notes:
Details of rules of origin under these agreements are provided in Chapter III (Table III.3).
ANZSCEP: New Zealand-Singapore Free Trade Agreement
JSEPA: Japan-Singapore Free Trade Agreement
ESFTA: European Union Free Trade Agreement
SAFTA: Singapore-Australia Free Trade Agreement
USSFTA: United States-Singapore Free Trade Agreement

Source: WTO Secretariat, based on the texts of Singapore's bilateral FTAs.

REFERENCES

Chin, A. (2001), 'Developments in the Air Transport Industry: Implications for Singapore Tourism', in Tan Ern Ser et al. (eds.), *Tourism Management and Policy: Perspectives from Singapore* (World Scientific).

Economic Review Committee Report (2002), Ministry of Trade and Industry, Singapore (http://www.mti.gov.sg).

Elek, A. (2003), 'Beyond Free Trade Agreements: 21st Century Choices for East Asian Cooperation', Pacific Economic Papers, No. 336 (Australia-Japan Research Centre, Australian National University).

Fernald, J. and B. Neiman (2003), 'Measuring Productivity Growth in Asia: Do Market Imperfections Matter?', Working Paper WP2003-15 (Federal Reserve Bank of Chicago).

Hertel, T. W., T. Walmsley and K. Itakura (2001), 'Dynamic Effects of "New Age" Free Trade Agreement Between Japan and Singapore' (mimeo, Centre for Global Trade Analysis, Purdue University, West Lafayette).

Lee, H. (2000), 'General Equilibrium Evaluation of Japan-Singapore Free Trade Agreement', in P. Drysdale and I. Kenichi (eds.), *East Asian Trade and Financial Integration: New Issues* (Melbourne: Asia Pacific Press).

Low, L. (2003), 'Multilateralism, Regionalism, Bilateral and Crossregional Free Trade Arrangements: All Paved with Good Intentions for ASEAN?', *Asian Economic Journal*, 17, 1, 65–86.

Ministry of Industry and Trade (2005), Economic Survey of Singapore 2004, Singapore (http://www.mti.gov.sg).

Sally, R. (2004), 'Southeast Asia in the WTO', Southeast Asia Background Series No. 5 (Institute of Southeast Asia, Singapore).

Soesastro, H. (2003), 'Dynamics of Competitive Liberalization in RTA Negotiations: East Asian Perspective', *PECC Trade Form* (Washington, DC).

Thangavelu, S. (2004), 'Singapore: TFP', in *Total Factor Productivity Growth: Survey Report* (Asian Productivity Organization, Tokyo).

Toh, M. H. and W. C. Ng (2002), 'Efficiency of Investments in Asian Economics: Has Singapore Over-invested?', *Journal of Asian Economics*, 13, 52–71.

Tongzon, J. (2003), 'US-Singapore Free Trade Agreement: Implications for ASEAN', *ASEAN Economic Bulletin*, 20, 2, 174–78.

3

Turkey: Trade Policy Review

Sübidey Togan

1. INTRODUCTION

𝕿 *HE Trade Policy Review: Turkey 2003*, the third of its kind, provides a comprehensive survey of trade policy developments and practices in Turkey. This paper discusses besides the principal issues highlighted in the report, an issue that has largely been neglected in Trade Policy Reviews. It is the sustainability of current account. Section 2 describes the main developments in Turkey's trade regime and trade performance, and Section 3 examines the trade policy under the headings of measures affecting imports, exports and foreign direct investment. Section 4 is on liberalisation of services, and Section 5 on sustainability of current account. The final section offers conclusions.

2. MAIN DEVELOPMENTS

Until the early 1980s Turkey was a fairly closed economy. At that time – as part of more wide-ranging economic reforms – the trade policy of protection and import substitution was replaced by a much more open trade regime.

a. Trade Agreements

Turkey acceded to the GATT in 1951 under the Torquay Protocol, has participated in all subsequent rounds of multilateral trade negotiations, and became an original Member of the World Trade Organisation (WTO) on 26 March, 1995. It is according to its trade partners at least MFN treatment, and has preferential trade agreements with a number of countries. It has amended legislation in the areas of intellectual property, safeguards, anti-dumping and countervailing measures. Turkey has made extensive commitments under the General Agreement on Trade in Services (GATS). Turkey is not a signatory to the Plurilateral Agreements that resulted from the Uruguay Round; it is an observer to the Plurilateral Agreements on Government Procurement and Trade in Civil Aircraft. It is attaching great importance to the Doha Development Agenda. To date Turkey has been involved in several cases under the WTO dispute settlement mechanism. Seven consultations have been requested regarding Turkey's trade measures and Turkey has been the complainant in two cases.

Turkey applied for associate membership in the EU – then the EEC – as early as 1959. The application resulted in an Association Agreement in 1963, whereby Turkey and the EU would conditionally and gradually create a customs union by 1995 at the latest. The customs union was seen as a step towards full membership at an unspecified future date. The EU unilaterally granted Turkey preferential tariffs and financial assistance, but the process of staged, mutual reductions in tariffs and non-tariff barriers was delayed in the 1970s because of economic and political conditions in Turkey. Turkey applied for full membership in 1987. The response in 1990 was that accession negotiations could not be undertaken at the time, since the EU was engaged in major internal changes and as well as in the transition of Eastern Europe and the Soviet Union. However, the EU was prepared to extend economic relations without explicitly rejecting the possibility of full membership at a future date.

Turkey joined the European Customs Union (CU) starting 1 January, 1996. According to the Customs Union Decision (CUD) of 1995, all industrial goods, except products of the European Coal and Steel Community (ECSC), that comply with the European Community norms could circulate freely between Turkey and the EU as of 1 January, 1996. For ECSC products, Turkey signed a free trade agreement (FTA) with the EU in July 1996, and, as a result, ECSC products have received duty-free treatment between the parties since 1999.

The CUD required Turkey to implement the European Community's Common Customs Tariffs (CCT) on imports of industrial goods from third countries as of 1 January, 1996, to adopt by 2001 all of the preferential trade agreements the EU has concluded over time, and to implement on the commercial policy side measures similar to those of the European Community's commercial policy. Adhering to the stipulations of the CUD, Turkey maintained rates of protection above those specified in the CCT for certain 'sensitive' products until 2001. In order to adopt the EU's preferential trade agreements, Turkey signed FTAs with the European Free Trade Association countries, Israel, and the Central and Eastern European countries. FTAs are being discussed with the Mediterranean countries. In addition, Turkey has adopted the EC competition law, established the Competition Board, adopted the EC rules on protection of intellectual and industrial property rights, established a Patent Office, and started to harmonise technical legislation concerning industrial products and the establishment of sound conformity assessment and market surveillance structures internally.

On 10–11 December, 1999, the European Council meeting held in Helsinki produced a breakthrough in Turkey-EU relations. At Helsinki, Turkey was officially recognised as a candidate state for accession, on an equal footing with other candidate states. It now has a so-called Accession Partnership with the EU, which means that the EU is working together with Turkey to enable it to adopt the *acquis communautaire*, the legal framework of the EU. In contrast to other candidate countries, Turkey did not receive a timetable for accession. After the approval of the Accession Partnership by the Council and the adoption of the Framework Regulation on 26 February, 2001, the Turkish Government announced its own National Programme for the adoption of the *acquis communautaire* on 19 March, 2001. Progress towards accession continues along the path set by the National Programme.

In late 2004 another milestone was reached with the recommendation of the Commission of the European Communities that the European Council endorse the launching of formal accession negotiations and establish a timetable. The Copenhagen European Council in December 2002 concluded that:

> if the European Council in December 2004, on the basis of a report and a recommendation from the Commission, decides that Turkey fulfils the Copenhagen political criteria, the European Union will open accession negotiations with Turkey without delay.

The December 2004 Council decided to start membership talks with Turkey on 3 October, 2005.

In addition to the Customs Union with the EU and the FTA with the EFTA, Turkey also participates in the Economic Cooperation Organisation (ECO) and the Black Sea Economic Cooperation (BSEC). The ECO is an intergovernmental regional organisation established in 1985 by Iran, Pakistan and Turkey for the purpose of sustainable socio-economic development of member states. In 1992, the Organisation was expanded to include Afghanistan, Azerbaijan, Kazakhstan, Kyrgyz Republic, Tajikistan, Turkmenistan and Uzbekistan. On 17 July, 2003, the ECO Trade Agreement (ECOTA) was signed between Afghanistan, Iran, Pakistan, Tajikistan and Turkey. The Agreement foresees the reduction of tariffs to a maximum of 15 per cent within a maximum period of eight years. ECOTA has binding provisions on state monopolies, state aid, protection of intellectual property rights, dumping and anti-dumping measures. On the other hand, the BSEC aims to improve and diversify economic and trade relations between its eleven members. The member countries are Albania, Armenia, Azerbaijan, Bulgaria, Georgia, Greece, Moldavia, Romania, the Russian Federation, Turkey and Ukraine. The BSEC Declaration was signed on 25 June, 1992, and on 7 February, 1997, a declaration of intent for the establishment of a BSEC free trade area was adopted. Recently, BSEC launched projects to eliminate non-tariff barriers on regional trade and to harmonise trade documents in the region.

b. Investment Framework

Foreign-owned firms had long been subject to special authorisations and sectoral limitations. In 2001 the Turkish government requested the Foreign

Investment Advisory Service of the World Bank to conduct a study on the business environment affecting foreign direct investment (FDI) firms in Turkey. The study was conducted in cooperation with the Undersecretariat for the Treasury. According to Foreign Investment Advisory Service (2001a and 2001b) seven major problems impeded the operations of FDI enterprises up until the early 2000s: (i) political instability, (ii) government hassle, (iii) a weak judicial system, (iv) heavy taxation, (v) corruption, (vi) deficient infrastructure and (vii) competition from the informal economy. On the basis of this work, a new Law on FDI and important amendments in various laws (Commercial Law and in the laws concerning the Employment of Foreigners, the Registry of Title Deeds and Public Procurement) were adopted by the Parliament in 2003. The new legislation removed the screening and pre-approval procedures for FDI projects, re-designed the company registration process on an equal footing for domestic and foreign firms, facilitated the hiring of foreign employees, included FDI firms in the definition of 'domestic tenderer' in public procurement, and authorised foreign persons and companies to acquire real estate in Turkey. Thus the new law guarantees national treatment and investor rights. According to the law a company can be 100 per cent foreign owned in almost all sectors of the economy. Acquisitions of more than 30 hectares by foreigners are subject to permission from the Council of Ministers, and establishments in the financial, petroleum and mining sectors require special permission, according to appropriate laws.

c. Trade Performance and Investment

Basic data on Turkey's merchandise trade are shown in Tables 1 and 2. The tables reveal that in 2004 Turkish merchandise exports amounted to US$63 billion and merchandise imports to $97.3 billion.[1] Exports to the EU15 made up 54.6 per cent of total exports, and imports from the EU made up 46.6 per cent of total imports.

Table 1 reveals that the three export commodities with the highest shares of total exports during 2003 were clothing, 21.1 per cent; textiles, 11.1 per cent; and automotive products, 10.4 per cent. The three import commodities with the highest shares of total imports were fuels, 16.7 per cent; other non-electrical machinery, 10.5 per cent; and automotive products, 9 per cent. Similarly, the three export commodities with the highest shares of exports to the EU were clothing, 30.2 per cent; automotive products, 13.4 per cent; and textiles, 10 per cent. The three commodities with the highest shares of imports from the EU were automotive products, 17.4 per cent; other non-electricial machinery, 15.5 per cent; and other semi-manufactures, 7.6 per cent.

During the period 1990–2003, Turkey's total exports grew at an annual rate of 9 per cent and total imports at the rate of 8.3 per cent. The export commodities

---

[1] All dollar amounts are US dollars unless otherwise indicated.

TABLE 1
Exports and Imports, Turkey

SITC	Commodity	Total Exports, 2003 (US$ millions)	Percentage Distribution, Total Exports	Annual Growth Rate of Exports, 1990–2003 (Per cent)	Exports to the EU 2003 (US$ millions)	Percentage Distribution, Exports to EU	Share of Exports to EU of Sectoral Exports	Annual Growth Rate of Exports to EU, 1990–2003 (Per cent)
	Agricultural Products							
0+1+4+22	Food	4,735	10.03	2.01	1,949	8.31	41.17	2.32
2-22-27-28	Agricultural raw materials	522	1.11	2.56	220	0.94	42.24	0.41
	Mining Products							
27+28	Ores and other minerals	572	1.21	4.23	246	1.05	42.95	2.56
3	Fuels	980	2.08	7.93	211	0.90	21.53	-0.31
68	Non-ferrous metals	457	0.97	8.64	222	0.94	48.45	9.03
	Manufactures							
67	Iron and steel	3,342	7.08	5.12	939	4.00	28.09	16.52
	Chemicals							
51	Organic chemicals	171	0.36	1.53	107	0.46	62.55	4.28
57+58	Plastics	545	1.15	9.20	112	0.48	20.50	5.40
52	Inorganic chemicals	230	0.49	5.99	80	0.34	34.68	5.38
54	Pharmaceuticals	220	0.47	10.28	72	0.31	32.64	17.99
53+55+56+59	Other chemicals	726	1.54	10.19	65	0.28	8.97	4.00
6-65-67-68	Other semi-manufactures	4,143	8.77	12.52	1,645	7.01	39.70	12.21
	Machinery and transport equipment							
71-713	Power-generating machinery	246	0.52	24.80	85	0.36	34.47	22.77
72+73+74	Other non-electrical machinery	1,566	3.32	18.16	537	2.29	34.29	17.73
75+76+776	Office machines and tel. equipment	1,978	4.19	17.99	1,569	6.68	79.30	17.27
77-776-7783	Electrical machinery and apparatus	2,076	4.40	16.83	999	4.26	48.14	14.64
78-785-786 +7132+7783	Automotive products	4,928	10.44	24.42	3,139	13.38	63.70	29.30
79+785+786+7131 +7133+7138+7139	Other transport equipment	1,542	3.27	20.70	853	3.63	55.31	23.07
65	Textiles	5,262	11.14	10.14	2,340	9.97	44.48	7.50
84	Clothing	9,962	21.10	7.21	7,079	30.17	71.07	5.94
8-84-86-891	Other consumer goods	2,675	5.67	16.37	954	4.06	35.66	12.44
9+891	*Other Products*	335	0.71	30.17	44	0.19	13.02	16.10
	Total	47,253	100	9.01	25,899	100	54.81	8.56

TABLE 1 Continued

		Total Imports, 2003 (US$ millions)	Percentage Distribution, Total Imports	Annual Growth Rate of Imports, 1990–2003 (Per cent)	Imports from EU 2003 (US$ millions)	Percentage Distribution, Imports from EU	Share of Imports from EU of Sectoral Imports	Annual Growth Rate of Imports from EU, 1990–2003 (Per cent)
	Agricultural Products							
0+1+4+22	Food	2,789	4.03	3.29	548	1.85	19.65	1.70
2-22-27-28	Agricultural raw materials	2,471	3.57	6.42	894	3.01	36.19	6.76
	Mining Products							
27+28	Ores and other minerals	2,262	3.26	4.58	670	2.26	29.61	-0.05
3	Fuels	11,575	16.71	8.06	460	1.55	3.97	7.71
68	Non-ferrous metals	1,411	2.04	9.55	308	1.04	21.80	4.23
	Manufactures							
67	Iron and steel	3,282	4.74	5.46	1,232	4.15	37.53	1.91
	Chemicals							
51	Organic chemicals	2,102	3.03	7.39	1,059	3.57	50.39	6.83
57+58	Plastics	2,837	4.09	12.80	1,645	5.54	58.00	11.57
52	Inorganic chemicals	543	0.78	2.82	178	0.60	32.78	0.99
54	Pharmaceuticals	2,302	3.32	17.09	1,546	5.21	67.14	17.05
53+55+56+59	Other chemicals	2,643	3.82	7.00	1,560	5.26	59.03	7.65
6-65-67-68	Other semi-manufactures	3,489	5.04	8.27	2,245	7.56	64.33	7.66
	Machinery and transport equipment							
71-713	Power-generating machinery	758	1.09	12.52	382	1.29	50.34	12.44
72+73+74	Other non-electrical machinery	7,250	10.46	5.21	4,607	15.52	63.54	4.18
75+76+776	Office machines and tel. equipment	4,166	6.01	10.95	1,618	5.45	38.83	12.15
77-776-7783	Electrical machinery and apparatus	2,065	2.98	6.82	1,175	3.96	56.93	5.75
78-785-786 +7132+7783	Automotive products	6,209	8.96	11.67	5,150	17.35	82.95	13.91
79+785+786+7131 +7133+7138+7139	Other transport equipment	1,012	1.46	1.80	711	2.40	70.29	4.88
65	Textiles	3,441	4.97	13.03	1,185	3.99	34.43	13.49
84	Clothing	422	0.61	24.93	204	0.69	48.26	21.68
8-84-86-891	Other consumer goods	3,540	5.11	10.07	1,910	6.44	53.96	9.27
9+891	*Other Products*	2,714	3.92	27.10	391	1.32	14.42	18.75
	Total	69,340	100	8.27	33,495	100	48.31	8.06

Note: SITC = Standard International Trade Classification. Source: Own calculations based on data provided by State Institute of Statistics.

with the highest annual growth rates were other products, 30.2 per cent; power-generating machinery, 24.8 per cent; and automotive products, 24.4 per cent. The import commodities with the highest growth rates were other products, 27.1 per cent; clothing, 24.9 per cent; and pharmaceuticals, 17.1 per cent. Similarly, the export commodities to the EU with the highest growth rates were automotive products, 29.3 per cent; other transport equipment, 23.1 per cent; and power-generating machinery, 22.8 per cent. The imported commodities from the EU with the highest growth rates were clothing, 21.7 per cent; other products, 18.8 per cent; and pharmaceuticals, 17.1 per cent.

A look at the EU's share of total sectoral exports reveals that highest shares of exports to the EU are held by office machines and telecommunications equipment, 79.3 per cent; clothing, 71.1 per cent; and automotive products, 63.7 per cent. Among the sectors considered, other chemicals, other products, and plastics have the lowest shares. The three sectors with the highest EU shares of sectoral imports are automotive products, 83 per cent; other transport equipment, 70.3 per cent; and pharmaceuticals, 67.1 per cent. Among the sectors considered, fuels, other products, and food have the lowest EU shares of sectoral imports.

Table 2 shows the evolution of Turkish trade with the EU over the period 1990–2004. The data reveal that with the formation of the customs union the share of imports from the EU of total imports went up from 47.2 in 1995 to 53 per cent in 1996, but then began to decrease, reaching 46.6 per cent in 2004. Comparison of the growth rate of Turkish imports from the EU prior to formation of the customs union with that observed after formation of the customs union shows that the average growth rate of imports has even declined, from 9.1 per cent during 1990–95 to –1.76 per cent during 1996–2002, and then increased to 39.5 per cent during 2003–04. The effect of the customs union on exports seems to be of limited importance initially. Whereas the annual average growth rate of Turkish exports to the EU was 7.5 per cent prior to formation of the customs union, it increased to 7.2 per cent over the period 1996–2002, and then to 36.6 per cent during 2003–04. Similarly, the share of exports to the EU of total exports increased from 51.2 per cent in 1995 to 54 per cent in 1999, but thereafter the share declined to 51.5 per cent in 2002, and then increased to 54.6 per cent in 2004. Finally, Table 2 reveals that Turkey has run a trade deficit with the EU during every year of the period 1996–2004 and that the deficit has been substantial by any standard. It reached $12.6 billion in 1997 and $11 billion in 2004.

These findings reveal that the formation of the customs union between Turkey and the EU did not lead initially to substantial increases in trade with the EU. Substantial increases in trade with the EU were achieved only during the period 2002–03. The reasons vary. First, the formation of the customs union did not lead to substantial reductions in trade barriers on the EU side, because the EU had abolished the nominal tariff rates on imports of industrial goods from Turkey on 1 September, 1971, long before the formation of the customs union. But at

TABLE 2
Trade with EU, 1990–2004

	Total Imports (US$ millions)	Imports from EU (US$ millions)	Growth Rate of Total Imports (Per cent)	Growth Rate of Imports from EU (Per cent)	Share of Imports from EU of Total Imports	Total Exports (US$ millions)	Exports to EU (US$ millions)	Growth Rate of Total Exports (Per cent)	Growth Rate of Exports to EU (Per cent)	Share of Exports to EU of Total Exports	Trade Balance with EU (US$ millions)	Real Exchange Rate
1990	22,302	9,898			44.38	12,959	7,177			55.38	−2,721	99.67
1991	21,047	9,987	−5.63	0.90	47.45	13,594	7,348	4.90	2.38	54.05	−2,639	96.66
1992	22,870	10,656	8.66	6.70	46.59	14,719	7,937	8.28	8.02	53.92	−2,719	100.94
1993	29,429	13,875	28.68	30.21	47.15	15,348	7,599	4.27	−4.26	49.51	−6,276	91.59
1994	23,270	10,915	−20.93	−21.33	46.91	18,105	8,635	17.96	13.63	47.69	−2,280	124.35
1995	35,708	16,861	53.45	54.48	47.22	21,636	11,078	19.50	28.29	51.20	−5,783	116.72
1996	43,627	23,138	22.18	37.23	53.04	23,224	11,549	7.34	4.25	49.73	−11,589	116.67
1997	48,559	24,870	11.30	7.49	51.22	26,261	12,248	13.08	6.05	46.64	−12,622	110.32
1998	45,921	24,075	−5.43	−3.20	52.43	26,974	13,498	2.72	10.21	50.04	−10,577	100.42
1999	40,687	21,417	−11.40	−11.04	52.64	26,589	14,349	−1.43	6.30	53.97	−7,068	94.30
2000	54,509	26,610	33.97	24.25	48.82	27,775	14,510	4.46	1.12	52.24	−12,100	85.17
2001	41,399	18,280	−24.05	−31.30	44.16	31,334	16,118	12.81	11.08	51.44	−2,162	106.33
2002	51,554	23,321	24.53	27.57	45.24	36,059	18,459	15.08	14.52	51.19	−4,863	96.11
2003	69,340	33,495	34.50	43.62	48.31	47,253	25,899	31.04	40.31	54.81	−7,596	88.23
2004	97,341	45,373	40.38	35.46	46.61	63,017	34,399	33.36	32.82	54.59	−10,974	83.93
Average 1990–95			8.31	9.13	46.62			9.90	7.46	51.96		
Average 1996–2002			1.26	−1.76	49.65			6.08	7.24	50.75		
Average 2003–04			37.44	39.54	47.46			32.20	36.56	54.70		

Source: State Planning Organisation (http://www.dpt.gov.tr); own calculations.

that time certain exceptions were made. The European Community had retained the right to charge import duties on some oil products over a fixed quota and to implement a phased reduction of duties on imports of particular textile products. Moreover, the trade in products within the province of the ECSC have been protected by the Community through the application of non-tariff barriers and, in particular, anti-dumping measures. With the formation of the customs union, quotas applied by the EU were abolished, but the EU retained the right to impose anti-dumping duties.

Second, not until 2003 did Turkey incorporate into its internal legal order the European Community instruments related to removal of technical barriers to trade that would allow Turkish industrial products to enter into free circulation in the EU. Serious efforts to harmonise technical legislation concerning industrial products and the establishment of sound conformity assessment and market surveillance structures internally by Turkey were made only recently.

Third, during the 1990s economic crises began to affect Turkey with increasing frequency. Periods of economic expansion alternated with periods of equally rapid decline. Turkey faced a currency crisis in 1994 and 2001, and was hit by two severe earthquakes in 1999. GDP shrank considerably in 1994, 1999 and 2001. As a result of these developments, the country saw substantial decreases in import demand during 1994, 1999 and 2001.

Fourth, with the substantial reductions in trade barriers on the Turkish side during 1996, the increase in imports was inevitable, so long as it was not accompanied by a real devaluation of the Turkish lira. As Table 3 reveals, there was no change in the real exchange rate during 1996, and it then began to appreciate until the currency crisis of 2001. The real appreciation of the Turkish lira stimulated the import growth and hampered the growth of exports, leading to higher trade balance deficits. Also during the period 2001–04, the euro appreciated against the US dollar, leading to increases in the dollar value of EU exports, which was then reflected in the higher dollar trade values of Turkish imports from the EU and of exports to the EU.

Table 3 showing the FDI inflows over the period 1999–2003 reveals that the level of FDI inflow into Turkey is too low relative to FDI flows to developing countries with similar levels of GDP per capita. In particular, the FDI flows to Central and Eastern European countries are much larger than those to Turkey. The table indicates that manufacturing and services have attracted almost all FDI inflows into Turkey, and that the EU is the largest investor in Turkey.

3. TRADE POLICY

The main factors influencing the Turkish trading system are the WTO Agreements and Turkey's current and future trade relations with the EU. Over the last

TABLE 3
Foreign Direct Investment in Turkey (US$ million)

	1999	2000	2001	2002	2003
Sectoral Breakdown					
Agriculture	0	9	0	0	0
Mining	13	3	3	2	12
Manufacturing	353	932	846	78	338
Services	447	763	2,439	510	196
Country Breakdown					
EU	386	1,172	2,613	455	426
Other OECD	258	210	280	60	117
Middle East	155	184	0	5	0
Others	14	141	395	70	3
Total FDI	813	1,707	3,288	590	546
Share of FDI in GNP (Per cent)	0.44	0.85	2.28	0.32	0.22

Source: Central Bank of Turkey.

decade Turkey has continued to progressively align its trade regime on that of the EU, and domestic legislation in Turkey has been amended to reflect both its EU and WTO commitments.

a. Measures Affecting Imports

Prior to the successful conclusion of the Uruguay Round, most favoured nation (MFN) tariffs in many sectors were not legally bound, and as such they could potentially be raised. This created a lack of security in market access, and produced detrimental trade effects. A major goal of the Uruguay Round of Multilateral Trade Negotiations was to increase the proportion of bound industrial tariffs, thus providing added protection to trade liberalisation commitments. As a result of the Uruguay Round negotiations, 46.3 per cent of tariff lines in Turkey are now bound (all tariff lines for agricultural products and some 36 per cent of the lines for non-agricultural products). In 2005 final bindings will range from zero to 225 per cent on agricultural products, and from zero to 102 per cent on non-agricultural goods. The simple average bound tariff rate is set to decline to 33.9 per cent in 2005.

On the other hand the applied tariff schedules of Turkey are rather complex, consisting of a large number of lists comprising about 19,400 tariff lines classified at the HS 12-digit level for different country groups and countries.[2] List I displays customs duties applied to imports of agricultural products, excluding fish and fishery products. List II shows customs duties to be applied to imports

[2] HS stands for the Harmonised Commodity Description and Coding System.

of industrial products and products covered by the ECSC. Lists III and IV lay down customs duties applied to imports of processed agricultural products. List V displays reduced customs duties applied to imports of certain products used as raw materials in fertiliser, chemical, plastics, textile and electrical machinery industry. Turkey's tariff comprises *ad valorem* (98.5 per cent of tariff lines) and non-*ad valorem* rates consisting of specific, mixed, compound and formula duties. Specific taxes (Mass Housing Fund levy) are applied on the imports of 550 fish and fishery products specified in List IV. The mixed, compound and formula duties apply mainly on processed agricultural commodities. Here we note that in line with the CUD, processed agricultural products imported into Turkey from the EU are subject to customs duties comprising an industrial and agricultural component. While all industrial components enjoy duty-free treatment, few agricultural components are subject to preferential treatment. MFN customs duties still apply to most agricultural components, where these components are calculated by multiplying the quantity of primary agriculture product used in processing, according to an agreed set of ratios, by the specific rate charge.

Table 4 shows the nominal protection rates (NPR) prevailing in 2004, where all non-*ad valorem* tariffs have been converted to *ad valorem* equivalents. In the table average tariffs for three groups of countries are listed. These are the EU, GSP countries, and countries for which the MFN tariffs apply. In addition the Turkish tariff schedule lists the tariff rates for countries Turkey has free trade agreements with such as EFTA countries, Israel, Romania, Macedonia and Bosnia & Herzegovina, also the GSP tariffs for the least developed countries.[3] But the tariff rates for these countries are not shown in the table. In the table the average NPRs are shown for 21 aggregated HS commodity sections such as animal products, chemical products, textiles and vehicles.

The table reveals that in trade with the EU the simple average NPR is 8.21 per cent and weighted average NPR 1.25 per cent. Here weighted averages have been calculated by weighting the nominal tariffs on the commodities by their shares in total imports. The simple average tariff rate on imports from the GSP countries is 10.47 per cent and the weighted NPR 2.62 per cent. Finally, the simple average MFN tariff is 11.97 per cent and the weighted average NPR 4.11 per cent.

In trade with the EU 17 out of a total of 21 sectors have zero NPRs. Concentrating in the following on weighted average NPRs we note that the highest tariff rate (49.98 per cent) applies in the case of 'live animals and animal products'. The NPR on 'vegetable products' is 38.78 and on 'edible oils' 23.26. On the other hand in the case of trade with GSP countries and with countries for which the MFN tariffs apply the NPRs on 'live animals and animal products', 'vegetable

---

[3] The list of GSP countries and the list of least developed countries are specified in Annex Table 3 to the import regime (see www.igeme.gov.tr).

TABLE 4
Nominal Protection Rates, 2004
(Per cent)

HS	Commodity	Number of Tariff Lines	Per Cent of Total 2003 Imports	Applied Mean Tariffs (Simple) EU	Applied Mean Tariffs (Weighted) EU	Applied Mean Tariffs (Simple) GSP	Applied Mean Tariffs (Weighted) GSP	Mean MFN Tariffs (Simple) Others	Mean MFN Tariffs (Weighted) Others
01–05	Live Animals; Animal Products	1,116	0.21	70.41	49.98	74.06	52.18	74.07	52.18
06–14	Vegetable Products	868	2.23	28.03	38.78	28.27	38.89	28.30	38.89
15	Edible Oils	243	0.51	19.10	23.26	19.45	23.30	19.58	23.34
16–24	Prepared Foodstuffs, Beverages and Tobacco	1,272	1.47	0.00	0.00	0.08	0.02	0.00	0.00
25–27	Mineral Products	457	14.48	0.00	0.00	0.08	0.02	0.62	0.42
28–38	Chemical Products	3,156	12.20	0.07	0.02	0.53	0.60	2.98	2.17
39–40	Plastics and Rubber	566	6.16	0.00	0.00	0.27	0.84	3.10	3.22
41–43	Leather and Travel Goods	294	1.33	0.00	0.00	0.45	0.37	2.20	1.81
44–46	Wood Products	329	0.57	0.00	0.00	0.58	1.50	1.98	3.10
47–49	Cellulose Products, Paper and Paper Products	444	1.79	0.00	0.00	0.00	0.00	0.00	0.00
50–63	Textile and Textile Articles	3,534	8.09	0.00	0.00	6.30	4.18	7.89	5.26
64–67	Footwear and Miscellaneous Manufactures	206	0.35	0.00	0.00	3.76	6.29	7.41	10.40
68–70	Articles of Stone, Ceramics, Glass and Glass Products	458	0.75	0.00	0.00	0.91	1.17	3.08	3.28
71	Precious and Semi-precious Articles	104	4.49	0.00	0.00	0.00	0.00	0.98	0.11
72–83	Base Metals and Articles of Base Metal	1,892	7.31	0.00	0.00	2.63	3.95	3.82	4.86
84–85	Machinery	2,744	25.17	0.00	0.00	0.19	0.48	1.84	2.21
86–89	Transport Equipment	528	9.42	0.00	0.00	1.80	3.74	4.39	7.76
90–92	Precision	746	2.38	0.00	0.00	0.09	0.10	1.74	1.29
93	Arms and Ammunitions	34	0.16	0.00	0.00	2.32	1.32	2.32	1.32
94–96	Miscellaneous Manufactured Articles	397	0.93	0.00	0.00	0.08	0.13	2.41	3.06
97	Art and Antiques	13	0.01	0.00	0.00	0.00	0.00	0.00	0.00
	Total	19,401	100	8.21	1.25	10.47	2.61	11.97	4.11

Source: Own calculations.

products' and 'edible oils' are not much different from the tariff rates applied on imports from the EU. The figures show that the agricultural sector is heavily protected in Turkey. In trade with the GSP countries the most protected non-agricultural three sectors are 'footwear' (6.29 per cent), 'textiles' (4.18 per cent) and 'base metals' (3.95 per cent). In the case of trade with MFN countries the most protected non-agricultural three commodities are 'footwear' (10.4 per cent), 'transport equipment' (7.76 per cent) and 'textiles' (5.26 per cent).

Table 5 shows the nominal protection rates for the agricultural commodities in more detail. The table reveals that in trade with the EU the simple average NPR is 42.5 per cent and weighted average NPR 19.8 per cent. The simple average tariff rate on imports from the GSP countries is 45.6 per cent and the weighted NPR 21.2 per cent. Finally, the simple average MFN tariff is 45.8 per cent and the weighted average NPR 21.4 per cent.

Concentrating on the case of agricultural commodities we note that in the case of trade with the EU the highest weighted average NPR (120.43 per cent) applies in the case of 'meat and edible offal'. The NPR on 'milk and dairy products' is 96.91 per cent and on 'edible fruits and citrus fruits' 90.24 per cent. On the other hand in the case of trade with GSP countries and countries for which the MFN tariffs apply the highest weighted average NPRs are imposed on 'meat and edible offal', 'milk and dairy products' and 'sugar and sweets'. These tariff rates are not much different from the tariff rates applied on imports from the EU. On the other hand the lowest tariff rates apply in the cases of 'vegetable plaiting materials', 'hides and skin', 'wool and animal hair' and 'cotton'.

Tariff preferences on agricultural products granted under Turkey's trade agreements, are subject to tariff quotas. The tariff quotas applied in trade with the EU cover 34 items at the HS six-digit level including live bovine animals and their meat, butter, cheese and flower bulbs.

Regarding duty and tax concessions on imports we note that these concessions in Turkey are granted through two main programmes: the General Investment Encouragement Programme and Aids Granted to Small and Medium-sized Enterprise Investments. Under both programmes feasible investment projects that are found to be eligible by the Undersecretariat of the Treasury can benefit from customs duty exemptions on all machinery and equipment to be used in the physical plant. In addition under the inward processing (IP) regime Turkish manufacturers/exporters can import materials free of duties. Goods imported under the IP scheme are intended for re-export from customs territory of Turkey in the form of compensating products. The system works through suspension of duties and VAT until exports are produced, or re-imbursement based on a drawback method. Under the drawback system, import duties and VAT have to be paid when the goods enter for free circulation into Turkey.

The above considerations reveal that Turkish NPRs are, except for agricultural commodities, rather very low. Hence one could state that tariffs for Turkey are

TABLE 5
Protection in Agriculture, 2004

HS Code	Description	Number of Tariff Lines	2003 Imports ($ million)	Applied Mean Tariffs (Simple) EU (Per cent)	Applied Mean Tariffs (Weighted) EU (Per cent)	Applied Mean Tariffs (Simple) GSP (Per cent)	Applied Mean Tariffs (Weighted) GSP (Per cent)	MFN Tariffs (Simple) Third Countries (Per cent)	MFN Tariffs (Weighted) Third Countries (Per cent)
I.	**Live animals and animal products**								
1	Live animals	120	11.85	54.16	2.19	54.16	2.19	54.16	2.19
2	Meat and edible offal	241	0.18	137.89	120.43	137.96	120.43	137.96	120.43
3	Fish and sea products	479	32.41	36.15	34.16	46.07	42.39	46.07	42.39
4	Milk and dairy products; eggs; honey	229	52.34	93.30	96.91	90.26	97.28	90.26	97.28
5	Other animal products	47	33.06	3.49	7.91	3.56	7.91	3.70	7.91
II.	**Vegetable products**								
6	Plants and floriculture products	52	15.70	18.76	5.30	19.22	6.41	19.22	6.41
7	Vegetable, plants, roots and tubers	168	27.57	20.52	18.63	20.58	18.74	20.58	18.74
8	Edible fruits; citrus fruits	202	80.34	42.49	90.24	42.49	90.24	42.49	90.24
9	Coffee, tea, spices	54	24.41	38.37	39.10	38.63	40.20	38.63	40.20
10	Cereals	64	696.67	36.25	56.41	36.28	56.41	36.28	56.41
11	Products of the milling industry	120	10.16	39.84	23.43	40.06	24.77	40.06	24.77
12	Oilseeds, various seeds/fruits; industrial plants	134	477.74	15.74	10.28	16.49	10.48	16.49	10.48
13	Vegetable lacquers, resins, balsams	47	38.07	0.85	0.69	1.58	0.90	2.11	0.98
14	Vegetable plaiting materials	27	3.36	0.00	0.00	0.00	0.00	0.00	0.00
III.	**Animal or vegetable oils and fats**								
15	Animal or vegetable oils and fats	243	313.92	19.10	23.26	19.45	23.30	19.58	23.34

IV.	**Foodstuffs, beverages, tobacco**									
	16	Products made from meat, fish, crustacea	146	0.80	95.63	60.40	101.11	75.43	101.11	75.43
	17	Sugar and sweets	68	34.10	72.47	89.67	84.07	92.77	84.19	92.78
	18	Cocoa and cocoa products	29	198.90	11.64	2.09	29.76	5.63	30.48	6.28
	19	Cereal products, wheat floor, pastries	88	51.78	6.97	10.45	23.38	31.06	23.52	31.06
	20	Foods made of vegetable, fruits and other plants	381	15.37	54.44	51.28	55.02	53.37	55.06	53.44
	21	Various foods	71	157.19	5.54	2.41	13.51	15.72	15.77	18.08
	22	Alcoholic and non-alcoholic beverages	201	15.76	25.99	1.49	38.77	6.22	39.63	8.42
	23	Residues of food industry; fodders	84	199.85	7.05	1.26	7.52	2.55	7.52	2.55
	24	Processed tobacco and substitutes	204	234.88	23.28	18.83	25.75	21.69	26.88	22.93
V.	**Hides, wool and cotton**									
	4101–4103 Hides and skin		95	440.48	0.00	0.00	0.00	0.00	0.00	0.00
	5101–5103 Wool and animal hair		119	49.70	0.00	0.00	0.00	0.00	0.00	0.00
	5201–5203 Cotton		33	674.84	0.00	0.00	0.00	0.00	0.00	0.00
Total			3,746	3,891.41	42.47	19.79	45.63	21.20	45.81	21.41

Source: Own calculations.

largely a non-issue in the non-agricultural sector. We therefore turn now to consideration of non-tariff barriers (NTBs).

In Turkey import prohibition applies for 11 broad product categories such as narcotics, arms and ammunitions, and ozone-depleting substances for reasons such as environment, public security, health and public morals. Imports of 13 broad product categories such as electricity, natural gas, radioactivity-related items, explosives, telecommunications-related items and some machinery are subject to licensing. Importers of these items must obtain permission from the relevant authorities. In addition to security, safety and environmental reasons, the restrictions are intended to protect consumers, e.g. for assuring the suitability of imported vehicles for highways. In addition, Turkey has been applying import quotas on certain textile and clothing products since 1 January, 1996, as a requirement for harmonising its import policy with that of the EU.

Regarding contingent protectionism Turkey has reported initiation of 46 anti-dumping investigations, and imposition of 33 anti-dumping measures during the period 1995–2002. As of the end of 2004 Turkey had 34 definitive anti-dumping duties in force. Most of the anti-dumping investigations were against China, the EU, Korea, Thailand and Chinese Taipei, and measures have affected mostly textiles and clothing, base metal products, plastics and rubber articles, and manufacturers such as light lighters and pencils. On the other hand Turkey has so far not taken any countervailing measures, and safeguard actions under GATT Article XIX.

Regarding technical barriers to trade (product standards) we note that there is a challenge for both Turkish firms and government policy. In the case of the latter, there are a large number of norms to apply. According to Annex II of the Decision 2/97 of the 1997 Turkey-EU Association Council, Turkey was supposed to incorporate into its internal legal order 324 instruments that correspond to various EEC or EC regulations and directives. Currently, Turkey has incorporated into its legal order only 203 of these 324 instruments. In the meantime, the number of instruments that Turkey has to incorporate into its legal order has increased to 560, and Turkey has incorporated 276 of them. Thus progress has been rather slow.

Turkey also must establish the so-called quality infrastructure, a generic term encompassing the operators and operation of standardisation, testing, certification, inspection, accreditation and metrology (industrial, scientific and legal). In the EU, national quality infrastructures that function according to the same principles and obey the same rules are a critical element of the free circulation of goods in the Single Market. Turkey, as a member of a customs union with the EU and as a candidate country, has to align its national quality infrastructure to the European one. Products manufactured in a future EU member state must satisfy to the same requirements prevailing in the EU, and conformity to these requirements must be demonstrated in the same 'harmonised' way and according to the same principles.

Recently, Turkey has taken major steps to align with the *acquis*. Law 4703 on the Preparation and Implementation of Technical Legislation on Products, which entered into force in January 2002, has been supplemented by secondary legislation. This framework law provides the legal basis for harmonisation with the EC legislation. It defines the principles for product safety and for implementation of the old and new approach directives, including the conditions for placing products on the market; the obligations of the producers and distributors, conformity assessment bodies and notified bodies; market surveillance and inspection; withdrawal of products from the market; and notification procedures.[4] The legislation on market surveillance, use and affixing of the CE conformity mark, working principles and procedures for the conformity assessment bodies and notified bodies, and notification procedures between Turkey and the EU for technical regulations and standards which apply to non-harmonised regulated areas entered into force during 2002.[5] Furthermore, Turkey has adopted all of the 23 new approach directives that require affixing the CE conformity marking, and 18 of the directives entered into force up to the present time. They cover commodities and product groups such as low-voltage equipment, toys, simple pressure vessels, construction products, electromagnetic compatibility, gas appliances, personal protective equipment, machinery, medical devices, non-automatic weighing instruments, telecommunications terminal equipment, hot-water boilers, civil explosives, lifts and recreational crafts.

Overall, then, Turkey has advanced the harmonisation of its technical legislation both on a sectoral (vertical) basis and at a horizontal level. It is in the process of establishing the necessary structures on conformity assessment and market surveillance. By now Turkey has the legal basis on which accreditation could be based. In order to assign the notified bodies that would deal with the certification of products, the ministries have established the criteria for the selection of such bodies for the products covered by certain new approach directives. Although in Europe, as in Turkey, accreditation is not mandatory to be appointed as a notified

---

[4] Law 4703 is based on Council Directive 92/59/EEC on general product safety, Council Regulation 85/C136/01 on the new approach to technical harmonisation and standards, and the Council resolution of December 1989 on the global approach to conformity assessment.

[5] The legislation on market surveillance was prepared using Council Directive 92/59/EEC on general products safety, the Council resolution of December 1989 on the global approach to conformity assessment, Council Directive 88/378/EEC on the approximation of the laws of the member states on the safety of toys, and on European Commission (2000). The legislation on working principles and procedures for the conformity assessment bodies and notified bodies was prepared using the material in chapter 6 of European Commission (2000). The legislation on the use and affixing of the CE conformity mark is based on Council Decision 93/465/EEC on the modules for the various phases of the conformity assessment procedures and the rules for affixing and use of the CE conformity marking. Finally, the legislation on notification procedures between Turkey and the EU for technical legislation and standards is based on Council Directive 98/34/EC laying down a procedure for the provision of information in the field of technical standards and regulations and the relevant section of Decision 2/97 of the EC-Turkey Association Council.

body, since the Turkish Ministries did not feel adequately prepared to select
notified bodies, they made accreditation one of the criteria for their selection by
signing protocols with the Turkish National Accreditation Body, TURKAK.[6]
However, the fact that TURKAK has been a member of the European Accreditation Agency since 2003 and yet has not signed any multilateral agreement with
the European partners makes its accreditation non-functional. Thus, even though
TURKAK has given accreditation to potential notified bodies, this accreditation
is meaningless in the eyes of national accreditation bodies of the EU.

Because of this the market is also reluctant to use TURKAK, because TURKAK
accreditation is not accepted within the EU. This situation presents Turkish conformity assessment bodies with a disadvantage. The relatively large Turkish firms
wishing to obtain CE marking for products exported to the EU market usually
contact local subsidiaries of European notified bodies that use their European
laboratories for testing. But for other Turkish companies this process seems to be
expensive and slow. The small and medium-sized enterprises (SMEs) that export
products find it particularly difficult to pay the high costs. In Turkey, marking
and certification parallel to the EU system are implemented only in the automotive sector.

Other than for the automotive sector, as of 2005 Turkey is suffering from a
lack of certification bodies. To make its conformity assessment compatible with
that in the EU, Turkey has opened up the certification, testing and calibration
market to other Turkish actors. However, Turkish firms are reluctant to enter the
market for conformity assessment bodies as long as uncertainties prevail regarding the acceptance of notified bodies by the European Commission. Some of the
Turkish firms in cooperation with the notified bodies in the EU have entered the
Turkish market. Over time competition will ensure lower costs for conformity
assessment. The expense, time and unpredictability incurred in obtaining ap-
provals can then be reduced by having products evaluated in Turkey once the
Turkish notified bodies are accepted by the European Commission and joint
ventures with notified bodies in the EU increase. These savings can be particularly important where rejection of products in the EU can create delays and
necessitate additional shipping or other costs.

Although, in principle, standards are voluntary in Turkey, in the absence of a
proper market surveillance system the technical ministries and the Undersecretariat
of Foreign Trade have turned the standardisation regime and licensing before
production into a mandatory regime in order to protect the market and the consumers. This pre-market control system gives the Turkish Standards Institute
(TSE) a great deal of power. It is emphasised that the TSE has misused its power

---

[6] Under a law published on 27 October, 1999, TURKAK is the national accreditation body in all
fields. But the regulations that gave the Turkish Standards Institute (TSE) and Turkish Scientific
and Research Council (TUBITAK) the power to accredit are still in force.

in several cases of imports and has created technical barriers to trade. The TSE asked for the technical files of the imported products when they entered the Turkish market, and the processing of the files took an unusually long time. There are also cases in which products bearing the CE marking were asked for further inspection. Yet the Turkish internal market is regulated largely through mandatory standards and marking issued by the TSE. Since 2004 products covered by directives on toy safety, medical devices, active implantable medical devices, low-voltage electrical equipment, electromagnetic compatibility and machinery are not subject to mandatory controls when imported and used in the internal market. But products covered by the remaining 12 new approach directives are subject to mandatory controls.

In Turkey, 500 standards are mandatory for the domestic market as well as for imports. For all of these the TSE occupies a monopoly position, and for 500 of them TSE certification is mandatory. For these mandatory standards, manufacturers mostly need first a TSE certificate and then a Ministry of Industry and Trade licence to put the products on the market.

As argued by numerous studies of the impacts of a customs union, abolition of such real trade costs are likely to generate significant gains for Turkey. Full implementation of the EU *acquis* on technical barriers to trade, with the accompanying institutional strengthening will constitute the major change over the status quo in terms of non-agricultural merchandise trade with the EU.

b. Measures Affecting Exports

In Turkey the exportation of certain commodities is subject to registration, and the exportation of some other commodities is prohibited for various reasons including environment, health or religious reasons. All other commodities can be exported freely. Exporters are required to register with the Exporters Association and their local Chamber of Commerce. A fee of 0.05 per cent of the f.o.b. value of exports is charged as a service commission. According to the regulations of the export regime, export prohibitions have been imposed on commodities such as game and wild animals, flower bulbs, ozone-depleting substances, wood and wood charcoal, antiques and archaeological works, and grapevine, fig, hazelnut, pistachio and olive plants. Although Turkey does in general not apply export quotas, Turkish exporters of certain textiles and clothing products are faced with quotas on the US and Canadian markets. Turkey does not auction its quotas. Quotas have been allocated mainly on the basis of past performance.

Regarding export incentives we note that as a result of the customs union between the EU and Turkey as well as Turkey's commitments *vis-à-vis* the WTO, Turkey has progressively revamped the incentives provided to exporters. Changes include the abolition of most direct export subsidies, streamlining its duty concessions programmes, elimination of corporate tax exemption, and the introduction of new export credit, guarantee and insurance programmes. Currently the following export subsidies are provided:

Cash subsidies are extended to a number of agricultural products and processed agricultural goods including cut flowers, frozen vegetables, frozen fruit and olive oil. Table 6 shows the subsidies extended to these commodities. From the table it follows that subsidies are quite substantial for various commodities, but that the applied subsidy rates cannot exceed specified maximum rates. These rates are set between 10 and 20 per cent of the value of exports, and between 27 and 100 per cent of the quantities exported. The commodities under subsidy cover 25.41 per cent of total agricultural exports.

Under duty concessions we note that under the General Investment Encouragement Programme and Aids Granted to Small and Medium-sized Enterprises Investments exporter/producers' feasible investment projects, that are found to be eligible by the Undersecretariat of the Treasury, can benefit from customs duty exemptions on all machinery and equipment to be used in the physical plant. Furthermore, exporters are exempt from a number of duties such as the stamp tax, and exporters can import duty free under the inward-processing regime scheme.

Preferential export credits are extended by the Turk Eximbank, which operates a large number of export credit, guarantee and insurance schemes. It supports exporters, export-oriented manufacturers and overseas investors with short-, medium- and long-term cash and non-cash credit programmes. Moreover, export receivables are discounted in order to promote sales on deferred payment conditions and to increase export trade volumes. During 2002 Turk Eximbank provided support to 14 per cent of Turkey's total exports. Turk Eximbank also offers a variety of insurance policies for Turkish exporters, investors and overseas contractors against commercial and political risks.

In addition to the above subsidies R&D projects that aim to increase the productivity in export industries can be subsidised up to 50 per cent of the cost of the project. Furthermore, projects related to technical barriers can be subsidised up to 50 per cent of the cost of the project, and subsidies are provided to export promotion activities of firms directed to the participation in trade fairs. According to a government decision of 1997 subsidies can be provided for the contracting of market research by exporters. Subsidies can also be provided for the organisation of educational activities such as seminars and conferences by exporters. In addition the government subsidises medium- and small-scale enterprises for their hiring of skilled personnel. The aim is to increase the productivity of the exporters concerned. Finally, Turkey subsidises activities related with the promotion of trademarks, opening of branch offices in foreign countries, patents and industrial designs.[7]

---

[7] The export subsidies summarised above are consistent with WTO rules.

TABLE 6
Cash Export Subsidies, 2004

HS	Commodity	Cash Subsidies	Maximum Subsidy Rate (Per cent)	Share of Exported Quantity Eligible for the Subsidy (Per cent)	Exports in 2003 (US$1,000)
0207	Meat and edible offal of poultry (excluding 02071391, 02071399, 02071491, 02072691, 02072699, 020734, 02073591, 02072791, 02072799, 02073599, 02073681, 02073685, 02073689)	$186/tonne	20	14	15,887
040700	Birds' eggs, in shell, fresh, preserved or cooked	$6/1,000 units	10	78	10,676
040900	Honey	$65/tonne	10	32	37,090
060310	Fresh cut flowers and flower buds of a kind suitable for bouquets	$205/tonne	20	37	14,816
070190	Potatoes	$20/tonne	15		16,607
070310190011	Onions	$17/tonne	15		15,050
0710	Vegetables (uncooked or cooked by steaming or boiling in water) (excluding 071010)	$79/tonne	20	27	39,188
0712	Dried vegetables, whole, cut, sliced, broken or in powder	$370/tonne	10	20	30,291
0811	Fruits and nuts, uncooked or cooked by steaming or boiling	$78/tonne	20	41	32,265
1509	Olive oil (including 15162091014 and 15162098011)	$180/tonne	10	100	162,125
1610099, 160231, 160232	Sausages made of poultry	$250/tonne	10	22	1,069
1604	Prepared or preserved fish	$200/tonne	15	100	10,520
1806	Chocolate and other food preparations containing cocoa	$119/tonne	10	48	129,795
1902	Pasta	$66/tonne	10	32	26,848
190530	Sweet biscuits; waffles (including 19059040, 19059045)	$119/tonne	10	18	66,648
2001, 2002, 2003, 2004, 2005, 2006, 2008	Vegetables, fruits, nuts and other edible parts of plants, tomatoes prepared or preserved. Fruits, nuts, and other edible parts of plants (excluding 200811, 20081911, 20081913, 20081919014, 200819190039, 200819190049, 20081951, 20081959, 20081993, 200819999, 20081995014, 20081995003, 20081995003, 20081995009)	$68/tonne	20	51	540,160
2007	Jams, fruit jellies, marmalades, fruit or net purée (excluding 20079920, 20079951, 20079998019)	$63/tonne	20	35	58,613
2009	Fruit juices (excluding 200990)	$134/tonne	20	17	72,584

Source: www.igeme.gov.tr

Export taxes apply at the rate of $0.04 per kg on shelled hazelnuts and $0.08 per kg on unshelled hazelnuts. Semi-processed leather is subject to an export tax at the rate of $0.5 per kg.

Since passage of the Turkish law on free zones in 1985, 20 zones have been established. The zones are open to a wide range of activity, including manufacturing, storage, packaging, trading, banking and insurance. Foreign products enter and leave the free zones without payment of any customs or duties. Income generated in the zones is exempt from corporate and individual income taxation and from the value-added tax, but firms are required to make social security contributions for their employees. Additionally, standardisation regulations in Turkey do not apply to the activities in the free zones, unless the products are imported into Turkey. In contrast to most other free zones, sales to the Turkish domestic market are allowed. Goods and revenues transported from the zones into Turkey are subject to all relevant import regulations. There are no restrictions on foreign firms' operations in the free zones.[8]

4. LIBERALISATION OF SERVICES

In 2003, the services contributed 63.6 per cent to GDP, and employed 47.9 per cent of the labour force. While exports of services amounted during 2003 to $19.0 billion, imports of services amounted to $8.5 billion. Among the services, tourism is a major net foreign exchange earner. The sector is dominated by several state-owned enterprises. Some of these companies still operate under monopoly, or hold exclusive rights in several branches of the sector.

Turkey has made, as emphasized above, extensive commitments under GATS. Its schedule covers 72 activities out of a total of 161 in nine sectors. Turkey maintains MFN exemptions under Article II of the GATS, reserving the right to offer more favourable treatment to some WTO members in some specific areas of business, communication, financial and transport services. It became a party to the Interim Agreement on Financial Services in 1995, the 1997 Information Technology Agreement, the 1997 Agreement on Telecommunications Services, and the 1997 Agreement on Financial Services.

Services are not covered by the customs union agreement between Turkey and the EU. As part of the pre-accession strategy for Turkey, negotiations have started between Turkey and the EU on liberalisation of services in line with the Turkey-EU Association Council Decision of 11 April, 2000. Since joining the EU will require Turkey to adopt and implement the whole body of EU legislation in all areas – the *acquis communautaire* – Turkey will have to liberalise further its

---

[8] Free zones are not consistent with the EU rules on state aid. Turkey during the pre-accession period has to make the necessary changes.

services sectors, and with accession it will be part of the European single market for services. Recently, Turkey has been implementing autonomous reforms in the various sectors of the economy such as banking, telecommunications, natural gas and electricity.[9]

5. SUSTAINABILITY OF CURRENT ACCOUNT

Figure 1 shows developments in the current-account-to-GDP over the period 1975–2004.[10] Turkey has faced currency crises in the late 1970s, 1994 and 2001. The figure indicates that the probability of a balance of payments crisis increases in Turkey as the current-account-deficit-to-GDP ratio increases above the critical level of 5 per cent.[11] In 2004 the annual current account deficit amounted to $15.4

FIGURE 1
Current-Account-to-GDP Ratio, 1975–2004

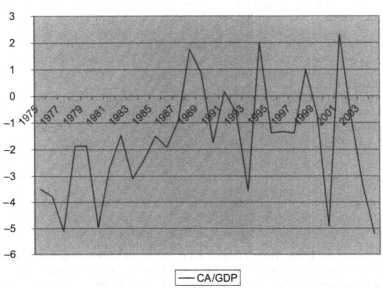

Source: Central Bank of Turkey.

---

[9] For consideration of reform efforts in the banking sector see Pazarbaşıoğlu (2005); for the telecommunications sector see Akdemir et al. (2005); for the natural gas sector see Mazanti and Biancardi (2005); for the electricity sector see Atiyas and Dutz (2005); and for the transport sector see Francois (2005).

[10] This section draws heavily on Togan and Ersel (2005).

[11] We do not state that large current account deficits are the only cause of the currency crises. During the periods prior to the crises current account deficits were financed mainly by short-term foreign borrowing. There were also other weaknesses in the Turkish economy. The 1994 and 2001 crises occurred when the country was facing large fiscal deficits, huge public debts, problems in the

billion, and the current-account-deficit-to-GDP ratio has increased to 5.1 per cent. The deficit is funded mainly by short-term funds, and foreign direct investment inflows remain weak. Total foreign debt of Turkey in 2004 reached $161.7 billion or 53.4 per cent of GDP, which reflects a significantly higher level of indebtedness than in other emerging countries.

Figure 2 shows the time path of the real exchange rate (RER) over the last two decades.[12] The figure reveals four episodes of RER developments. After the foreign exchange crisis of the late 1970s, the government pursued a policy of RER depreciation.[13] The policy continued until 1988. After 1988 the governing political party changed the policy of RER depreciation. RER started to appreciate.[14] In

---

banking sector, and high inflation rates. Budget deficit measured by the public sector borrowing requirements-to-GNP ratio amounted to 10.9 per cent during 1991–93, and to 10.4 during 1994–2003. Inflation rate during 1990–2000 fluctuated between 54.9 and 106.3 per cent, and average inflation rate amounted to 75.2 per cent. There were distortions created by the state banks, which had a substantial share in the banking sectors' total assets. These banks faced unrecovered costs from duties carried out on behalf of the government, and they covered their financing needs from markets by borrowing at high interest rates and short maturities. Currency and maturity mismatches on the balance sheets of the banks had left the public authorities little leeway for using either interest-rate or exchange rate adjustments to restore balance without undermining the stability of the banking sector. In addition Turkey lacked in the banking sector competent supervisory authorities and a regulatory framework. Thus Turkey before the 2001 crisis had neither resolved its fiscal problems, nor attained price stability and a sound banking sector. There were also major problems with governance in general.

[12] When constructing real exchange rate indices one is faced with four decisions: choice of the price index, choice of the currency basket, choice of weights and choice of mathematical formula. In the formulation of the real exchange rate we use CPI as CPI data are available on a monthly basis for a large number of countries. Choice of currency basket is composed of countries which are major competitors of Turkey in world markets as well as major suppliers of imported commodities to Turkey. The countries considered consist of: in Western Europe: Belgium, France, Germany, Greece, Italy, Netherlands, Portugal, Spain, Switzerland and the UK; in America: Brazil, Canada, Mexico and the US; in the Central and Eastern European and Commonwealth of Independent States Countries: Czech Republic, Hungary, Poland, Russia; in Asia: China, Indonesia, Japan, Korea, Malaysia, Taiwan and Thailand; and in the Middle Eastern and North African countries: Egypt, Tunisia and Morocco. For weights assigned to different countries and formula used for estimation of RER we use the approach developed by Zanello and Desruelle (1997).

[13] Until the end of the 1970s, Turkey followed a fixed and multiple exchange rate policy while experiencing relatively high inflation rates. The policy led to a loss of competitiveness and eventually to the foreign exchange crisis of the late 1970s. The GNP shrank by 0.5 per cent in 1979 and by 2.8 per cent in 1980. With the stabilisation measures of 1980, Turkey devalued its lira by about 100 per cent and eliminated the multiple exchange rate system. After May 1981, the exchange rate was adjusted daily against major currencies to maintain the competitiveness of Turkish exports. Multiple currency practices were phased out during the first two years of the 1980 stabilisation programme, and the government pursued a policy of depreciating the RER – on average by about 6 per cent annually over the period 1980–88.

[14] A drawback of the RER depreciation policy pursued during the 1980s was the decline in real wages, measured in terms of foreign currency. By the second half of the 1980s, popular support for the government had begun to fall off. In the local elections of March 1989, the governing political party suffered heavy losses. To increase political support, the government conceded substantial pay increases during collective bargaining in the public sector. Pressure then built up in the private sector to arrive at similarly high wage settlements, and real wages began to increase and the RER

1989 foreign exchange operations and international capital movements were liberalised entirely.[15] According to the government, the appreciation of the RER experienced after 1989 stemmed from market forces. During the 1990s, Turkey's public finances had deteriorated considerably. The large public sector deficits were financed by borrowing from the market at very high real interest rates.[16] Significant capital flowed into the country because it was offering not only high real interest rates but also the prospect of steady real appreciation of the exchange rate. Thus the government's implicit commitment to the RER appreciation insured the private sector, domestic and foreign, against currency risk. It encouraged capital inflows from abroad and lending to the public sector, giving rise to the phenomenon of large, arbitrage-related, short-term capital inflows. The appreciation of the RER carried on under various coalition governments until 1994 when the country was faced with another currency crisis. The RER depreciated sharply in April 1994, but thereafter it started to appreciate again. The appreciation of the RER carried on until February 2001, when the country was

---

started to appreciate. To clarify the relation between RER and real wages let $p^* E/p$ be the RER where p^* denotes the GDP deflator in the foreign country, E the exchange rate measured as domestic currency units per unit of foreign currency and p the GDP deflator in the home country, and $py = wL + rK$ the nominal GDP where y stands for real GDP, w the nominal wage rate, L total employment, r the return on capital and K the stock of capital. Expressing the capital income in the above equation as $rK = \lambda(wL)$, where λ stands for the mark-up rate, the RER can be written as $\dfrac{Ep^*}{p} = \dfrac{(y/L)Ew^*(1 + \lambda^*)}{(y^*/L^*)(1 + \lambda)w}$, where (y/L) denotes labour productivity in the home country, (y^*/L^*) labour productivity in the foreign country, λ^* the mark-up rate in the foreign country and w^* the wage rate in the foreign country. Thus, developments in the RER depend on developments in the productivity ratio $\dfrac{\rho}{\rho^*}$, relative wage ratio $\dfrac{w}{Ew^*}$, and on the relative mark-up ratio $\dfrac{(1 + \lambda)}{(1 + \lambda^*)}$. Hence, for constant values of productivity ratio and relative mark-up ratio, an increase in the relative wage ratio $\dfrac{w}{Ew^*}$ implies appreciation of the RER.

[15] Turkey opened the capital account in 1989 before it had taken measures to upgrade banking and financial market supervision and regulation, adopt international auditing and accounting standards, strengthen corporate governance and shareholder rights, and modernise bankruptcy and insolvency procedures.

[16] Real interest rate is defined as $r_t = \left[\left\{ \dfrac{\left[1 + \left(\dfrac{i_t}{100} \right) \right]}{1 + \left(\dfrac{\pi_t}{100} \right)} \right\} - 1 \right] * 100$, where i_t denotes the annual rate of interest on government bonds and treasury bills, attained as the weighted average rate in auctions during the month t weighted by total sales during the month, and π_t denotes the expected annual rate of inflation at time t over the period t to $t + 12$. In the calculations of the real interest rate, we set the expected annual rate of inflation at time t over the period t to $t + 12$ equal to the actual annual rate of inflation over the period t to $t + 12$. The average level of real interest rates over the period January 1991 to March 1993 amounted to 9 per cent, and between February 1994 and October 2003 to 25.5 per cent.

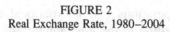

FIGURE 2
Real Exchange Rate, 1980–2004

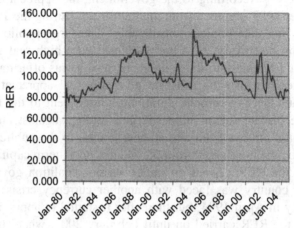

Source: The author.

faced with yet another currency crisis. After the sharp depreciation of the RER from February 2001 to April 2001, it began to appreciate, in particular after October 2001. It has appreciated during October 2001 and October 2004 by about 30 per cent. With the appreciation of the RER considerable economic recovery was observed in 2002 and thereafter.

The above considerations reveal how important current account sustainability is for a country like Turkey.[17] Here our basic presumption is that if the current account is not sustainable, then the country is expected to face an exchange rate collapse or an external debt default. Starting from the notion that under current account sustainability the country must satisfy its lifetime budget constraint, we say that the current stance of policies are sustainable if the continuation of the current government policy stance and private sector behaviour into the future does not entail a drastic policy shift or lead to a currency or balance of payments crisis.

To clarify the concept of sustainability of the current account we make use of the balance of payments relation and show that current-debt-to-GDP ratio, d_t, equals the expected discounted present value of foreign debt outstanding in period $t + n$ relative to GDP, $\Gamma_t \delta_{t,n} d_{t+n}$, plus the sum of all discounted non-interest current account plus net FDI flows to GDP ratio between period t and period $t + n$, $\Gamma_t \sum_{i=1}^{n} \delta_{t,i} A_{t+i}$, where $\delta_{t,k}$ denotes the 'k-periods ahead' discount factor used

---

[17] The purpose of this section is to emphasise the relations between current account sustainability, real exchange rate, and domestic aggregate demand policies. Our purpose is not to discuss the factors leading to currency crises in general. These factors were mentioned briefly in footnote 11 above.

to calculate the present value of assets and liabilities in period $t + k$ for period t, $\Gamma_t x_{t+k}$ the period t expectation of the variable x in period $t + k$, $A_t = tb_t + fdi_t - \Delta r_t$, tb_t the non-interest-current-account-to-GDP ratio, fdi_t the FDI-to-GDP ratio, and Δr_t the change in reserves-to-GDP ratio.[18] To translate the intertemporal budget constraint into a practically more relevant requirement we consider the budget constraint for a limited period of time n^* and add the sustainability condition that the discounted debt/GDP ratio at the end of period $t + n^*$ should not exceed the debt/GDP ratio at time t.[19]

But this sustainability condition, while useful, is not easy to assess in practice. Even under initial negative A_t values over the next few years the current account can be said to be sustainable if during the latter periods large positive non-interest-current-account-to-GDP and FDI-to-GDP and thus A_{t+i} values are assumed. Consider the year 2004. During that year we had the following values for the variables under consideration: $d_{2004} = 53.45$ per cent, $tb_{2004} = -3.54$ per cent,

---

[18] Consider the balance of payments relation, which can be written as $TB_t^\$ - i^*D_{t-1} + FDI_t + D_t - D_{t-1} - \Delta R_t = 0$ where $TB^\$$ denotes the non-interest current account, i^* the foreign rate of interest, D the stock of foreign debt, FDI the net foreign direct investment, R the foreign exchange reserves of the country, and ΔR_t the change in reserves. Also, $(TB_t^\$ - i^*D_{t-1}) = Current\ Account_t$ and $(FDI_t + D_t - D_{t-1}) = Capital\ Account_t$. All variables are measured in terms of foreign currency. If $d_t = \dfrac{E_t D_t}{p_t y_t}$ is the foreign-debt-to-GDP ratio, $tb_t = \dfrac{E_t TB_t^\$}{p_t y_t}$ the non-interest-current-account-to-GDP ratio, $fdi_t = \dfrac{FDI_t E_t}{p_t y_t}$ the FDI-to-GDP ratio, and $\Delta r_t = \dfrac{(\Delta R_t) E_t}{p_t y_t}$ the change-in-reserves-to-GDP ratio, the equation determining the time path of d_t can be written as $d_t = -tb_t + \dfrac{(1 + r^*)(1 + \eta)}{(1 + g)} d_{t-1} - fdi_t + \Delta r_t$ where r^* denotes the foreign real rate of interest and η the rate of depreciation of the RER. The equation reveals that the external-debt-to-GDP ratio decreases with increases in the non-interest-current-account-to-GDP ratio tb, the FDI-to-GDP ratio fdi, and the growth rate of GDP g. By contrast, the debt-to-GDP ratio increases with increases in the foreign real interest rate r^*, rate of depreciation of the RER η, and changes in the reserves-to-GDP ratio Δr. Following the approach of von Hagen and Harden (1994), we solve this expression forward for n periods and obtain $d_t = \Gamma_t \delta_{t,n} d_{t+n} + \Gamma_t \sum_{i=1}^{n} \delta_{t,i} A_{t+i}$ where $\delta_{t,k} = \prod_{i=1}^{k} \dfrac{1 + g_i}{(1 + r_i^*)(1 + \eta_i)}$ and $A_t = tb_t + fdi_t - \Delta r_t$. Here, $\delta_{t,k}$ can be interpreted as the 'k-periods ahead' discount factor used to calculate the present value of assets and liabilities in period $t + k$ for period t. $\Gamma_t x_{t+k}$ denotes the period t expectation of the variable x in period $t + k$. The equation shows that current-debt-to-GDP ratio equals the expected discounted present value of foreign debt outstanding in period $t + n$ relative to GDP, plus the sum of all discounted A_t's between period t and period $t + n$. Theoretically, the intertemporal budget constraint requires that $\lim \Gamma_t \delta_{t,n} d_{t+n} \le 0$ as n becomes very large, so that foreign debt remains bounded relative to GDP. If the intertemporal budget constraint were violated, private investors would realise that the government's liabilities would eventually exceed its revenue-raising capabilities. As a result, the price of the debt of the country would fall to zero, and the country would see itself barred from international capital markets.

[19] Symbolically, the current account is said to be not sustainable if $S(n^*) = d_t - \Gamma_t \delta_{t,n} d_{t+n} = \Gamma_t \sum_{i=1}^{n} \delta_{t,i} A_{t+i} < 0$.

$fdi_{2004} = 0.62$ per cent, $\Delta r_{2004} = 1.44$ per cent, $A_{2004} = -4.35$ per cent, $g_{2004} = 8.9$ per cent, $\eta_{2004} = -6.45$ per cent, and $r^*_{2004} = 5.2$ per cent. If the value of A_{2004+i} over the next few years, say three years, were to remain negative the present value $\Gamma_t \sum_{i=1}^{n} \delta_{t,i} A_{t+i}$ could turn out to be positive if one were to assume sufficiently large positive future non-interest-current-account-to-GDP and FDI-to-GDP values over the latter periods, namely from 2008 onwards. Current account will then turn out to be sustainable. The analysis thus depends on the assumptions one makes about the evolution of A_{2004+i} over time.

In the following we assume the continuation of the present policies into the future. In particular we introduce the following assumptions. We assume that $n^* = 10$, and that the government, private sector and rest of the world will not change the policies they pursue in period 2004 over the time period 2005 and 2014. In addition, we assume that there will be no accumulation/decumulation of international reserves and that the country will neither depreciate nor appreciate the RER over the next ten years so that $\Delta r_{t+i} = 0$ and $\eta_{t+i} = 0$ for $i = 1, \ldots, 10$. We suppose that the values of tb_{t+i} and fdi_{t+i} for $i = 1, \ldots, 10$ will remain unchanged at their initial values of tb_{2004} and fdi_{2004}. Furthermore, we assume that real GDP will grow at the average rate of 4.1 per cent annually and that foreign real interest rate equals 6.86 per cent over the next ten years.[20] Finally, we assume that $\Delta r_{2004} = 0$ so that $A_{2004} = -2.92$ per cent rather than the actual value of $A_{2004} = -4.36$ per cent. We then calculate the value of debt-to-GDP ratio in 2014 using the difference equation (1) and then the value of the sustainability measure (3).

When over the next ten years A_{2004+i} stays constant at -2.92 per cent, current account in 2004 turns out to be unsustainable in the sense that the actual debt-to-GDP ratio in 2004 falls short of the expected discounted present value of foreign debt outstanding in period 2014 by 25.31 per cent. The sustainability of the current account requires that the value of the sustainability measure be increased so that it becomes positive. This goal can be achieved either through an increase in the non-interest-current account-to-GDP ratio tb_t or through an increase in the FDI-to-GDP ratio fdi_t during the period 2005–14 or through a combination of

---

[20] A look at Turkey's annual GDP growth rate over the period 1980–2004 reveals that the average growth rate of GDP amounted to 4.1 per cent during 1980–89 and again 4.1 per cent during 1990–2004. Hence, for the growth rate of GDP over the time period 2004 to 2014 we take the figure of 4.1 per cent. On the other hand, we determine the foreign interest rate from eurobond issues of the Turkish Treasury. The average rate of return on Turkish US$ eurobonds during the time of issue was 10.13 per cent in 1998, 12.08 per cent during 1999, 11.61 per cent in 2000, 11.35 per cent in 2001, 10.66 per cent in 2002, 10.08 per cent in 2003 and 8.06 per cent in 2004. By deflating the nominal return figures by US CPI inflation rates observed during the following period we obtain as the average figure for the time period 1998–2004 7.84 per cent, and for the time period 2002–04 6.86 per cent. In the calculations we set the value of foreign real interest rate as 6.86 per cent. We would like to thank Tekin Çotuk of the Undersecretariat of the Treasury for providing the data on Turkish eurobonds.

increases in both the non-interest-current-account-to-GDP and FDI-to-GDP ratios. For Turkey to achieve the minimal condition for external sustainability, the value of A_t during each time period of the interval 2005–14 would have to be 0 per cent. Thus Turkey has to increase the sum of its non-interest-current-account-to-GDP ratio and its FDI-to-GDP ratio during each period of the interval 2005–14 by at least 2.92 per cent.

Suppose first that fdi_t during the time period 2005–14 remains constant at its 2004 level of 0.62 per cent. Economic theory tells us that non-interest-current-account-to-GDP ratio can be increased by decreasing aggregate demand for domestic goods and services and/or by depreciating the RER. Decreasing the aggregate demand for goods and services requires that the country uses contractionary policies. But, Turkey as of the beginning of 2005 is already in the midst of a determined campaign to turn around decades of weak performance due to pervasive structural rigidities and weak public finances. Aiming for more ambitious fiscal objective than the constant primary surplus of 6.5 per cent of GNP will be very painful after so many failed stabilisation attempts. The alternative is to depreciate the RER and keep the RER around its 'long-run equilibrium level' over time. To determine the extent of depreciation in the RER required for achieving current account sustainability we consider the elasticity of the ratio of non-interest-current-account-to-GDP with respect to the RER,

$$\theta = \left(\frac{dNICA/GDP}{dRER} \frac{RER}{NICA/GDP} \right).$$

Then starting from initial trade balance we derive that

$$\theta = (\eta_{im} + \eta_{exp} - 1),$$

where η_{im} and η_{exp} denote the import and export elasticities with respect to the RER. Estimates based on estimated Turkish import and export equations range quite widely. Here we consider the estimates of Tansel and Togan (1987) who determine the export price elasticity as 0.933 and import price elasticity as 0.472. Thus, $\theta = 0.405$. Considering the ratio of exports-to-GDP of 19.6 per cent, the parameter values imply that a reduction of the ratio of non-interest-current-account-to-GDP of 1 per cent requires a depreciation of the RER by 12.6 per cent. Thus sustainability of the current account requires that the RER be depreciated by 36.8 per cent.

Note that the above results were derived under the condition that $A_{2004+i} = 0$ for $i = 1, \ldots, 10$. Solving the difference equation determining the time path of foreign-debt-to GDP ratio dt given in footnote 18 for the value of foreign debt-to-GDP ratio in 2014 with the values of $tb_{2004+i} = -0.62$ per cent, $fdi_{2004+i} = 0.62$ per cent, $\Delta r_{2004+i} = 0$ per cent, $g_{2004+i} = 4.1$ per cent, $r^*_{2004+i} = 6.86$ per cent and η_{2004+i}

= 0 per cent we note that the debt-to-GDP ratio increases from its value of 53.45 per cent in 2004 to 69.43 per cent in 2014. The increase in debt-to-GDP ratio is thus perfectly compatible with the sustainability condition specified above.

An alternative specification of the sustainability condition requires that the ratio of the stock of foreign liabilities to GDP stay constant over time at its initial value in time period 2004. In that case, the equation determining the time path of the debt-to-GDP ratio d can be solved for the equilibrium value of the sum of tb and fdi, under the assumption that $\Delta r = 0$, as:

$$(tb + fdi) = -\left[\frac{(g - r^* - \eta - r^*\eta)}{(1 + g)}\right] d,$$

where η denotes the rate of depreciation of the RER, g the growth rate of real GDP and r^* the foreign real interest rate. Considering the same parameter values as before, the equilibrium value of $(tb + fdi)$ is determined to be 1.42 per cent.[21] Because in 2004 the actual value of $(tb_t + fdi_t)$ equalled −2.92 per cent, Turkey needs to increase the sum of its non-interest-current-account-to-GDP and FDI-to-GDP ratios over time by 4.34 per cent. Suppose again that fdi_t over time stays constant at its 2004 level of 0.62 per cent. Then the increase in tb_t, and thus in A_t over time, can be achieved by depreciating the RER by 54.7 per cent.

Finally, following the suggestion of Reinhart, Rogoff and Savastano (2003), we consider a case in which the country tries to decrease its ratio of stock of foreign liabilities to GDP from its initial value of 53.45 per cent to 40 per cent over a period of ten years. In that case, Turkey has to increase the sum of its non-interest-current-account-to-GDP ratio and its FDI-to-GDP ratio over time by 5.53 per cent. This change, under the assumption that fdi_t over time stays constant at its 2004 level, requires that the RER be depreciated by 69.7 per cent.

Once Turkey is able to attract higher levels of FDI into the country, it does not need to depreciate its currency by as much as 36.8 or 69.7 per cent in order to attain sustainability in its current account.[22] With increases in the FDI-to-GDP ratios, the depreciation rate of the RER required to attain sustainability in the current account decreases. When the FDI-to-GDP ratio increases to 3 per cent of

[21] We assume as before that η equals 0 and set the values of the parameters as $g = 0.041$, $r^* = 0.0686$ and $d_{2004} = 0.5345$ for the year 2004.
[22] The formulation of the sustainability problem through equation (1) assumes that FDI is a surer and safer form of external financing. Thus the analysis is the paper assumes that current account deficits financed mainly by FDI inflows does not lead to problems of sustainability of current account. But if FDI takes the form of purchases of stocks and if these shares can be liquidated easily in domestic markets, then it is possible to take the money out of the country as in other forms of investment. In those cases FDI makes no difference and there is no reason to separate FDI flows in equation (1). Under these conditions sustainability of the current account will require higher rates of depreciation of the RER than those obtained above.

GDP, then the system becomes sustainable under the approach of von Hagen and Harden (1994) when the RER is depreciated by 6.7 per cent. On the other hand, when the ratio of the stock of foreign liabilities to GDP stay constant over time at its initial value in time period 2004, the system becomes sustainable when the RER is depreciated by 24.7 per cent. Finally, to reduce the debt-to-GDP ratio to 40 per cent over a period of ten years, the RER needs to be depreciated by 39.7 per cent.

Finally, in order to determine the robustness of the analysis we consider pessimistic and optimistic scenarios. Under the pessimistic scenario we assume that $g = 0.031$ and $r^* = 0.0786$ and under the optimistic scenario we have $g = 0.051$ and $r^* = 0.0586$. Under the pessimistic (optimistic) scenario when the FDI-to-GDP ratio stays constant at 0.62 per cent of GDP over the period 2005–14, the system becomes sustainable under the approach of von Hagen and Harden (1994) when the RER is depreciated as before by 36.8 per cent. On the other hand, when the ratio of the stock of foreign liabilities to GDP stay constant over time at its initial value in time period 2004, the system becomes sustainable when the RER is depreciated by 67.9 (41.6) per cent. Finally, to reduce the debt-to-GDP ratio to 40 per cent over a period of ten years, the RER needs to be depreciated by 81.6 (58.1) per cent. When the FDI-to-GDP ratio increases over time from its value of 0.62 per cent, the required rate of depreciation of the RER in order to attain sustainability in the current account decreases with increases in the FDI-to-GDP ratio.

The sustainability analysis reveals that the exchange rate as of the beginning of 2005 is overvalued. According to Eichengreen and Choudhry (2005) the standard advice in such a situation would be: (i) increasing exchange rate flexibility, (ii) maintaining capital account restriction, (iii) strengthening prudential supervision, (iv) sterilising inflows, (v) loosening monetary policy, (vi) tightening fiscal policy, and (vii) negotiating a programme with the IMF. Currently, the Turkish exchange rate regime is an independent float. The Central Bank of Turkey (CBT) intervenes in the foreign exchange market in a strictly limited fashion to prevent excessive volatility without targeting a certain trend level. Regarding the second point we note that Turkey is committed not to impose any restrictions to capital account transactions. Regarding the third point it should be stressed that the soundness of the banking system is considered by Turkey as an important element for attaining a sustainable regime for capital movements. The country has been trying to develop effective systems of supervision and the necessary administrative capacity to enforce the rules in particular since the 2001 financial crisis. It realises that both domestic and international banks operating in the country should be sound and stable institutions.[23] Regarding the fourth point we note that

---

[23] However, the country still faces problems in the real sector. There is a need to strengthen corporate governance, and there is also a large informal sector in the economy, where accounting practices need to be improved.

the CBT has purchased foreign exchange through market-friendly auctions: the mechanism through which the CBT purchased foreign exchange and how much it was going to purchase daily were set in advance and announced. Whenever the reverse dollarisation process and capital inflows stopped, the CBT also stopped opening purchase auctions. In other words, it has not been aggressive in reserve accumulation. Through foreign exchange purchase auctions, the CBT purchased (as mentioned by Özatay, 2005) US$0.8 billion in 2002, $5.7 billion in 2003, and $4.1 billion in 2004. CBT did not open purchase auctions in nine months in 2002, six months in 2003, and seven months in 2004. During 2005 CBT intends to have daily auctions where it will buy foreign exchange between minimum and maximum amounts. These preannounced amounts have been set as $15 million and $45 million daily.

Regarding the fifth point it should be emphasised that Turkey is following an implicit inflation targeting policy, and will introduce inflation targeting explicitly in 2006. Monetary policy will be used for attaining the inflation target. Regarding the sixth point, we note that Turkey is following tight fiscal policy. It is committed to keep the primary surplus at 6.5 per cent of GDP over the next three years. Aiming for a more ambitious fiscal objective than the constant primary surplus of 6.5 per cent of GDP will be very painful. Finally, Turkey has negotiated recently another three-year stand-by arrangement with the IMF. Thus Turkey has been trying to follow the policies under (i), (iii), (vi), (vii) and also partially (iv).

If Turkey intends to reverse the appreciation of the RER and attain sustainability in the current account there seem to be, in principle, three feasible policy alternatives: (1) taking measures to increase FDI inflow into Turkey, (2) changing the exchange rate regime from independent float to crawling bands or managed float, and (3) imposing restrictions on capital account transactions.[24]

6. CONCLUSION

The Trade Policy Review: Turkey 2003 (TPR) is a valuable document, a compendium of information on various aspects of Turkey's economic policy and performance. The TPR praises Turkey for its trade policies pursued through a wide network of bilateral and regional trade agreements, with a view to bringing its trade regime into line with its customs union on industrial products with the EU. While commending Turkey for conforming to the commitments to the multilateral trading system, the report points out among others the following issues for improvement. With regard to macroeconomic policies, it highlighted the importance of attaining macroeconomic stability. It stressed the need to speed up

---

[24] See Togan and Ersel (2005) for a discussion of these points.

privatisation. With regard to trade policies, the report states that only 46.3 per cent of tariff lines are bound. Turkey, by increasing the percentage of bound tariff lines and then decreasing the average level of bound tariff rates, will introduce more predictability to its trade regime. In addition, the report stresses that agriculture and services are highly protected in Turkey. According to TPR, Turkey will benefit from further liberalisation of agricultural and services sectors. Finally, Turkey needs to take measures to increase foreign direct investment flows. In addition to the points emphasised in the TPR, we believe that Turkey needs to pay attention to the issue of sustainability of the current account.

REFERENCES

Akdemir, E., E. Başçı and G. Locksley (2005), 'A Comparative Analysis of Turkish Telecommunications Sector', in B. Hoekman and S. Togan (eds.), *Turkey: Economic Reform and Accession to the European Union* (The World Bank, forthcoming).

Atiyas, I. and M. Dutz (2005), 'Competition and Regulatory Reform in the Turkish Electricity Industry', in B. Hoekman and S. Togan (eds.), *Turkey: Economic Reform and Accession to the European Union* (The World Bank, forthcoming).

Commission of the European Communities (2004), 'Regular Report on Turkey's Progress Towards Accession – 2004,' COM(2004) 656 final (Brussels).

Dutz, M., M. Us and K. Yılmaz (2005), 'Foreign Direct Investment Challenges: Competition, the Rule of Law, and EU Accession', in B. Hoekman and S. Togan (eds.), *Turkey: Economic Reform and Accession to the European Union* (The World Bank, forthcoming).

Eichengreen, B. and O. Choudhry (2005), 'Managing Capital Inflows: Eastern Europe in an Asian Mirror', paper presented at the Turkish Central Bank Conference on Macroeconomic Policies for EU Accession (Ankara, 6–7 May).

European Commission (2000), 'Guide to the Implementation of Directives based on the New Approach and the Global Approach', (Brussels).

Foreign Investment Advisory Service (2001a), 'Turkey: A Diagnostic Study of the Foreign Direct Investment Environment' (World Bank and the Treasury of Turkey, Ankara).

Foreign Investment Advisory Service (2001b), 'Turkey: Administrative Barriers to Investment' (World Bank and the Treasury of Turkey, Ankara).

Francois, J. (2005), 'Accession of Turkey to the EU: Implications for the Transportation Sector', in B. Hoekman and S. Togan (eds.), *Turkey: Economic Reform and Accession to the European Union* (The World Bank, forthcoming).

Mazzanti, M. R. and A. Biancardi (2005), 'Institutional Endowment and Regulatory Reform in Natural Gas', in B. Hoekman and S. Togan (eds.), *Turkey: Economic Reform and Accession to the European Union* (The World Bank, forthcoming).

Organisation for Economic Co-operation and Development (2004), *OECD Economic Surveys: Turkey* (Paris: OECD).

Özatay, F. (2005), 'Monetary Policy Challenges for Turkey in European Union Accession Process', paper presented at the Turkish Central Bank Conference on Macroeconomic Policies for EU Accession (Ankara, 6–7 May).

Pazarbaşıoğlu, C. (2005), 'Costs of European Union Accession: The Potential Impact on Turkish Banking Sector', in B. Hoekman and S. Togan (eds.), *Turkey: Economic Reform and Accession to the European Union* (The World Bank, forthcoming).

Reinhart, C., K. Rogoff and M. Savastano (2003), 'Debt Intolerance', *Brookings Papers on Economic Activity*, 1–74.

Tansel, A. and S. Togan (1987), 'Price and Income Effects in Turkish Foreign Trade', *Weltwirtschaftliches Archiv*, **123**, 521–34.

Togan, S. and H. Ersel (2005), 'Macroeconomic Policies for Turkey's Accession to the EU', in B. Hoekman and S. Togan (eds.), *Turkey: Economic Reform and Accession to the European Union* (The World Bank, forthcoming).

von Hagen, J. and I. J. Harden (1994), 'National Budget Process and Fiscal Performance', *European Economy. Reports and Studies 3. Towards Greater Fiscal Discipline*, 311–93.

Zanello, A. and D. Desruelle (1997), 'A Primer on the IMF's Information Notice System', IMF Working Paper WA/97/71 (Washington, DC: International Monetary Fund).

4

2004 Trade Policy Review – The United States

Thomas J. Prusa

1. INTRODUCTION

THE World Trade Organisation's (WTO) Trade Policy Review plays a fundamentally important role in the auditing and surveillance of national trade policies. In simplest terms a Trade Policy Review (TPR) gives WTO members an opportunity to monitor and comment on each Member's trade policies. Each TPR contains two parts: a policy statement prepared by the government under review, and a detailed report prepared independently by the WTO Secretariat. These two reports, together with the proceedings of the Trade Policy Review Body, are published after the review meeting.

Reviews are conducted on a regular, periodic basis. The largest traders like the United States, the European Union, Japan and Canada are examined every two years. The next 16 countries in terms of their share of world trade are reviewed every four years. The smaller traders and least-developed countries are reviewed every six years (or sometimes longer).

There are several objectives to the TPR. First, Member countries believe that regular monitoring increases the transparency and understanding of trade policies and practices. In turn the transparency and clarity resulting from the TPR will encourage Members to adhere to the negotiated rules and fulfil their commitments. (Whether this belief is borne out is something I will discuss below.) Second, the TPR provides Member countries with a unique opportunity to discuss and comment on other Members' trade policies. It is not that Member countries are talking trade policy that make the TPR special – one can hardly walk down the hall at the WTO without engaging in some type of policy discussion. Rather, what makes the TPR distinctive is that the policy discussion is neither directly related to a specific negotiation nor part of a specific policy dispute. In a sense, the TPR can be thought of shining a bright light on a country's trade policies and rules with the belief being that the bright light improves the quality of public and intergovernmental debate on the issues. Third, the TPR process enables a multilateral assessment of the effects of each Member's policies on the world trading system.

The TPR plays an especially important role for smaller countries. Large traders like the United States and the European Union (or OECD members more generally) hardly need the WTO to monitor what other countries are doing. Large countries have devoted considerable legal and economic resources to keeping tabs on other Members. Developing countries, on the other hand, have not made such investments and hence are likely the greatest beneficiaries of the system. In a sense, the TPR essentially solves a public good problem – WTO members would like to monitor other Members' policies but apparently few believe the private gain exceeds the private costs. WTO Members correctly realised, however, that substantial benefits accrue to the overall trading system that are not internalised by individual members.

In early 2004 the WTO concluded its seventh TPR of the United States. In many respects the United States is the 900-pound gorilla in the WTO. By virtue of its economic size the United States' macroeconomic and trade policies have a profound influence on the world trading system. Its size, its historical role in the founding and development of the GATT/WTO, and its ongoing leadership in widening the scope of the WTO also mean that US policies carry greater weight than the typical country. While the old maxim 'when the US sneezes the rest of the world catches a cold' still holds, perhaps as significant is the fact that US policies often serve as the template for those adopted by other Members. As a role model US policies and actions (whether good or bad) are often adopted by other Members. Thus, shining a bright light on US trade policies tells us more than just what the US has done, it is a strong indicator of what to expect from other Members.

This review was conducted during 2002–03, an extraordinary period for the United States. In a 12-month period the United States (i) went into a recession for the first time in more than a decade, (ii) experienced the terrorist attacks on 11 September, 2001, (iii) passed a farm Bill which increased government farm outlays by about 80 per cent, (iv) experienced a sharp fall in stock prices, (v) endured numerous corporate scandals, and (vi) initiated and (mostly) enacted the largest safeguard action in history.

Considering the magnitude of these events, the US argues that its economic performance is remarkable given the lacklustre performance of many of its trading partners. Feeble growth in foreign demand is also a main justification for US dumping and safeguard protection. The open US market is an easy dumping ground for foreign producers. The US's bulging trade deficit is partly due to the fact that the economic growth of its major trading partners is below trend. Despite the strains created by the trade deficit, the US maintains that it has largely resisted protectionist pressures and is fully committed to the multilateral trading system of the WTO.

The WTO Secretariat's report acknowledges the robustness of the US economy and the vital role the US plays in the ultimate success of the WTO. Nevertheless, the TPR paints a less sanguine picture of US macroeconomic and trade policies. The discussion and analysis in the TPR are both highly complementary and also highly critical of the US. This criticism of the US is especially blunt at the end of the report – the final 50 pages contain a long list of frank opinions of the US's actions by Members.

In this article, I will not make any attempt to summarise all the rhetoric, tables, figures and trends included in this very comprehensive TPR. For the most part, most of the facts are widely known and are not subject to any real dispute. The US is unanimously acknowledged as having an open and transparent system. Despite the many external and internal challenges the WTO report notes that the US economy has remained amongst the world's most competitive, and has continued to support global growth by keeping its import market largely open. The TPR also emphasises that recent US macroeconomic policy has been directed, increasingly successfully, towards recovering and sustaining growth, with benefits to the global economy, including through trade transmission. The report also recognises the high level of and the continuing impressive growth in US labour productivity.

Instead, I have chosen to focus on the key policy issues that are the primary sources of tension between the US and other WTO Members: (1) US agricultural policy, (2) US contingent protection, (3) US steel safeguard action, and (4) the proliferation of regional and bilateral trade agreements. Each of the issues were relevant for the immediate 2002–03 self-study, and each are likely to have continuing implications for how the US relates to other Members.

2. KEY ISSUES

a. Issue No. 1: Agricultural Policy

The United States is among the world's largest agricultural producers and exporters. Because of its size, both as a market and as an exporter, its agricultural policies greatly influence world trade and prices. The 1996 US farm bill introduced direct and decoupled payments and moved away from the long-established price support mechanisms. Under the 1996 bill, a schedule of declining fixed payments was put in place.

In a marked U-turn, the 2002 farm bill increased loan rates for some crops and introduced a counter-cyclical payments programme for crops; both policies have production-enhancing impacts. The bill authorises increases in support for farm programme crops (wheat, feed grains, rice and cotton) when world market prices decline. These counter-cyclical payments would be additional to continued underlying support through fixed payments. This is a hugely costly bill with government expenditure authorisations totalling more than $170 billion over ten years. Estimates are that the 2002 payments increase total farm payments over the 1996 basis by about 80 per cent.

Not surprisingly, the US agricultural policy discussion focuses on other aspects of the bill. First, the US argues that the support package was designed to be decoupled from production, does not subsidise exports, and is considered (by the US) 'minimally market distorting'. Second, the US emphasises that the 2002 farm bill was the first US farm bill to explicitly recognise that spending had to be contained within international WTO obligations. Despite the mandate, there appears to be a significant probability that farm spending will go above WTO limits.

The divergent views on US agriculture policy reflect serious disagreement between the US and other Members. Reviewing the TPR one finds that Member countries devote dozens of pages to questions and comments on the farm bill. By contrast, the US devotes less than one page of its discussion of all agriculture policy.

There are at least three serious problems with the US's position. First, the legislation goes against the spirit of reducing farm subsidies and runs counter to the US's long-standing calls for reductions in farm support. An 80 per cent increase in farm subsidies is hardly what Members expected from a country that claims the mantle of WTO leadership and regularly demands other Members reduce their subsidy payments.

Second, the bill puts the US in the awkward position of having to defend another questionable trade policy.[1] Despite the US's insistence that the farm bill is WTO consistent, the position is tenuous at best. Certainly if a Member were to bring the policy before the DSB the US farm bill would be an extremely tough policy to defend. The US bill essentially provides price insurance to farmers. If prices are high, small payments are made; if prices fall, larger payments are given. It is hard to imagine a panel determining that such price insurance does not distort domestic production. Moreover, given the demand elasticity for agricultural products, price effects of even modest increases in production will be significant. Moreover, given that the US exports approximately 40 per cent of its corn, wheat, rice and soybean production, one would expect farmers in other countries to be affected. It should be stressed, however, that given Japan's and the EU's own agricultural entanglements it is unclear what Member(s) would challenge the US's farm policy. Poor developing countries are the most grievously affected parties but these countries rarely initiate WTO disputes; hence, the fact that many other Members also have questionable agricultural policies may spare the US farm bill from further WTO scrutiny.

Third, the US had not notified the WTO of any domestic agricultural support payments since 2000, a suspiciously long lag which creates even more doubts

---

[1] The US has been subject to more WTO disputes than any other WTO Member (p. xviii).

about the legality of US agricultural policy. One might argue that the holdup is simply due to bureaucratic delay, but one can only wonder if there is more to the delay. For the twelve months ending September 2000 the US reported that it provided over $17 billion in agricultural support. The US's WTO farm support ceiling is only $19 billion. Given the marked increase in support incorporated in the 2002 farm bill it would seemingly not take much for the US to run foul of the ceiling. Numerous countries commented on the fact that the US is precariously close to its support ceiling. Members have asked how the United States intends to monitor expenditures during each reporting period so that action, if necessary, could be taken within the reporting period to ensure that the United States complies with its annual commitment level. It is more than a little ironic that the US stresses the openness and transparency of its system but then fails to report even the fairly simple calculation of farm support payments.

b. Issue No. 2: Contingent Protection

Contingency measures are a key form of protection against imports into the United States. The active use of anti-dumping (AD) and countervailing duty (CVD) measures has likely made the unfair trade statutes the US's largest trade impediment (Gallaway, Blonigen and Flynn, 1999). As measured by the number of AD filings, the US is the world's heaviest AD user (Prusa, 2005). The TPR reveals that US AD activity was fairly stable from 1980 to the late 1990s, but surged by 25 per cent over the last five years. For example, in 2001 the US initiated more AD investigations than in any year since 1992. By contrast, CVD activity has significantly lessened over time; in recent years the US initiates only a handful of cases annually.

The US's long-standing position is that trade remedies are an integral part of the current rules-based international trading system. The US does not believe the AD and CVD statutes need significant changes but only need 'clarification and improvement'. The TPR makes it clear that the US's position is not universally held. WTO Members raised a number of issues with the US's contingent protection procedures, many which related to specific cases. Overall, however, two recurring themes emerge: (i) AD imposes greater costs on foreign suppliers than the US publicly recognises, and (ii) the US refuses to amend their statutes even after the Dispute Settlement Body determines that particular provisions are WTO inconsistent.

(i) Costs

The language in the TPR seems to indicate that Members recognise that the true impact of AD/CVD protection is greater than generally acknowledged. This is a view held by most academics, but the TPR's bluntness is surprising. For one thing, the spectre of AD/CVD actions creates uncertainty for foreign suppliers.

Thus, even if a case is never initiated, foreign suppliers are intimidated by the prospect of an expensive, highly unpredictable legal proceeding. Additionally as the TPR notes, preliminary duties are almost always applied. This means that trade patterns are distorted before any serious evidence that an injurious, unfair action has occurred. The *investigation* distorts trade.[2] Member countries are concerned that the law is more unfair than the underlying unfair trade that it was designed to protect against.

(ii) Illegal rules and methods

Trading partners aggressively questioned the rules and methods used by the United States concerning AD and CVD investigations and measures. Perhaps the single biggest issue over which Members expressed dismay involves the US's refusal to change its AD and CVD statutes even after the WTO Dispute Settlement Body has found them to be in violation of the WTO agreement. The WTO rulings against the Anti-dumping Act of 1916 and the Continued Dumping and Subsidy Offset Act (often referred to as the Byrd Amendment) are two prime examples of the US's intransigence.

The Unfair Competition Act, better known as the Anti-Dumping Act of 1916, contained provisions pertaining to international price discrimination remedies. It allowed remedies far in excess of what is permissible under WTO rules, providing not only for criminal punishment for any violation, but also allowing any person harmed by a violation of the Act to sue for treble damages. The WTO rejected the 1916 Act more than three years before the TPR report, and yet as of the report's publication the US had still refused to repeal the law.

The Continued Dumping and Subsidy Offset Act of 2000 (CDSOA) is even a more blatant rejection of the US's WTO commitments. The Byrd Amendment introduced a system under which AD and CVD duties assessed are distributed to members of the affected US industry who supported the petition for investigation. Under the CDSOA, 'affected domestic producers' may receive a portion of the assessed AD or CVD duties to cover certain qualifying expenditures. The CDSOA defines 'affected domestic producer' as any manufacturer, producer, farmer, rancher or worker representative who was a petitioner or interested party in support of the petition with respect to which an anti-dumping duty order or a countervailing duty order has been entered; qualifying expenditures encompass most fixed and some variable costs. Allocations under the CDSOA are distributed on an annual basis.

As of the date of the TPR report CDSOA had resulted in disbursements totalling almost $1 billion (i.e., about $250 million per year). While disbursements thus far have been relatively modest the amounts sought are anything but humble: in 2001

---

[2] Staiger and Wolak (1994) find that about half of an AD/CVD's ultimate protection occurs when the preliminary duty is levied.

US companies filed 894 separate claims seeking in total $1.2 trillion (Ikenson, 2004). In 2002 the number of claims jumped to 1,089 totalling $1.4 trillion. Said differently, in 2001 and 2002 the companies seeking Byrd payouts have requested payouts close to 10 per cent of gross US domestic product. The requested payouts are so ludicrously large that one cannot help but be reminded of the US's accounting scandals over the past decade.

Moreover, none of these totals include any revenue collected in cases where the parties are still engaged in legal appeals. For instance, in the softwood lumber, a dispute that both NAFTA and WTO panels have rejected, reportedly more than $4 billion in revenue has been collected but not yet distributed. If the US were to distribute the softwood lumber money, the Byrd dispute would rival the Foreign Sales Corporation dispute in size.

In a prominent case the European Union and ten other countries – Australia, Brazil, Canada, Chile, India, Indonesia, Japan, Mexico, South Korea and Thailand – sought consultations with the United States over the Byrd Amendment. Failing resolution, a WTO dispute settlement panel was appointed to adjudicate the matter. In late 2001 WTO Members challenged the CDSOA and in July 2001 requested the establishment of a Panel. A Panel Report was issued in September 2002; the United States appealed the case, and in January 2003 the Appellate Body affirmed the Panel's findings that the CDSOA was inconsistent with the WTO Agreement. The Appellate Body determined that the 'offsets' under the CDSOA were a non-permissible specific action against dumping or a subsidy and that they nullified or impaired benefits accruing to the complaining parties.[3] The 'reasonable period of time' for implementation was determined by arbitration and expired in December 2003.

Despite the WTO decision, there appears to be little chance that the Byrd Amendment will be repealed in the near future, if ever. At first glance, the US's defiance is perplexing since it is widely acknowledged that it was only enacted by deft political manoeuvring by Senator Byrd. The CDSOA was never directly voted on but rather was slipped in an omnibus appropriations bill at the 11th hour without any debate. With such chicanery at the origin of the bill and with overwhelming foreign opposition, it would seem obvious that Congress would repeal the Act.

---

[3] Interestingly, the Appellate Body ruled that CDSOA was not an incentive to file petitions since the AD Agreement does not speak to what an industry's motivation might be in filing a case. While this may be correct legally, it is certainly not economically. Under US law a case can only be initiated if at least 25 per cent of the domestic industry supports the case and at least 50 per cent of the domestic industry does not oppose the case (firms can declare 'no position' toward the case). Following the passage of the Byrd Amendment it is now common practice for 'sign-up' sheets to be posted on the Internet warning firms that unless they support the case they will be entitled to no Byrd payout. Does the payout matter? In the recent shrimp case it was estimated that the typical payout could be more than ten times the annual wages of an average shrimper.

Amazingly, the opposite has happened. Congress has drawn a line in the sand over this issue. The WTO decision regarding CDSOA has become the poster child for those in Washington who believe the WTO is biased against the US and overreaches by attempting to extend obligations to the US that were not explicitly negotiated. A former counsel to the Senate Finance Committee has suggested that the only way the issue will ever be resolved is if complainants adopt their own versions of the Byrd Amendment.

c. Issue No. 3: Steel Safeguard Action

Safeguard investigations are carried out under Sections 201–204 of the US Trade Act of 1974. Domestic industries seriously injured or threatened with serious injury by increased imports may petition the US International Trade Commission (USITC) for import relief. The USITC determines whether an article is being imported in such increased quantities that it is a substantial cause of serious injury, or threat thereof, to the US industry producing an article like or directly competitive with the imported article. If the USITC makes an affirmative determination, it recommends to the President relief that would address the serious injury or threat thereof, and facilitate the adjustment of the domestic industry to import competition. The President makes the final decision whether to provide relief and the form and amount of relief within 60 days from receipt of a USITC report. Since a safeguard measure requires Presidential action, an affirmative determination of injury is a necessary but not sufficient condition for its application. Because of the requirement that the President must make the final decision, safeguard actions have largely fallen out of favour – US industries have realised that the more easily granted anti-dumping protection can offer nearly the same protection as a safeguard protection.

The US initiated only one safeguard investigation since 2000 but in size, scope and resulting controversy and trade tensions that one case generated was enormous. The steel safeguard (initiated in June 2001) was the largest safeguard investigation in US history, covering more products, tariff line-items and countries than any previous case.

What made the case even more unique was the fact that it was initiated by the President. While self-initiations are possible under US law, the President has initiated a safeguard investigation only a handful of times since 1950.[4] Another unusual aspect of the case was its scope. Typically a safeguard action involves a single, well-defined product. For instance, the four most recent safeguard cases prior to the steel safeguard case involved wheat gluten, lamb meat, steel wire rod

---

[4] The move was widely interpreted as a political move. The potential political gain to the President was substantial as three key swing states, West Virginia, Ohio and Pennsylvania, are home to large steel-making facilities.

and circular welded carbon quality line pipe – all precisely specified investigations. By contrast, the steel safeguard case encompassed essentially all steel products. For perspective, the USITC organised its investigation by dividing the steel safeguard investigation into 34 separate products.

In October 2001, the USITC issued affirmative determinations of serious injury with respect to about half of the steel product categories. In March 2002, the President announced the decision to impose safeguard measures with regard to twelve steel products. The measures announced by the President consisted of tariffs ranging from 8 to 30 per cent and a tariff rate quota for steel slab. In most cases, the tariff imposed was higher than the consensus recommendation of the USITC. In an attempt to quell the domestic firestorm following the decision and in the hope of appeasing foreign governments 727 steel products (usually defined by a specific tariff line-item) affected by the measures were excluded.[5] In March 2003 the tariff levels were adjusted downward and the tariff quota was expanded. The safeguard measures on steel products applied to all countries, except Israel and Jordan, Canada and Mexico (NAFTA partners), and most developing countries with a market share of less than three per cent for each product.

To no one's surprise, the US safeguard measures applied in March 2002 were immediately challenged at the WTO by the EU, Japan, Korea, China, Switzerland, Norway, New Zealand and Brazil; it was agreed to refer all the complaints to a single panel. The Panel Report, issued in July 2003, concluded that the safeguard measures imposed by the United States were inconsistent with the Agreement on Safeguards and GATT 1994. In particular, the United States had acted inconsistently (i) by failing to demonstrate that 'unforeseen developments' had resulted in increased imports causing serious injury to the relevant domestic producers; (ii) with respect to the facts supporting its determination of 'increased imports'; (iii) by failing to provide a reasoned and adequate explanation for most products that a 'causal link' existed between any increased imports and serious injury to the relevant domestic producers; and (iv) by failing to comply with the requirement of 'parallelism' between the imports for which the conditions for safeguard measures had been established, and the imports which were subjected to the safeguard measure. In response to the WTO decision, ongoing domestic opposition by steel consumers, and the threat of retaliatory tariffs by affected parties, the US terminated the safeguard case in November 2003.

---

[5] A couple of comments are in order on the exclusion issue. First, to my knowledge the number of exclusions constitutes another record. The fact that over 700 products were ultimately excluded gives a sense of the vast scope of the action. Second, almost all of the excluded products involved very small import volume. A half a dozen exclusions accounted for approximately half of all the excluded import volume. Interestingly, these few large-volume exclusions all involved steel products that were purchased by US steel mills, not steel consumers. With the exception of products destined for use in US steel mills, no exclusions involved large volume.

There are three important lessons that can be learned from this escapade. First, when in doubt domestic politics trumps WTO commitments. Despite that the US almost surely knew its decision was inconsistent with its WTO obligations, it still enacted the safeguard measures. Why do I say that the US 'knew' its decision would be overturned by the WTO? Every US safeguard action since the completion of the Uruguay Round has been found to be inconsistent with the WTO agreement. Moreover, every reason cited by the DSB in its steel safeguard report had been cited in one (or more) prior decisions. Given this history and the direct relevance for the steel case, US policymakers could have anticipated what the WTO's decision would be.

Second, until amended it appears that the US safeguard provision is inconsistent with the WTO safeguard agreement. The dilemma is that the USITC bases its decisions on US law, not the WTO agreement. The safeguard agreement is not part of the Doha agenda; therefore, the burden for resolving the inconsistencies between the US statute and the WTO statute lies with the US Congress. Unfortunately, if Congress's intransigence over the Byrd Amendment is an indication, there is very little prospect that the US will amend its safeguard provisions. It appears that, in the long run, the WTO Members will have to negotiate directly with the US if there is a desire to have the US comply with the WTO.

Third, the time it takes for the WTO DSB to reach a final decision regarding the consistency of a safeguard action largely neutralises the effectiveness of the review. The time required for the DSB to make its decision (and for the affected country to exhaust all of its appeals) means that countries can enact measures for a period of two to three years before Members can retaliate. In the previous safeguard cases that were found inconsistent by the DSB, the US did not end the measures until more than 30 months had passed. The fact that the steel safeguard measures were ended after only 18 months was due to the sustained outcry by domestic steel users as much as it was due to the threat of retaliation; again, this suggests that domestic politics trumps WTO rules.[6] Given that the WTO allows automatic compensation if a safeguard action remains in place for more than 36 months, safeguard cases have a practical life of only three years even without the DSB decision. Given the time required for the DSB to sanction retaliation, the WTO dispute process only slightly shortens the period of protection.

d. Issue No. 4: Regional Trade Agreements

More than any other country the United States has aggressively pursued a series of regional and bilateral initiatives to promote free trade. Over the review

---

[6] If it had chosen to do so, the US could have appealed against the WTO decision and delayed foreign retaliation by another 6 to 12 months.

period the US concluded bilateral agreements with Singapore and Chile, and a regional agreement with the Central American countries of Guatemala, Honduras, El Salvador and Nicaragua (known as the Central American Free Trade Area or CAFTA).[7] The US was also in the final stages of negotiations of bilateral agreements with Australia and Morocco and had announced its intent to negotiate six more FTAs: the US-Southern Africa Free Trade Agreement, and agreements with Thailand, Panama, Colombia, Peru and Bahrain.

The number and variety of regional and bilateral negotiations occurring simultaneously left numerous Members perplexed. If the US successfully negotiates so many FTAs, won't the end result be similar to what could have been achieved in a multilateral forum? Was the US pursuing regional and bilateral agreements at the expense of the multilateral approach favoured by the WTO. Were regional agreements diverting attention away from successfully completing the Doha Round?

The US's position reflects five principles. First, the US presumes these regional and bilateral agreements could act to accelerate and deepen multilateral liberalisation. Second, the US believes that the regional agreements create a climate for 'competitive liberalisation' and encourage countries to come to the negotiating table. Third, the US sees regional and bilateral agreements as a way to lock-in broader reform agendas among the participants. Fourth, the US emphasises that all negotiations are done in accordance with WTO rules on such agreements. Finally, the US states repeatedly that the Doha Round remains a priority in US liberalisation efforts.

It is clear that the current US embrace of regional and bilateral agreements reflects an important shift in its thinking. The Clinton administration's philosophy was that all lateral agreements, whether be multi-, uni-, tri-, plurilateral were beneficial. The current US position goes further. The current US view is that regional and bilateral agreements act as an incubator and catalyst for multilateral liberalisation. In other words, the countries with whom the US is negotiating need the regional agreement in order to prepare themselves for multilateral liberalisation. To support this view the US reminds Member countries that between 1934 and 1945, the United States entered into 32 reciprocal trade agreements, many of which had clauses that foreshadowed those currently in the GATT.

Members' comments on this issue reflect grave doubt about the ultimate effect of these agreements. Four key criticisms were expressed. First, despite US protestations to the contrary, many countries expressed concerns that negotiating and administrative resources were being distracted and diverted away from the multilateral process. Even if one assumes that the US has the capacity to

---

[7] Since the TPR was published Costa Rica and the Dominican Republic have also joined CAFTA.

engage in multiple simultaneous negotiations, it is not at all clear that its bilateral and regional partners have the capacity to do so. Members are concerned about the capacity of potential partners to participate in multiple agreements. In effect, the US's embrace of bilateral and regional agreements hinder progress toward multilateral liberalisation because other countries cannot focus on Doha.

Second, there was a fear that trade and regulatory structures based on preferential agreements could hinder trade. At one level this fear could be interpreted as a standard trade diversion argument. Countries that did not belong to the free-trade arrangement would find their competitiveness *vis-à-vis* the US market lessened. But, at another level it appears that many Members believe that the asymmetry between the United States and the separate bilateral partners might lead to agreements that might liberalise less than a multilateral agreement. For example, as part of a 'grand deal' the US might liberalise its sugar sector. But as part of CAFTA, the US sees no need to surrender its sugar protection. And, once the CAFTA deal is done, CAFTA countries might be less motivated to push for liberalised sugar trade.

Third, there is also a risk that the growing number of preferential tariff schemes could greatly complicate the US trading regime. In a few years it may be impossible to calculate average tariff rates for the US. The NAFTA agreement suggests the problem. In 2002, 54 per cent of total US imports from Canada entered under the NAFTA regime, and 45 per cent entered at MFN rates. For Mexico, the import figures were 62 per cent under the NAFTA regime and 37 per cent at MFN rates. The US suggests that trade taking place outside of the NAFTA regime largely reflects zero MFN rates. Alternatively, such trade may reflect exporters availing themselves of low MFN rates rather than zero-duty NAFTA rates, if, for example, the margin of preference offered under NAFTA is not sufficiently attractive to offset the cost of complying with rules of origin requirements. In other words, many Mexican and Canadian firms opt to pay a tax rather than fill-out the necessary paperwork. The costs associated with complying with rules of origin will only increase as the number of country-specific rules of origin increase. Moreover, the greater is the trade that enters under the MFN regime, the lower is the 'cost' to the US of signing the bilateral agreement (as the primary benefit to its partners is preferential access).

Fourth, as more and more regional and bilateral agreements are signed, Members felt it was inevitable that vested interests will develop that actively discourage multilateral liberalisation. These vested interests may appear within the US but also within its regional and bilateral partner countries. For example, once a US firm has committed resources to build a production facility in Chile, that firm has a commercial interest in having other foreign competitors, say India, to continue to face higher MFN tariffs (McLaren, 1997).

3. CONCLUDING THOUGHTS

The fervent belief of WTO Members is that transparency and clarity are cornerstones of an effective trading system. The hope is that the transparency and clarity resulting from the TPR will encourage Members to adhere to the negotiated rules and fulfil their commitments.

Much of the discussion and comments regarding US trade policy over the most recent period casts doubt on whether this view is valid. The US steel safeguard action is the most obvious example of the failure of the system. Given prior WTO decisions, there could be little doubt that the steel safeguard decision was inconsistent with the US's WTO obligations. Not only did this fact not impact US decision-makers, but even in this TPR the US continues to argue that its safeguard statute is WTO consistent and that the steel safeguard decision fully complied with WTO rules.

The US intransigence with respect to repealing the Byrd Amendment is another example. More than two years have passed since the WTO DSB definitively ruled against the US and yet there is no indication that Congress has any intention of repealing the statute. The discussion in the TPR leaves no doubt that all other Members unambiguously oppose the US and, yet again, the shining light of the TPR appears to have no impact on US policies. If the experience with the Foreign Sales Corporation is any indication, it will take the imminent threat of large trade sanctions before Congress is motivated to repeal the provision.

At the end of the day, one cannot read the TPR without having a greater sense of the complexities of modern trade policy and trade policy negotiations. In most easily measured dimensions, the United States has among the world's most liberal and transparent trading systems. However, in countless less tangible dimensions, the United States gives the impression that it loves the rhetoric of free and open trade as long as one is referring to its partners. If the US is to truly be the leading advocate for free trade, it must be willing to drop its pretence that all aspects of its rules are WTO consistent.

REFERENCES

Gallaway, M. P., B. A. Blonigen and J. E. Flynn (1999), 'Welfare Costs of US Antidumping and Countervailing Duty Laws', *Journal of International Economics*, **49**, 2, 211–44.

Ikenson, D. (2004), ' "Byrdening" Relations: US Trade Policies Continue to Flout the Rules', *Center for Trade Policy Studies Free Trade Bulletin No. 5* (Cato Institute).

McLaren, J. (1997), 'Size, Sunk Costs, and Judge Bowker's Objection to Free Trade', *American Economic Review*, **87**, 3, 400–20.

Prusa, T. J. (2005), 'Anti-dumping: A Growing Problem in International Trade', *The World Economy*, **28**, 5, 683–700.

Staiger, R. W. and F. A. Wolak (1994), 'Measuring Industry Specific Protection: Antidumping in the United States', *Brookings Papers on Economic Activity: Microeconomics*, 51–118.

5

Agricultural Liberalisation and the Least Developed Countries: Six Fallacies

Arvind Panagariya

1. INTRODUCTION

𝕿 ODAY, agriculture remains the most distorted sector of the world economy. The Uruguay Round Agreement on Agriculture took a major step forward by bringing the sector within the purview of the multilateral trading rules but its success in opening up the sector to global competition was at best limited. Therefore, agricultural liberalisation is rightly the top priority in the Doha negotiations. On that much there is general agreement among informed analysts.

There remains considerable confusion, however, on who protects agriculture and how much, which countries stand to benefit from the liberalisation most, and whether there are potential losers and if so what might be done about it. Because many of the potential exporters of agricultural products happen to be developing countries and many potential importers developed countries, liberalisation in this area has an obvious North-South dimension. But beyond this simple generalisation, the public-policy discourse remains fogged by a number of fallacies.

These fallacies probably originated at the beginning of this millennium with the World Bank leadership (as distinct from its technical and research staff) – most notably the outgoing President James Wolfensohn and his former Chief Economist Nicholas Stern – filling the media waves with the allegations that agricultural protectionism was almost exclusively a developed-country problem, that this protection represented hypocrisy and double-standard on the part of the developed countries, that it hurt the poorest countries most, and that it constituted

The author is grateful to Jagdish Bhagwati for comments on an earlier draft of this paper.

the principal barrier to the latter's development. But today, the fallacies have been embraced more widely, including by the leadership of other international organisations such as the International Monetary Fund (IMF) and the Organisation of Economic Co-operation and Development (OECD), the non-governmental organisations (NGOs) such as Oxfam, and numerous journalists. Remarkably, on this set of issues, we can scarcely distinguish the view of such mainstream international institutions as the World Bank, the IMF and the OECD from that of the institutions that instinctively blame the rich countries for the ills of the poor countries including various United Nations agencies, South-South Centre and a host of anti-globalisation NGOs. Indeed, even the hardnosed financial newspapers such as the *Economist* and some of the prominent globalisation critics among academics, most notably Nobel Laureate Joseph Stiglitz, have ended up giving a nod to some of the fallacies.

In this paper, I propose to carefully identify and debunk these fallacies.[1] In Section 2, I identify six fallacies relating to agricultural barriers and explicitly document their existence in some of the most powerful public-policy circles. In Section 3, I take apart each of the fallacies. In Section 4, I make some concluding remarks; in particular, I recall that economists have studied the possible adverse impact of developed-country agricultural protection on the developing countries for more than four decades. But while advocating free trade policies in agriculture in the developed countries, these pioneering and widely read economists did not fall victim to the fallacies that the leadership of international organisations, NGOs and the press have embraced today.

2. THE FALLACIES AND EVIDENCE

At least six distinct fallacies, each having an important bearing on either the conduct of the Doha negotiations or the appropriate development strategy for the poor countries, can be identified:

Fallacy 1: Agricultural border protection and subsidies are largely a developed-country phenomenon.

Fallacy 2: Developed-country agricultural subsidies and protection hurt the poorest developing countries most.

Fallacy 3: Developed-country subsidies and protection hurt the poor, rural households in the poorest countries.

Fallacy 4: Developed-country agricultural protection and subsidies constitute the principal barrier to the development of the poorest developing countries.

---

[1] See an earlier article by Bhagwati and Panagariya (2002) and Panagariya (2003a) for the discussion of several fallacies related to trade liberalisation more generally.

Fallacy 5: Agricultural protection reflects double standard and hypocrisy on the part of the developed countries.

Fallacy 6: What the donor countries give with one hand (aid), they take away with the other (farm subsidies). In effect, the benefits of aid to the poorest countries are more than offset by the losses from the developed-country subsidies.

Perhaps the clearest single source spelling out many of these fallacies is the 'Declaration by the Heads of the IMF, OECD and World Bank on the Eve of the Cancún Ministerial Meeting of the WTO' issued on 4 September, 2004, and available on the OECD website at the time of writing (Kohler et al., 2003). The statement has seven paragraphs in all.

In the first paragraph, the statement begins with the relatively benign assertion that:

the Doha negotiations are a central pillar of the global strategy to achieve the Millennium Development Goals: a strategy to reduce poverty by giving poor people the opportunity to help themselves.

In the second paragraph, it becomes more expansive, however:

Ambitions for Cancún must be commensurate with these objectives. We need a decisive break with trade policies that hurt economic development. Donors cannot provide aid to create development opportunities with one hand and then use trade restrictions to take these opportunities away with the other – and expect that their development dollars will be effective.

In the third paragraph, the Declaration crucially states:

Agriculture is of particular importance to the economic prospects of many developing countries, and reforming the current practices in global farm trade holds perhaps the most immediate scope for bettering the livelihoods of the world's poor. Yet, developed countries impose tariffs on agriculture that are 8 to 10 times higher than on industrial goods. Many continue to use various forms of export subsidies that drive down world prices and take markets away from farmers in poorer countries. In every sector except agriculture, these same countries long ago agreed to prohibit export subsidies. Agricultural support costs the average household in the EU [European Union], Japan, and United States more than a thousand U.S. dollars a year. Much of this support depresses rural incomes in developing countries while benefiting primarily the wealthiest farmers in developed countries, and does little to accomplish the environmental and rural community goals that developed countries strive to pursue.

The highly publicised Oxfam (2002a) report 'Rigged Rules and Double Standards' that the NGO has aggressively pushed (including free hard copies to the faculty at the US universities), conveys a similar message in its executive summary:[2]

---

[2] According to a fascinating account of the activities and reach of Oxfam by Greg Rushford (2004) in the *Rushford Report*, the NGO spends *annually* some $500 million and has approximately 4,000 employees worldwide. This makes Oxfam only a little less than half of the World Bank along some dimensions. The latter had 9,300 employees worldwide and an annual operating budget of $1.4 billion at the time of writing.

In their rhetoric, governments of rich countries constantly stress their commitment to poverty reduction. Yet the same governments use their trade policy to conduct what amounts to robbery against the world's poor. When developing countries export to rich country markets, they face tariff barriers that are four times higher than those encountered by rich countries. Those barriers cost them $100bn a year – twice as much as they receive in aid.

The report further states:

Lack of market access is not an isolated example of unfair trade rules, or of the double standards of Northern governments. While rich countries keep their markets closed, poor countries have been pressurized by the International Monetary Fund and World Bank to open their markets at breakneck speed, often with damaging consequences for poor communities.

In the summary of yet another briefing paper entitled 'Stop the Dumping! How EU Agricultural Subsidies are Damaging Livelihoods in the Developing World', Oxfam (2002b) offers the following message:

European Union agricultural subsidies are destroying livelihoods in developing countries. By encouraging over-production and export dumping, these subsidies are driving down world prices of key commodities, such as sugar, dairy, and cereals. Reforming a system in which Europe's large landowners and agribusinesses get rich on subsidies, while smallholder farmers in developing countries suffer the consequences, is an essential step towards making trade fair.

The argument that developed countries give with one hand and take it away with the other has found a dramatic expression in the *Human Development Report 2003*, published by the United Nations Development Programme (UNDP, 2003, p. 155). In Chapter 8 entitled 'Policy, Not Charity: What the Rich Countries Can Do to Help Achieve the Goals', the report prominently displays a chart that shows that the EU gave $913 per EU cow in subsidies but just $8 per person in aid to sub-Saharan Africa in the year 2000.[3] This comparison has been reproduced over and over again by journalists, NGOs and the heads of some international institutions, as a quick search on the Internet would reveal.

In the book *Globalization and its Discontents*, which has captured the attention of many anti-globalisation NGOs and developing-country policy makers, Stiglitz (2002, p. 6) expresses a similar view:

The critics of globalization accuse Western countries of hypocrisy, and the critics are right. The Western countries have pushed poor countries to eliminate trade barriers, but kept up their own barriers, preventing developing countries from exporting their agricultural products and so depriving them of desperately needed export income.

---

[3] In so far as I am able to ascertain, the example on the subsidies to rich-country cows originated in a lecture delivered by the then World Bank Chief Economist Nicholas Stern (2002) at the Centre for Economic Studies (CES) after being named 'Distinguished CES Fellow 2002'. In the speech, Stern said, 'But many of the barriers to expanding the trade of developing countries are not within their control. OECD countries continue to maintain major obstacles to imports from developing countries, notwithstanding pledges to remove or reduce them . . . For example, the average European cow receives $2.50 per day in government subsidies and the average Japanese cow receives $7.50 in subsidies, while 75 per cent of people in Africa live on less than $2 per day.'

Finally, even the *Economist* magazine, which can usually be trusted to demand the highest standards of proof and is known for its careful analytic approach to policy issues, has fallen prey to the dominant rhetoric. For example, in its lead editorial in the latest double issue (*Economist*, 18–31 December, 2004), it identifies agricultural liberalisation among the three main policy issues likely to dominate the policy agenda during 2005. It describes agricultural products as 'crucial to many poor economies, whose exports are treated harshly by America, Japan and the European Union'. In the concluding paragraph, it goes on to uncritically embrace the evidence and argument produced by Oxfam:

> Trade liberalization, by contrast, ought to be a simple choice for poverty-fighting politicians. Oxfam, a campaigning group, estimates, for example, that a 1 per cent increase in Africa's share of world exports would be worth five times as much as the continent's share of aid and debt relief . . . Thus, what deal, if any, is struck at the WTO meeting next December may provide the truest test of whether the will really exists to make poverty history.

3. DEBUNKING THE FALLACIES

Let me now turn to a critical examination of each of the six fallacies I have identified and explain why and where its proponents have got the facts or the analysis wrong. As a starting point, a sharp distinction must be drawn among the poorest developing countries identified as the Least Developed Countries (LDCs) by the United Nations; the Cairns Group developing countries; and other developing countries. The first group contains virtually all countries in sub-Saharan Africa; Afghanistan, Bangladesh, Bhutan, Cambodia, Lao, Maldives and Nepal in Asia; and Haiti in Central America. The second group contains Argentina, Brazil, Chile, Colombia, Costa Rica, Indonesia, Malaysia, Philippines, South Africa, Thailand and Uruguay, which are mostly if not exclusively middle-income developing countries and have a strong comparative advantage in agriculture. The third group contains other developing countries that include the relatively poor countries such as India that do not qualify as LDCs under the United Nations criteria as also the more prosperous developing countries such as China and the Republic of Korea that are not members of the Cairns Group.

Among developing countries, the major beneficiaries of agricultural liberalisation by the developed countries will be the countries in the second group, which have pushed the hardest for the liberalisation. The Cairns Group of countries was largely behind the inclusion of agricultural liberalisation in the Punta del Este Declaration that launched the Uruguay Round negotiations and has been the principal driving force behind the push for agricultural liberalisation since then. The other set of major beneficiaries of agricultural liberalisation would be the developed countries themselves that bear the efficiency costs of protection and the costs of transfers to the importing countries resulting from the production and export subsidies that lower the international agricultural prices for the importers.

As I will discuss shortly, the poorest countries – the LDCs – will actually be hurt by this liberalisation.[4]

a. Fallacy 1: Agricultural Border Protection and Subsidies are Largely a Developed-country Phenomenon

It is true that agriculture is heavily protected and subsidised in the developed countries. But the frequent implication that, by contrast, developing countries do not heavily protect or subsidise agriculture is false. Indeed, if we go by the tariff rates as measures of protection, the extent of protection in the major developing countries is greater than in the developed countries.

Thus, consider Table 1, excerpted from the World Trade Organisation (WTO) (2001, Table III.3). The table shows the proportion of duty-free items in agriculture and the simple average of the *ad valorem* tariff rates in agriculture in a number of countries in various parts of the world.[5] Two estimates of the latter are shown, one by the OECD and the other by the World Bank. Because many countries employ per-unit rather than *ad valorem* tariff rates for some products, they have to be converted into the latter before the average rate is calculated. The differences in these calculations account for the small, occasional differences in the average rates calculated by the OECD and World Bank.

According to these tariff rates, the protection levels in the developing countries are hardly lower than those in the developed ones. The proportion of duty-free items is clearly higher in the developed than in the developing countries. In the United States and EU15, more than a quarter of the agricultural products enter free of duty. In Canada, this proportion is even higher at 43 per cent. On the other hand, with the exception of Malaysia, even the Cairns Group of developing countries, which have a strong comparative advantage in agriculture, allow duty-free less than three per cent of agricultural products.

This comparison broadly carries over to the average tariff levels. Thus, the average bound tariff rates according to the World Bank estimates in the United States and EU are nine and 20 per cent, respectively. The most protectionist developed countries are Iceland, Norway and Switzerland with average tariff rates of 72, 50 and 47 per cent, respectively. The most protectionist developing countries listed in Table 1 are Colombia and India with average tariff rates of 105 and 101 per cent, respectively. Again, even many of the Cairns Group of developing countries exhibit high levels of protection. I have already mentioned Colombia as one of

---

[4] In what follows, unless stated otherwise, the expression 'poor countries' should be interpreted to refer to the LDCs.

[5] The country coverage in my Table 1 is the same as in the WTO table. The latter, in addition, provides information on industrial tariffs for the same group of countries. My concern in this paper being solely with agricultural tariffs, I suppress this information.

TABLE 1
Post-Uruguay-Round Bound Tariffs on Imports of Agriculture (Per cent)

Country	Share of Duty-free Tariff Lines	Simple Average (OECD Estimate)	Simple Average (World Bank Estimate)
North America			
Canada	42.9	4.6	8.8
United States	27.9	5.5	9.0
Latin America			
Argentina	0.1	32.8	32.5
Brazil	2.0	35.3	35.2
Colombia	0.0	88.3	105.6
Mexico	0.1	42.9	25.1
Venezuela	0.0	55.4	67.7
Western Europe			
EU15	26.5	19.5	20.0
Iceland	21.1	48.4	72.1
Norway	23.4	123.7	50.4
Switzerland	28.2	51.1	46.9
Turkey	0.0	63.9	74.3
Eastern Europe			
Czech Republic	30.5	13.3	18.9
Hungary	8.4	22.2	6.7
Poland	2.9	52.8	38.3
Romania	0.0	98.6	130.2
Asia/Pacific			
Australia	32.6	3.3	2.5
Bangladesh	0.0	83.8	
India	1.6	124.3	101.0
Indonesia	0.0	47.2	59.9
Japan	31.0	11.7	29.7
Korea, Rep. of	2.2	62.2	39.6
Malaysia	14.2	13.6	39.0
New Zealand	50.6	8.7	0.7
Philippines	0.0	35.3	46.9
Sri Lanka	0.0	50.0	50.0
Thailand	0.7	34.6	43.2
Africa			
Tunisia	0.0	116.7	15.1

Source: World Trade Organisation (2001, Table III.3).

the two most protected developing countries. But Argentina, Brazil, Indonesia, Malaysia, Philippines and Thailand are all highly protected with average tariff rates that considerably exceed those of the United States, Canada and EU15.

While the bound rate is the right one to consider in the context of multilateral liberalisation, some may argue that the bound rates give a distorted view of the actual level of protection in the case of the developing countries since their actual, applied rates are far below their bound rates. Therefore, Table 2, which

TABLE 2
Actual and Bound Tariff Rates

Country	Definition*	Actual		Bound (Final)**
		Rate	Year	
Developed				
Australia	HS	1.2	1998	3.3
Canada	WTO	24.7	1998	?
Japan	WTO	26.3	1996	25.3
Poland	WTO	34.2	1999	55.5
United States	WTO	10.7	1999	8.2
Developing				
Bangladesh	HS	25.1	1999/2000	188.3
Bolivia	HS	10.0	1998	40.0
Egypt	WTO	64.9	1998	84.1
Indonesia	HS	8.6	1998	47.3
Israel	HS	21.9	1999	74.9
Jamaica	HS	20.2	1997	100.0
Kenya	WTO	16.7	1999	100.0
Mali	HS	28.7	1997	60.0
Papua New Guinea	HS	22.0	1999	45.0
Peru	WTO	17.8	1999	31.1
Romania	HS	32.3	1999	112.0
Singapore	HS	0.0	1999	9.6
Trinidad and Tobago	HS/WTO	19.1 (HS)	1998	100.0 (WTO)
Thailand	HS	32.1	1999	32.0
Uruguay	HS	13.0	1998	35.2

Notes:
* Sectoral tariff averages vary with the definition used. The HS definition of agriculture (HS 01-24) includes fishing and forestry, while the definition of agricultural products used for the purpose of the Uruguay Round negotiations (WTO definition) excludes fish and fishing products (HS 03 and parts of HS 16) and includes items regarded as agricultural from HS 29, 33, 35, 38, 41, 43, 50, 51, 52 and 53 (Annex 1 of the Agreement).
** Developed-country Members have to implement reduction commitments over a six-year period commencing in 1995 while developing-country Members have the flexibility to implement reduction commitments over a period of up to ten years commencing in 1995. Least-developed-country Members are not required to undertake reduction commitments.

Source: WTO (2001, Table III.5).

reproduces WTO (2001, Table III.5), shows the applied tariff rates for a group of developing and developed countries. The gap between developed and developing countries is now less but the general point that in terms of the average tariff rates the developing countries protect as much as or more than the developed countries remains valid.

Some may further argue that developed countries also impose tariff quotas that may have a protective effect. But this contention is incorrect since the tariff quotas are meant to be liberalising measures. In negotiating the Agreement on Agriculture, it was feared that the member countries might replace the non-tariff border measures by prohibitive tariffs thereby eliminating even the existing market access. Therefore, it was agreed that countries should guarantee the level of market access already achieved through a quota with a within-quota tariff rate that was sufficiently lower than its MFN tariff binding to maintain at least the existing level of imports. Furthermore, in the case of the products that a country did not import at all or imported in minuscule quantities, the Agreement on Agriculture introduced *de minimus* imports through a tariff quota such that a lower tariff rate than the MFN rate would be applied to imports up to *de minimus* quantity. A removal of the tariff quotas while maintaining the current tariff rates would reduce, not increase, agricultural imports.

Finally, consider the issue of subsidies. Here the sins of the developed countries are well documented. But the lack of availability of data does not permit a comparison with the developing countries. The available information suggests, however, that the developing countries are not altogether innocent here. Countries such as Brazil, Mexico, South Africa, Venezuela, India, the Republic of Korea and Thailand have had sizeable agricultural subsidies. Some of the developing-country subsidies are not subject to reduction commitments because of the 'Special & Differential' treatment but that hardly makes them non-distortionary. The subsidies in the so-called Blue Box under the Special & Differential provisions for the developing countries include such measures as price supports and input subsidies and are just as distortionary as the developed-country subsidies.

Pretending that the developing countries have low protection in agriculture when the evidence is to the contrary does the countries themselves no good. It only strengthens the hand of the protectionists within those countries by making it easier to claim that they do not need to liberalise. And if they then succeed, it only hurts the countries since their ability to export depends not just on the openness of the partner country markets but on their own openness as well.

b. Fallacy 2: Developed-country Agricultural Subsidies and Protection Hurt the Poorest Countries (i.e., LDCs) Most

Of all the fallacies I have listed, this is the most crucial one to debunk not just because it enjoys the near-universal acceptance but also because a proper understanding of the effects of developed-country liberalisation in agriculture has important implications for how best to assist the LDCs in their quest for development. The argument behind the assertion is that protection and subsidies by the developed countries together depress the world prices and limit market access of the LDCs thereby impacting adversely the quantity as well as value of their exports.

Two key points explain why this argument is seriously flawed and is, indeed, wrong. First, protection and output and export subsidies by the developed countries depress the world prices of agricultural products. As importers, LDCs have access to these low prices. Once the subsidies and protection are eliminated,

FIGURE 1
An EU Output Subsidy

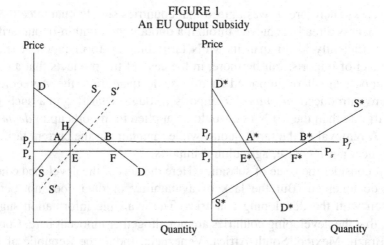

the world prices would rise and hurt the importers. For many LDCs that are large importers of agricultural products, these losses could be substantial.

Second, under the Everything But Arms (EBA) initiative of the European Union, LDCs have quota- and duty-free access to the EU market.[6] This means that they can sell their exports at the internal EU price that is kept artificially high to protect the EU producers. In effect, the LDC sellers enjoy the same protection under the EBA as the EU producers. With some exceptions, the EU internal price is far more lucrative than the price that is likely to obtain in the absence of tariffs and subsidies.

Let me elaborate on these points. In the left-hand panel of Figure 1, DD and SS respectively show the EU demand and supply curves for an agricultural commodity, say, wheat. In the right-hand panel, D*D* and S*S* respectively show the demand and supply curves of the rest of the world for the same commodity. Under free trade, the EU is an importer of wheat with the price settling at P_f. At this price, the EU demand for imports, AB, equals the rest of the world supply of exports, A*B*. Here subtracting its total supply from its total demand at each price yields the EU demand for imports. Likewise, subtracting its total demand from its total supply at each price yields the rest of the world supply of exports.

An output subsidy by the EU shifts its supply curve down to S′S′, where the vertical distance between SS and S′S′ represents *per-unit* output subsidy. At the original price P_f, the EU supply is now larger and its demand for imports smaller than AB (= A*B*). The resulting excess supply of wheat in the world market pushes the world price of wheat down. The new equilibrium is reached at price P_s with EU demand for imports, EF, equalling once again the rest of the world

---

[6] Currently, there are three exceptions: bananas, rice and sugar where quotas exist. But the quotas are slated to end between 2006 and 2008.

supply of exports, E*F*. The gross price received by the EU producers equals P_s plus EH, where EH is per-unit output subsidy.

It is immediate that since the EU output subsidy, which lowers the EU demand for imports and thus works like a tariff, *improves* the EU terms of trade: the import price of wheat drops. From the viewpoint of the exporting countries, the terms of trade get worse and the rest of the world *as a whole* is left worse off. But it is important to remember that the right-hand panel in Figure 1 represents the *combined* position of the rest of the world that includes both exporters and importers of wheat other than the EU. The effects of the subsidy on these two groups are asymmetric, with the importers actually made better off in the post-subsidy equilibrium since they are able to buy wheat at the lower world price. Because their benefits are more than offset by the losses of the exporters, the rest of the world as a whole loses.

An export subsidy is often painted as impacting the rest of the world the same way as the output subsidy but actually works differently. In this case, it is the EU that is hurt as a whole while the rest of the world benefits. But as before, the world price of wheat falls so that the exporters of wheat in the rest of the world are hurt and importers benefit, with the gains of the latter more than offsetting the losses of the former this time around. This is shown in Figure 2, which assumes that the EU is a net exporter of wheat in the free trade equilibrium.

In the initial, free trade equilibrium, the price is P_f, with the EU exporting AB and the rest of the world importing A*B* such that AB = A*B*. The way an export subsidy works is that the producers can avail of the subsidy only if they export. This creates a wedge between the price at which they are willing to export and the one at which they are willing to sell in the domestic market, with the wedge equalling the subsidy per unit. Therefore, in the new equilibrium, the internal price in the EU rises to P_d while the world price falls to P_s. The price in

FIGURE 2
An Export Subsidy by the EU

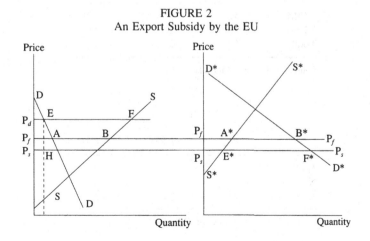

the rest of the world drops to P_s, with imports expanding to E^*F^*. In the EU, the internal price being P_d, the demand drops to E along the demand curve while production rises to point F along the supply curve. Producers sell EF (= E^*F^*) in the world market at P_s but receive the same gross price as in the domestic market once we add the export subsidy. As already noted above, the importers of wheat in the rest of the world are better off overall and the exporters worse off.

Those who argue that the removal of the output and export subsidies in the rich countries, represented by the EU in Figures 1 and 2, would benefit the poor countries implicitly assume that the latter are exporters of agricultural products. But as I have argued forcefully in Panagariya (2003a, 2003b and 2004a), in reality a large number of the developing countries and the vast majority of the LDCs are net agricultural importers. To restate this point, consider Tables 3 and 4, taken from Valdes and McCalla (1999), which indicate the importer and exporter status of various developing countries with respect to food and agricultural products.

The World Bank divides the total of 148 developing countries into 63 Low Income Countries (LIC), 53 Lower Middle Income Countries (LMIC) and 33 Upper Middle Income Countries (UMIC). Based on the 1995–97 data on agricultural exports and imports, Valdes and McCalla further divide these countries into Net Food Importing (NFIM) and Net Food Exporting (NFEX) Countries on the one hand and Net Agricultural Importing (NAIM) and Net Agricultural Exporting (NAEX) on the other.

According to Table 3, as many as 48 out of 63 Low Income Countries are net importers of food. Even among the Low Middle Income Countries, 35 out of 52 are net food importers. In so far as the subsidies apply with potency to food

TABLE 3

	LIC	LMIC	UMIC
NFIM	48	35	22
NFEX	15	17	11
Total	63	52	33

Source: Valdes and McCalla (1999).

TABLE 4

	LIC	LMIC	UMIC
NAIM	30	32	23
NAEX	33	20	10
Total	63	52	33

Source: Valdes and McCalla (1999).

FIGURE 3
A Developing Country Turning from a Net Importer to Exporter

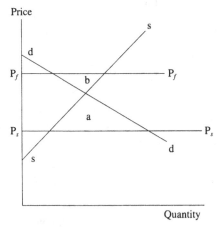

items, their removal will raise the world prices of the latter and hurt the real incomes of the importing countries.

Table 4 classifies the three groups of countries according to their net position in agriculture as a whole rather than just food. Here more Low Income Countries appear as exporters – 33 versus only 15 when we consider only food items. But the picture is more pessimistic if we focus on the LDCs only. At the time Valdes and McCalla wrote, there were 48 LDCs in the world. Of these, as many as 45 were net food importers and 33 net agricultural importers.

Some analysts argue, however, that the importers need not necessarily lose from the increase in agricultural prices that will follow the removal of the production and output subsidies by the EU (and other developed countries) because many of them will become exporters of the products at the higher prices. But two arguments can be offered why this assertion is unpersuasive. The first argument, discussed immediately below with the help of Figure 3, is a 'likelihood' argument. The second one, discussed next, is logically tight and especially applicable to the LDCs.

In Figure 3, dd and ss respectively denote the demand and supply curves of a developing country that initially imports wheat. The world price of wheat in the presence of the production subsidy, given to their producers by the developed countries, is P_s. The developing country imports wheat and makes net gains from trade equalling the triangular area marked 'a'. The removal of the subsidy by the developed countries raises the price to the free trade level indicated by P_f. At this higher price, the developing country turns into an exporter of wheat. The gains from trade are now given by the triangular area 'b', which is smaller than area 'a'. Thus, the country loses on a net basis despite turning its status from importer to exporter. Only if the world price increases sufficiently to make area 'b' larger

FIGURE 4
Under the EBA, LDC Exporters Sell at P_t and Buy at P_s; Under Free Trade They Will Have to
Buy and Sell at P_f

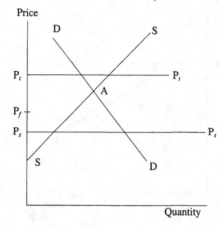

than area 'a' will the country make a net gain from the removal of the developed country subsidy.

Indeed, the complete and realistic story from the viewpoint of the LDCs is even more pessimistic. In many products, under free trade, the EU would be an importer. Yet, through a combination of export and output subsidies on the one hand and import tariff on the other, it maintains a regime in which it ends up being an exporter of the product. Thus, in Figure 4, let DD be the EU demand curve and SS its supply curve of wheat. By assumption, under free trade, the EU would be an importer with the price settling at P_f in the spirit of Figure 1. But an export subsidy combined with a tariff turns the EU into an exporter of the product.[7] Specifically, suppose it gives an export subsidy equal to P_tP_s per unit, complemented by a tariff at the same or higher rate. These measures push the external (world) price down to P_s (since the EU is a large exporter in the world market, the expansion of its exports depresses the world price) and the internal price up to P_t.

If we now start with the export subsidy and tariff in the initial equilibrium and consider their removal, the outcome will be similar to that in Figures 1 and 2. As there, the importers of the product will lose from the price rise and exporters will benefit. The key complication that we have not introduced so far and may now be considered is that in so far as the LDCs are concerned, under the EBA, they are currently allowed to export to the EU at its *internal* price; that is, at P_t. And those that import the product get to buy it at the lower world price P_s. When the subsidy and tariff are removed, both the EU and the world price converge to P_f, which is

---

[7] To avoid clutter, I suppress the production subsidy now but the reader can readily include it by imagining that SS represents the production subsidy inclusive supply curve and modifying the remainder of the analysis accordingly.

lower than P_t that the LDC exporters received and higher than P_s that the LDC importers paid earlier. Both exporting and importing LDCs are hurt from the liberalisation.

The assertion that importers of agricultural products can benefit from the tariff-export-subsidy removal by turning into exporters can now be seen to have no logical basis in the case of the LDCs. Under the EBA, in the initial, distorted equilibrium, the importing LDCs face the price P_t if it wants to export rather than import the product. If it is unable to export at that price, it surely cannot export at the lower, free trade, price, P_f. Needless to say that the analysis of Figure 4 is readily modified to include an output subsidy. All that is needed is to interpret SS as the supply curve inclusive of the output subsidy (similarly to S'S' in Figure 1) and P_f as the world price with output subsidy but no other intervention.

Indeed, the danger that the LDCs will lose from the developed-country liberalisation is even greater than that suggested by the analysis based on Figures 1–4 above. This is because, in anticipation of the liberalisation under the Doha Round, the politics within the developed countries is already pushing the import barriers up in the form of Sanitary and Phytosanitary (SPS) measures. This process will escalate in the post-Doha world. And in so far as the LDCs are at a much greater disadvantage than their counterparts in the Cairns Group and the developed world at overcoming these highly sophisticated technical barriers, they are in danger of losing even some of their existing market access.

Given the above dissection of agricultural liberalisation from the viewpoint of the LDCs, how do we explain the ruckus at Cancún over the cotton subsidies? Recall that some of the poorest countries were at the forefront of the demand for the removal of these subsidies. The answer is that this case *is* consistent with the popular rhetoric of the developed-country subsidies hurting the poor countries. But it is also an exception. Cotton happens to be a product in which the EU does not have major producer interests to protect so that its internal price is close to the world price. Therefore, the EBA is not much help in this product. Indeed, by far the largest subsidy on this product is given by the United States, followed by China, a developing country herself. But even in this exceptional case, I may note that by far the largest LDC in terms of population, Bangladesh, is a substantial importer and stands to lose from the end to the cotton subsidies.

A powerful example of the flaw in the populist view that the developed-country subsidies in agriculture hurt the poor developing countries (including but not limited to the LDCs) was provided recently by the WTO dispute settlement case on the EU export subsidies on sugar. The case was brought by Brazil, a middle-income developing country, which is also a member of the Cairns Group. The subsidised exports in this case had allowed the EU to import sugar from the African, Caribbean and Pacific (ACP) countries and India at its internal price. Not surprisingly, rather than support Brazil in its challenge and celebrate the ruling, these latter countries sided with the EU and saw the ruling as hurting their interests.

We may also ask how it is that many studies have shown or claim to show that the developed-country agricultural liberalisation promises large benefits to the LDCs. The answer is that, to my knowledge, with one exception, no study has considered in isolation the impact of the developed-country liberalisation in just agriculture on the LDCs while taking the role of the EBA into account.[8] For example, following my article in the *Financial Times* (Panagariya, 2004b), William Cline (2004) of the Institute for International Economics claimed in a letter that even if net agricultural importing countries lose from the rise in the prices of agricultural products following the removal of the subsidies, his model shows that they will benefit from improved prices of their manufactures exports. But given the structure of the problem as expounded above in Figure 1, this is not plausible unless one is considering, not just agricultural liberalisation, but the entire package including the liberalisation of textiles and apparel and footwear by the developed countries, which is altogether a different question.[9]

Thus, for example, if we think in terms of a three-good model – an exportable agricultural product, an importable agricultural product and an industrial good that may be exported or imported – my analysis above shows that agricultural liberalisation by the developed countries will lower the LDC price of the exportable agricultural product and raise that of the importable agricultural product in terms of the industrial product. Both of these changes represent an unambiguous deterioration of the LDC terms of trade.

Some studies also fail to identify the LDCs that lose because they lump them with other countries in the region that gain sufficiently that the region as a whole gains. Yet another common practice is to lump the developing-country liberalisation with the developed-country liberalisation. In so far as there are major gains from the liberalisation by the developing countries including LDCs themselves, the net effect of the package on the LDCs may be positive even if the effect of the rich-country liberalisation in isolation is negative. While these are all legitimate and interesting exercises in their own right, they do not allow us to conclude that developed-country protection and subsidies in agriculture hurt the LDCs.

c. Fallacy 3: Developed-country Subsidies and Protection Hurt the Poor, Rural Households in the Poorest Countries

This fallacy is to be distinguished from the previous one in that it focuses on the fortunes of a specific group within the developing countries rather than

---

[8] Researchers W. Yu and T. V. Jensen (2003) of the Danish Research Institute of Food Economics, who study the effect of EU liberalisation in agriculture taking into account the EBA do find that such liberalisation hurts the poor countries.

[9] See my reply to Cline (Panagariya, 2004c) in this context.

the countries as a whole. The essential argument behind the assertion is that even if the developed-country subsidies benefit an LDC that is predominantly an agricultural importer, they hurt the poor farmers within it since the latter earn their living by producing import-competing agricultural goods. In effect, the low price of farm goods results in a low value of the farmers' product at the margin.

For the LDCs, the logic behind this argument is hardly tight. Recall that the current regime keeps the prices of agricultural exports facing LDCs high and of the imports low relative to the respective levels that would prevail under a liberalised regime. If the LDC now happens to specialise in the production of the exportable products, the wages of the farmers vary directly with the prices of those products. The higher price of exports thus helps raise the farm wages. Indeed, in so far as the farmers may be consuming predominantly the imported agricultural products (recall that the vast majority of the LDCs are net food importers), the low import prices are to *their* benefit as well.

It is, of course, entirely possible to construct cases in which the current EU regime hurts the wages of the LDC farmers. In so far as an LDC produces both exportable and importable agricultural products, the net effect of the higher price of the former and lower price of the latter in terms of a third good, say manufactures, can be to lower the real wage. In non-LDC developing countries producing importable agricultural products, this outcome is even more likely.

But from the policy perspective, this outcome begs the question why no institution including the World Bank, IMF, OECD and Oxfam has advised the LDCs to impose countervailing duties on the subsidised imports till today. If the objective happens to be to maximise the incomes of the poor farmers in the LDCs, the better option would be to leave the EU protection and subsidies intact and encourage the LDCs to impose countervailing duties on their subsidised agricultural imports. Under this scenario, the internal price of the imported products would still rise without the deterioration in the terms of trade and the country will be able to generate extra revenues to affect further transfers to the poor. Those who make the above assertion have become prisoners of their own rhetoric and therefore failed to think through the available policy options.

d. Fallacy 4: Developed-country Agricultural Protection and Subsidies Constitute the Principal Barrier to the Development of Many Poor Countries

This is perhaps the most dangerous of the six assertions considered in this paper. For one thing, the premise underlying the assertion is just not true. Despite the protection that remains, developed-country markets are sufficiently open that countries with good internal policies can readily expand their exports. As economist Robert Baldwin (1982) has demonstrated, protection is almost always porous so that determined exporters are able to find ways to enter their partner-country markets. The exporters in the Far Eastern countries amply illustrated this in the 1960s and 1970s. Despite barriers in the industrial countries, those exporters found ways to expand their export sales. On the other hand, countries such as India that persisted in their belief that the world markets could not be relied upon languished. Today, countries such as Chile have found ways to expand even their agricultural exports to the United States. Sugar may be off limits but many fruits and vegetables are not. And in so far as the LDCs are concerned, as I have already explained at length, they have virtually free access to the EU agricultural market under the current regime.

As was true in the 1960s and 1970s, it is true today that much more serious barriers to development are the internal policies. The inability of the LDCs to export to the developed-country market is largely (though, admittedly, not exclusively) the result of the supply-side constraints that are of their own making. The sooner we recognise this fact the more urgently will the countries and international institutions focus their attention on how best to overcome these constraints. Telling the countries that the developed countries are responsible for their woes may make one popular but it does the countries no good. It only encourages complacency towards domestic policy reform in these countries and without those reforms no amount of opening up by the developed countries will kick off growth.

e. Fallacy 5: Agricultural Protection Reflects Double Standard and Hypocrisy on the Part of the Developed Countries

The argument often made is that the developed countries have opened markets where they have comparative advantage but retained barriers on the products in which the developing countries have comparative advantage. This is said to be especially true of agriculture, which was kept essentially out of the discipline of the General Agreement on Tariffs and Trade (GATT) until the Uruguay Round and is still the most protected sector. Again, such assertions betray basic misunderstanding of the history of trade negotiations. The continuing protection of agriculture in the developed countries is the result of two distinct forces.

First, by and large, the developing countries opted out of the multilateral negotiations in the 1960s and 1970s. Because they made no liberalisation commitments in the multilateral rounds prior to the Uruguay Round, they got no liberalisation commitments from the developed countries in the products of their export interest. The developed countries negotiated liberalisation among them and therefore liberalised largely in products of mutual interest to them. In so far as the Most Favoured Nation (MFN) principle extended this liberalisation to all GATT members, countries capable of exporting the liberalised products got a 'free ride'. That liberalisation was in part behind the phenomenal success of the Far Eastern countries in the 1960s and 1970s.

From one perspective, the position taken by the developing countries as a group may have been worse than that of indifference. In the 1960s and 1970s, they were wedded to the import-substitution-industrialisation (ISI) policies, did not want to rely on agricultural exports, and actually pursued policies that repressed agriculture.[10] In addition, in so far as agricultural subsidies led to surpluses that were shipped to the poor countries as 'food aid', as under the PL480 programmes of the United States, principal recipients of such aid did not see the subsidies as harmful to their interests. Therefore, whatever demands they made on the developed countries on moral grounds did not include demands for market access in agriculture. As a part of the demands for the so-called New International Economic Order (NIEO) following the successful OPEC oil price hike in 1973, their demands included the *stabilisation* of agricultural prices and the transfer of specific, labour-intensive manufacturing industries to the South but not an end to the subsidies and protection in agriculture.

The second force at work was internal to the developed countries themselves. Domestic politics in the Quad countries – the United States, European Community, Canada and Japan – favoured protection to farmers. The pro-protection lobbies in this sector were far more powerful than the export interests. As such, whereas the export lobbies carried the day in manufacturing, the same did not happen in agriculture. Thus, the internal politics and the absence of external pressure for a liberal regime rather than hypocrisy and wickedness combined to perpetuate a protectionist regime in agriculture.

f. Fallacy 6: What the Donor Countries Give with One Hand, They Take Away with the Other

This argument is often backed up by the example, noted earlier and highlighted in the UNDP Human Development Report, 2003, that Europeans gave only $8 per person in aid to Africa while giving as much as $913 per European cow in subsidies in 2000. Of course, a direct comparison of these numbers, while shocking, is downright silly. To begin with, all countries spend a lot more on internal redistribution of income than on the international redistribution. Developing countries themselves pursue policies aimed at the redistribution of income in ways that is comparable to the subsidy to the European cows.

But more to the point, a proper comparison should be between the harmful impact of the subsidies and the grant-in-aid equivalent worth of aid. As I have already argued in the context of Fallacy 2 above, in so far as the LDCs are concerned, the current tariff-subsidy regime works to their advantage in that it gives their exporters access to the high internal EU price and offers their importers

---

[10] Victoria Curzon Price (2004) has made this point recently.

the low international price. But even for the exporter countries that do not have access to the EU internal price and therefore suffer on account of the low international price at which they must sell, we must compute the loss to them from the deterioration in the terms of trade caused by the developed-country subsidies and protection. That loss is likely to be only a small fraction of the subsidies given to all European cows, acres, men and exports.

Symmetrically, what commonly passes as 'aid' in the public-policy discourse is not all grants-in-aid. Even the World Bank International Development Agency (IDA) funds take the form of loans at concessional terms so that only a fraction of the dollar flow is grants-in-aid. In addition, one must make the correction for conditionality that may accompany aid. If, for instance, aid is tied to a specific project or a specific market in which it must be spent, its real value further declines. The real value of the 'aid' flow is thus likely to be less than the nominal value.

4. CONCLUDING REMARKS

There are compelling reasons to reject the view, popularised by many international organisations, NGOs and the media, that developed-country subsidies and protection hurt the poorest countries, the LDCs; that agricultural protection is principally a developed-country problem; that developed-country protectionism and subsidies constitute the principal barriers to the development of Africa; and that the developed-country protection in agriculture is the result of their hypocrisy and wickedness.

First, such simplistic assertions may make one popular with the poorly informed but they do no good to the poor themselves. If we persist in making these assertions and the poor eventually find out that the liberalisation under the Doha Round ended up harming their interests, they would be disenchanted with liberalisation and we would have compromised the cause of free trade in the long run.

Second, without recognition of the detrimental effects of the liberalisation on the LDCs, we will fail to design compensation mechanisms and safety nets necessary to smooth out the adjustment to the more liberal regime. Developed countries have the necessary resources to come up with their own safety nets but the poor countries lack them and depend on the international transfers bilaterally or through such institutions as the World Bank.[11] Also important here is the needed focus on

---

[11] Following pointed criticisms by Bhagwati and Panagariya (2002), the heads of the IMF and World Bank, Kohler and Wolfensohn (2003), have belatedly recognised the merit of liberalisation by both developing and developed countries under the Doha Round and the need for such adjustment assistance. In turn, Bhagwati and Panagariya (2003) have welcomed the conversion of the two institutions in favour of trade liberalisation by the developing countries as well.

the creation of capacity for satisfying the SPS measures that are likely to become even more ubiquitous in the developed countries in the forthcoming years.

Finally, unless we point out to the poor countries that to take advantage of a more open and competitive world trading system they too must open up rather than seek exemption from such liberalisation, we will condemn them to the same fate they currently suffer. Opening just the developed-country markets will not be enough; the poor countries must generate the proper supply response through the reform of their own policy regime, which includes but is not limited to their own opening up.

Before I conclude, let me recall that there has been a longstanding tradition of the study of the implications of the developed-country agricultural policies for the developing countries among economists. Around four decades ago, Richard Snape (1963) and Harry Johnson (1966) produced quantitative estimates of the effects of sugar protection and the associated quota regime in the developed countries on developing countries and suggested how the latter could be assisted through better policies in the developed countries and a move towards free trade. Based on the calculations he undertook, Johnson reached two conclusions (1966, pp. 41–42):

> The first, and firmer, is that the prevalence of sugar protection has substantial effects both in wasting resources and in reducing the earnings of the less developed countries that have a comparative advantage in sugar production. According to the rough estimates presented here, replacement of the present national system of protection by deficiency payments (scientific protectionism) would increase the export earnings of these countries by something in the neighborhood of half a billion dollars, and free trade would increase their export earnings from the seven major countries alone by something in the neighborhood of three quarters of a billion dollars . . . Free trade would free resources that would go automatically or could be contributed as foreign aid to the less developed countries to an amount in the neighborhood of half a billion dollars (to be compared with the current foreign aid total of all countries and international organizations of about ten billion dollars, a figure probably nearly double the net transfer of real resources actually involved).

In stating the second conclusion, Johnson drew a sharp distinction between the developing countries that benefited from access to the developed-country internal price through sugar quotas and those exporting at the world price. Two years earlier, Raul Prebisch had argued in UNCTAD (1964) that developed countries give the other sugar exporters the same price that they give their own producers and the quota beneficiary countries. Johnson suggested that free trade offered a better deal for all. Thus, he wrote:

> Secondly, and less surely owing to lack of quantitative information on the effects of existing preferences for the important group of less developed countries, it appears that the abandonment of sugar protectionism in favor of free world competition in sugar could increase the resources available to the less developed countries by more than could a Prebisch-type policy of 'internationalizing' sugar protection. Moreover, in contrast to the latter policy, which would merely transfer resources from developed to less developed countries through an increase in prices, a policy of free trade would make additional resources available without cost to anyone, [footnote] as a consequence of the increased efficiency of resource allocation it would produce.

Even back then, Johnson was cognisant of and sensitive to the adjustment costs that may accompany the free trade policy. In the footnote to the last sentence above, he added the qualification:

> In the short run, there would be some costs involved in shifting resources out of sugar production, but it is reasonable to assume that resources are mobile enough in the developed countries to absorb a shift out of sugar production without intolerable social strains.

The global community would do well by accepting an augmented version of Johnson's solution even today: free trade in both developed and developing countries that increases efficiency, and increased aid from developed to the developing countries, especially the LDCs, that can be used among other things to offer adjustment assistance to those free trade would temporarily displace.

REFERENCES

Baldwin, R. (1982), 'The Inefficacy of Trade Policy', Frank D. Graham Memorial Lecture, *Essays in International Finance* (Princeton University, No. 150, December).

Bhagwati, J. and A. Panagariya (2002), 'Wanted: Jubilee 2010. Dismantling Protection', *OECD Observer*, No. 231/232, 27–29.

Bhagwati, J. and A. Panagariya (2003), 'World Bank and IMF Show Welcome Revisions to Stance on Developing Countries and Trade', *Financial Times*, Letters (23 December).

Cline, W. (2004), 'Global Agricultural Free Trade Would Benefit, Not Harm, LDCs', *Financial Times*, Letters (9 August).

Curzon Price, V. (2004), 'Place of Non-discrimination in a Rapidly Integrating World Economy', Trade Policy Analyses Series (Cordell Hull Institute, July).

Johnson, H. G. (1966), 'Sugar Protectionism and the Export Earnings of Less Developed Countries: Variations on a Theme by R. H. Snape', *Economica*, **33**, New Series No. 129, February, 34–42.

Kohler, H. and J. D. Wolfensohn (2003), 'We Can Trade Up to a Better World', *Financial Times*, Comments (12 December).

Kohler, H. J. D. Wolfensohn and D. J. Johnston (2003), 'Declaration by the Heads of the IMF, OECD and World Bank' (4 September, posted at http://www.oecd.org/document/9/0,2340,en_2649_201185_11813577_1_1_1_1,00.html).

Oxfam (2002a), 'Rigged Rules and Double Standards: Trade, Globalization and the Fight Against Poverty' (executive summary and introduction, posted at http://www.maketradefair.com/en/index.php?file=26032002105641.htm).

Oxfam (2002b), 'Stop the Dumping! How EU Agricultural Subsidies are Damaging Livelihoods in the Developing World', Oxfam Briefing Paper, No. 31 (posted at http://www.oxfam.org.uk/what_we_do/issues/trade/bp31_dumping.htm).

Panagariya, A. (2003a), 'Think Again: International Trade', *Foreign Policy* (November–December), 20–28.

Panagariya, A. (2003b), 'Trade Liberalization and Food Security: Conceptual Links', in *Trade Reforms and Food Security* (Food and Agricultural Organisation of the United Nations, Rome), Chapter 3, 25–42.

Panagariya, A. (2004a), 'Alternative Perspective on "Subsidies and Trade Barriers" by Kym Anderson', in B. Lomborg (ed.), *Global Crises, Global Solutions* (Cambridge: Cambridge University Press).

Panagariya, A. (2004b), 'The Tide of Free Trade Will Not Lift All Boats', *Financial Times*, Comment (4 August).

Panagariya, A. (2004c), 'Higher Food Prices Will Indeed Hit Poor', *Financial Times*, Letters (12 August).

Rushford, G. (2004), 'Oxfam's Janus Face', *The Rushford Reports* (November), 1–8.

Snape, R. H. (1963), 'Some Effects of Protection in the World Sugar Industry', *Economica*, **30**, New Series No. 117, February, 63–73.

Stern, N. (2002), 'Dynamic Development: Innovation and Inclusion', Munich Lectures in Economics (Centre for Economic Studies, Ludwig Maximilian University, Munich, 19 November).

Stiglitz, J. (2002), *Globalization and its Discontents* (New York: W. W. Norton & Company).

UNDP (United Nations Development Program) (2003), *Human Development Report 2003: Millennium Development Goals: A Compact among Nations to End Human Poverty* (New York: Oxford University Press).

United Nations Conference on Trade and Development (1964), *Towards a New Trade Policy for Development* (Geneva).

Valdes, A. and A. F. McCalla (1999), 'Issues, Interests and Options of Developing Countries', presented at the joint World Bank and WTO Conference on Agriculture and the New Trade Agenda in the WTO 2000 Negotiations (Geneva, Switzerland, 1–2 October).

World Trade Organisation (2001), 'Market Access: Unfinished Business', Special Studies No. 6 (Geneva).

Yu, W. and T. V. Jensen (2003), 'Tariff Preferences, WTO Negotiations and the LDCs – The Case of the "Everything But Arms" Initiative', Working Paper No. 04/03 (Danish Research Institute of Food Economics (FOI)).

6

Agricultural Trade Reform and the Doha Development Agenda

Kym Anderson and Will Martin

1. WHY ALL THE FUSS OVER AGRICULTURE?

𝔄GRICULTURE is yet again causing contention in international trade negotiations. It caused long delays to the Uruguay Round in the late 1980s and
1990s, and it is again proving to be the major stumbling block in the World Trade
Organisation's Doha Round of multilateral trade negotiations (formally known
as the Doha Development Agenda, or DDA). For example, it contributed substantially to the failure of the September 2003 Trade Ministerial Meeting in
Cancún to reach agreement on how to proceed with the DDA, after which it took
another nine months before a consensus was reached on the Doha work programme, otherwise referred to as the July Framework Agreement (WTO, 2004).

It is ironic that agricultural policy is so contentious, given its small and declining importance in the global economy. The sector's share of global GDP has
fallen from around one-tenth in the 1960s to little more than one-thirtieth today.
In developed countries the sector accounts for only 1.8 per cent of GDP and only
a little more of full-time equivalent employment. Mirroring that decline, agriculture's share of global merchandise trade has more than halved over the past three
decades, dropping from 22 to nine per cent. For developing countries its importance has fallen even more rapidly, from 42 to 11 per cent (Figure 1).

Since policies affecting this declining sector are so politically sensitive, there
are always self-interested groups suggesting it be sidelined in trade negotiations –
as indeed it has in numerous sub-global preferential trading agreements, and was

This paper is based on a programme of World Bank research on the implications of the Doha
Agenda for developing countries. The authors are grateful for the collaboration of all their co-
contributors to that project, especially Dominique van der Mensbrugghe and Tom Hertel, and for
funding from the UK's Department for International Development. The views expressed are the
authors' alone.

FIGURE 1

The Declining Share of Agriculture and Food in World and Developing[a] Countries' Merchandise
Exports, 1970 to 2003 (Per cent)

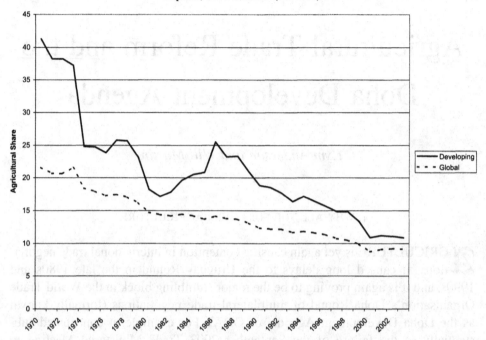

Note:

[a] Developing countries here do not include East Asia's newly-industrialised economies of Hong Kong, Korea,
Singapore and Taiwan.

Source: COMTRADE data in the WITS database (see www.wits.worldbank.org).

in the GATT prior to the Uruguay Round.[1] Today the groups with that inclination
include not just farmers in the highly protecting countries and net food importing
developing countries but also those food exporters receiving preferential access
to those markets including holders of tariff rate quotas, members of regional
trading agreements, and parties to non-reciprocal preference agreements including all least-developed countries. However, sidelining agriculture in the Doha
Round would do a major disservice to many of the world's poorest people, namely
those in farm households in developing countries. It is precisely *because* agricultural earnings are so important to a large number of developing countries that the
highly protective farm policies of a few wealthy countries are being targeted by

---

[1] The rules of the GATT are intended, in principle, to cover all trade in goods. However, in
practice, trade in agricultural products was largely excluded from their remit as a consequence of a
number of exceptions. Details are to be found in Josling, Tangermann and Warley (1996) and in
Anderson and Josling (2005).

them in the WTO negotiations. Better access to rich countries' markets for their farm produce is a high priority for them.[2]

Some developing countries have been granted greater access to developed-country markets for a selection of products under various preferential agreements. Examples are the EU's provisions for former colonies in the Africa, Caribbean and Pacific (ACP) programme and more recently for Least Developed Countries under the Everything But Arms (EBA) agreement. Likewise, the United States has its Africa Growth and Opportunity Act (AGOA) and Caribbean Basin Initiative (CBI). These schemes reduce demands for developed-country farm policy reform from preference-receiving countries, but they exacerbate the concerns of other countries excluded from such programmes and thereby made worse off through declining terms of trade – and they may even be worsening rather than improving aggregate global and even developing-country welfare.

Apart from that, many in developing countries feel they did not get a good deal out of the Uruguay Round. From a mercantilistic view, the evidence seems to support that claim: Finger and Winters (2002) report that the average depth of tariff cut by developing countries was substantially greater than that agreed to by high-income countries. As well, developing countries had to take on costly commitments such as those embodied in the SPS and TRIPS agreements (Finger and Schuler, 2001). They therefore are determined in the Doha Round that they get significantly more market access commitments from developed countries before they contemplate opening their own markets further.

Greater market access for developing countries' exporters, and especially for poor producers in those countries, is to be found in agriculture (and to a lesser extent in textiles and clothing). This can be seen from a glance at Table 1. It shows that developing-country exporters face an average tariff (even after taking account of preferences) of 16 per cent for agriculture and food, and 9 per cent for textiles and clothing, compared with just 2.5 per cent for other manufactures. The average tariff on agricultural goods is high not just in high-income countries but also in developing countries, suggesting even more reason why attention should focus on that sector (along with textiles) in the multilateral reform process embodied in the DDA.

If agriculture were to be ignored in the Doha negotiations, there is the risk that agricultural protection would start rising again. That is what happened throughout the course of industrial development in Europe and Northeast Asia (Anderson, Hayami and others, 1986; and Lindert, 1991). It was only with the establishment

---

[2] According to the UN's Food and Agriculture Organisation, 54 per cent of the economically active population is engaged in agriculture in developing countries, which is nearly five times larger than the sector's measured GDP share (FAO, 2004, Table A4). While some of that difference in shares is due to under-reporting of subsistence consumption, it nonetheless implies that these people on average are considerably less productive and hence poorer than those employed outside agriculture.

KYM ANDERSON AND WILL MARTIN

TABLE 1

Average Applied Import Tariffs, by Sector and Region, 2001

(Per cent, *ad valorem* equivalent)

Exporting Region:	Importing Region:		
	High-income Countries[b]	Developing Countries[a]	World
Agriculture and food			
High-income countries[b]	18	18	17.8
Developing countries[a]	14	18	15.6
All countries	16	18	16.7
Textiles and wearing apparel			
High-income countries[b]	8	15	12.0
Developing countries[a]	7	20	9.3
All countries	8	17	10.2
Other manufactures			
High-income countries[b]	2	9	4.1
Developing countries[a]	1	7	2.5
All countries	1	8	3.5
All merchandise			
High-income countries[b]	3	10	5.4
Developing countries[a]	3	10	4.9
All countries	3	10	5.2

Notes:

[a] These import-weighted averages incorporate tariff preferences provided to developing countries, unlike earlier versions of the GTAP database.

[b] High-income countries include the newly industrialised East Asian customs territories of Hong Kong, Korea, Singapore and Taiwan as well as Europe's transition economies that joined the EU in April 2004.

Source: Anderson, Martin and van der Mensbrugghe (2005a, Table 12.2).

of the World Trade Organisation, in 1995, that agricultural trade was brought under multilateral disciplines via the Uruguay Round Agreement on Agriculture (URAA).

That URAA was ambitious in scope, converting all agricultural protection to tariffs, and limiting increases in virtually all tariffs through tariff bindings. Unfortunately, the process of converting non-tariff barriers into tariffs (inelegantly termed 'tariffication') provided numerous opportunities for backsliding that greatly reduced the effectiveness of the agreed disciplines (Hathaway and Ingco, 1996). In developing countries, the option for 'ceiling bindings' allowed countries to set their bindings at high levels, frequently unrelated to the previously prevailing levels of protection. Hence agricultural import tariffs are still very high in both rich and poor countries, with bound rates half as high again as MFN applied rates (Table 2).

As well, agricultural producers in some countries are supported by export subsidies (still tolerated within the WTO only for agriculture) and by domestic support measures. Together with tariffs and other barriers to agricultural imports, these measures support farm incomes and encourage agricultural output to varying

TABLE 2
Agricultural Weighted Average Import Tariffs, by Region, 2001
(Per cent, *ad valorem* equivalent, weights based on imports)

	Bound Tariff	MFN Applied Tariff	Actual Applied Tariff[a]
Developed countries	27	22	14
Developing countries	48	27	21
of which: LDCs	*78*	*14*	*13*
World	37	24	17

Note:
[a] Includes preferences and in-quota TRQ rates where relevant, as well as the *ad valorem* equivalent of specific tariffs. Developed countries include Europe's transition economies that joined the EU in April 2004. The 'developing countries' definition used here is that adopted by the WTO and so includes East Asia's four newly industrialised tiger economies, which is why the 21 per cent shown in column 3 is above the 18 and 14 per cent shown in the first column of Table 1.

Source: Jean, Laborde and Martin (2005, Table 4.2).

FIGURE 2
Agricultural Producer Support in High-income Countries, by Value, Per Cent and Type of Support,
1986 to 2003 ($ billion and percentage of total farm receipts from support policy measures)

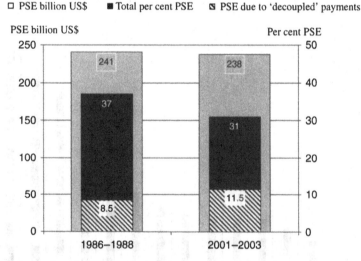

Source: PSE estimates from the OECD's database (see www.oecd.org).

extents. The market price support component also typically raises domestic consumer prices of farm products. Figure 2 shows the value and the percentage of total farm receipts from these support policy measures, called the Producer Support Estimate or PSE by the OECD secretariat.[3] For OECD members as a

---

[3] Until recently the PSE referred to the Producer Subsidy Equivalent. For more about the concept and its history, see Legg (2003).

group, the PSE was almost the same in 2001–03 as in 1986–88, at about $240 billion per year. But because of growth in the sector, as a percentage of total farm receipts (inclusive of support) that represents a fall from 37 to 31 per cent. Figure 2 also shows that there has been a significant increase in the proportion of that support coming from programmes that are somewhat 'decoupled' from current output such as payments based on area cropped, number of livestock, or some historical reference period.

Agricultural protection levels remain very high in these developed countries, especially when bearing in mind that 1986–88 was a period of historically very low international food prices and hence above-trend PSEs. And, as Figure 3 shows, the PSEs have fallen least in the most-protective OECD countries. By contrast, tariff protection to OECD manufacturing has fallen over the past 60 years from a level similar to that for OECD agriculture today (above 30 per cent nominal rate

FIGURE 3

Agricultural Producer Support in High-income Countries, by Country, 1986 to 2003

(Percentage of total farm receipts from support policy measures)

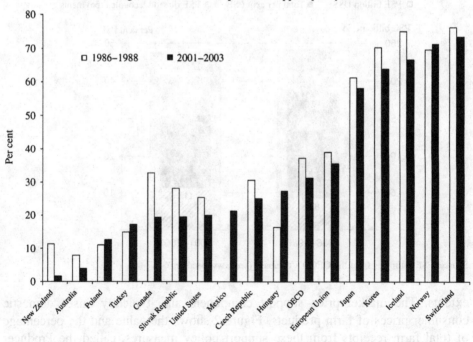

Notes:

[1] Czech Republic, Hungary, Poland and the Slovak Republic data are for 1991–93 in the first period.

[2] Austria, Finland and Sweden are included in the OECD average for both periods but also in the EU average for the latter period.

Source: PSE estimates from the OECD's database (see www.oecd.org).

of protection) to only one-tenth of that now. This means far more resources have been retained in agricultural production in developed countries – and hence fewer in developing countries – than would have been the case if protection had been phased down in both agriculture and manufacturing simultaneously.

Nonetheless, the achievements of the Uruguay Round Agreement on Agriculture provide some scope for optimism about what might be achieved via the WTO as part of the DDA and beyond. The current Doha Round has the advantage over the Uruguay Round of beginning from the framework of rules and disciplines agreed in that previous Round. In particular, it has the three clearly identified 'pillars' of market access, export subsidies and domestic support on which to focus. True, it took more than three years to agree on a framework for the current negotiations, reached at the end of July 2004 (WTO, 2004), but now that July Framework Agreement is likely to guide the negotiations for some time. It therefore provides a strong basis for undertaking *ex ante* analysis of various options potentially available to WTO members during the Doha negotiations.

This paper summarises a recent study (Anderson and Martin, 2005) that builds on numerous analyses of the Doha Development Agenda and agricultural trade, including five very helpful books that appeared in 2004. One, edited by Aksoy and Beghin (2004), provides details of trends in global agricultural markets and policies, especially as they affect nine commodities of interest to developing countries. Another, edited by Ingco and Winters (2004), includes a wide range of analyses based on papers revised following a conference held just prior to the aborted WTO Trade Ministerial meeting in Seattle in 1999. The third, edited by Ingco and Nash (2004), provides a follow-up to the broad global perspective of the Ingco and Winters volume: it explores a wide range of key issues and options in agricultural trade reform from a developing-country perspective. The fourth, edited by Anania, Bohman, Carter and McCalla (2004), is a comprehensive tenth-anniversary retrospective on the Uruguay Round Agreement on Agriculture as well as a look ahead following also numerous unilateral trade and subsidy reforms in developed, transition and developing economies. And the fifth focuses on implications for Latin America (Jank, 2004).

All of those 2004 studies were completed well before the July Framework Agreement was reached in the early hours of 1 August, 2004, and before the public release in December 2004 of the new Version 6 database of the Global Trade Analysis Project (GTAP) at Purdue University. That Version 6 database is a major improvement over the previous version for several reasons. One is that it includes global trade and protection data as of 2001 (previously 1997). Another is that protection data are available, for the first time, as bound as well as applied tariffs, non-reciprocal as well as reciprocal tariff preferences, the *ad valorem* equivalents of specific tariffs (which are plentiful in the agricultural tariff schedules of many high-income, high-protection countries), and the effects of agricultural tariff rate quotas. In addition, key trade policy changes to the start of 2005 have been added for our analysis, namely, the commitments associated with accession to the WTO by such economies as China and Taiwan (China), the implementation of the last of the Uruguay Round commitments (most notably the abolition of quotas on trade in textiles and clothing at the end of 2004), and the eastward enlargement of the European Union from 15 to 25 members in April 2004.

Hence what distinguishes the present study from the above 2004 studies and other books with similar titles is that (a) its *ex ante* analysis focuses on the core aspects of the July Framework Agreement from the viewpoint of agriculture and developing countries, taking account also of what might happen to non-agricultural market access and the other negotiating areas, and (b) it does so in an integrated way by using the new GTAP Version 6 database (amended to account for key protection changes to early 2005) and the latest version of the World Bank's global, economy-wide Linkage model, details of which are documented in van der Mensbrugghe (2004).[4]

2. WHAT QUESTIONS ARE ADDRESSED IN THIS STUDY?

Among the core questions addressed in this study, following an intense programme of integrated research during the latter half of 2004 by a complementary set of well-informed scholars from four continents, are the following:

- What is at stake in this Doha Round, in terms of efficiency gains foregone by the various regions of the world because of current tariffs and agricultural subsidies?
- How much are each of the three 'pillars' of agricultural distortions (market access, export subsidies and domestic support) contributing to those welfare losses, compared with non-agricultural trade barriers?
- How might the demands for Special and Differential Treatment for developing and least-developed countries be met without compromising the potential gains from trade expansion for those economies?
- What are the consequences, in terms of opening up to imports, of alternative formulas for cutting bound agricultural tariffs?

---

[4] This analysis is vastly more sophisticated than the *ex ante* analyses undertaken for the Uruguay Round. At that time there were very few economy-wide global models, so primary reliance was on partial equilibrium models of world food markets (see, e.g., World Bank, 1986; Goldin and Knudsen, 1990; and Tyers and Anderson, 1992); estimates of protection rates were somewhat cruder and less complete; and analysts grossly over-estimated the gains because they did not anticipate that tariffication would be so 'dirty' in the sense of creating large wedges between bound and MFN applied tariff rates, nor did they have reliable estimates of the tariff preferences enjoyed by developing countries or the *ad valorem* equivalent of specific tariffs. Some of these limitations also applied to *ex post* analyses of the Uruguay Round (see, e.g., Martin and Winters, 1996).

- In the case of products whose imports are subject to tariff rate quotas, what are the trade-offs between reducing in-quota or out-of-quota tariffs versus expanding the size of those quotas or the in-quota tariffs?
- To what extent would the erosion of tariff preferences, that necessarily accompanies MFN trade liberalisation by developed countries, reduce the developing countries' interest in agricultural and other trade reform?
- What should be done about agricultural export subsidies, including those implicit in export credits, food aid and arrangements for state trading enterprises?
- Based on recent policy changes in key countries, how might domestic farm support measures be better disciplined in the WTO?
- What are the consequences of reducing the domestic support commitments made in the Uruguay Round, in terms of cuts to the actual domestic support levels currently provided to farmers?
- In particular, how might reductions in cotton subsidies help developing-country farmers in West Africa and elsewhere?
- What difference does it make to expand market access for non-agricultural products at the same time as for farm goods under a Doha agreement?
- Which developing countries would have to reduce their farm output and employment as a result of such a Doha agreement?
- Taking a broad brush, and in the light of past experience and our understanding of the political economy of agricultural policies in rich and poor countries, how might reform of those policies best be progressed during the DDA negotiations?
- What would be the overall market and welfare consequences by 2015, for various countries and regions as well as globally, of the alternative Doha reform commitments considered in addressing each of the above questions?

3. WHAT HAVE WE LEARNED?

In addressing the above questions, the following are among the key messages that emerge from our study.

The potential gains from further global trade reform are huge. Global gains from trade reform post-2004 are estimated to be large even if dynamic gains and gains from economies of scale and increased competition are ignored. Freeing all merchandise trade and agricultural subsidies is estimated to boost global welfare by nearly $300 billion per year by 2015 (Table 3), plus whatever productivity effects that reform would generate.[5]

---

[5] There is strong evidence that trade reform in general is also good for economic growth and, partly because of that, for poverty alleviation (Winters, 2004; Dollar and Kraay, 2004; and Winters, McCulloch and McKay, 2004).

TABLE 3
Impacts on Real Income from Full Liberalisation of Global Merchandise Trade,
by Country/Region, 2015

(Impacts in 2015 relative to the baseline, in 2001 dollars)	Real Income Gain ($ billion)	Income Change Due Just to Change in Terms of Trade ($ billion)	As Per Cent of Baseline Income in 2015
Australia and New Zealand	6.1	3.5	1.0
EU25 plus EFTA	65.2	0.5	0.6
United States	16.2	10.7	0.1
Canada	3.8	−0.3	0.4
Japan	54.6	7.5	1.1
Korea and Taiwan	44.6	0.4	3.5
Hong Kong and Singapore	11.2	7.9	2.6
Argentina	4.9	1.2	1.2
Bangladesh	0.1	−1.1	0.2
Brazil	9.9	4.6	1.5
China	5.6	−8.3	0.2
India	3.4	−9.4	0.4
Indonesia	1.9	0.2	0.7
Thailand	7.7	0.7	3.8
Vietnam	3.0	−0.2	5.2
Russia	2.7	−2.7	0.6
Mexico	3.6	−3.6	0.4
South Africa	1.3	0.0	0.9
Turkey	3.3	0.2	1.3
Rest of South Asia	1.0	−0.8	0.5
Rest of East Asia	5.3	−0.9	1.9
Rest of LAC	10.3	0.0	1.2
Rest of ECA	1.0	−1.6	0.3
Middle East and North Africa	14.0	−6.4	1.2
Selected SSA countries	1.0	0.5	1.5
Rest of Sub-Saharan Africa	2.5	−2.3	1.1
Rest of the World	3.4	0.1	1.5
High-income countries	201.6	30.3	0.6
Developing countries – WTO definition	141.5	−21.4	1.2
Low- and middle-income countries	85.7	−29.7	0.8
Middle-income countries	69.5	−16.7	0.8
Low-income countries	16.2	−12.9	0.8
East Asia and Pacific	23.5	−8.5	0.7
South Asia	4.5	−11.2	0.4
Europe and Central Asia	7.0	−4.0	0.7
Middle East and North Africa	14.0	−6.4	1.2
Sub-Saharan Africa	4.8	−1.8	1.1
Latin America and the Caribbean	28.7	2.2	1.0
World total	**287.3**	**0.6**	**0.7**

Source: Anderson, Martin and van der Mensbrugghe (2005a, Table 12.4).

Developing countries could gain disproportionately from further global trade reform. The developing countries (as defined by the WTO) would enjoy 45 per cent of the global gain from complete liberalisation of all merchandise trade, well above their share of global GDP. Their welfare would increase by 1.2 per cent, compared with an increase of just 0.6 per cent for developed countries. The developing countries' higher share is partly because they have relatively high tariffs themselves (so they would reap substantial efficiency gains from reforming their own protection), and partly because their exports are more concentrated in farm and textile products whose tariffs in developed-country markets are exceptionally high (Table 1) – notwithstanding non-reciprocal tariff preferences for many developing countries, which contribute to the losses associated with terms of trade deterioration shown in the middle column of Table 3.

Benefits could be as much from South-South as from South-North trade reform. Trade reform by developing countries is just as important economically to those countries as is reform by developed countries, including from agricultural liberalisation (Table 4b). Hence choosing to delay their own reforms or reforming less than developed countries, and thereby holding back South-South trade growth, could reduce substantially the potential gains to developing countries.

Agriculture is where cuts are needed most. To realise that potential gain from opening up goods markets, it is in agriculture that by far the greatest cuts in bound tariffs and subsidies are required. This is because of the very high rates of assistance in that sector relative to other sectors. Food and agricultural policies are responsible for more than three-fifths of the global gain foregone because of merchandise trade distortions (column 1 of Table 4a) – despite the fact that agriculture and food processing account for less than ten per cent of world trade and less than four per cent of global GDP. From the point of view of welfare of developing countries, agriculture is at least as important as it is for the world as a whole: their gains from global agricultural liberalisation represent almost two-thirds of their total potential gains, which compares with just one-quarter from textiles and clothing and one-ninth from other merchandise liberalisation (Table 4b).

Subsidy disciplines are important, but increased market access in agriculture is crucial. Extremely high applied tariffs on agricultural relative to non-farm products are the major reason for food and agricultural policies contributing 63 per cent of the welfare cost of current merchandise trade distortions. Subsidies to farm production and exports are only minor additional contributors: four and one percentage points respectively, compared with 56 points due to agricultural tariffs.[6] This is even truer for developing countries than for developed ones

---

[6] This result is very similar to that reported from a partial equilibrium study by Hoekman, Ng and Olarreaga (2004). In our initial empirical analysis we also included crude estimates of implicit forms of farm export subsidisation such as via food aid, export credits or state trading enterprises, but even that was not enough to raise that export subsidy share above one per cent.

TABLE 4

Effects on Economic Welfare of Full Trade Liberalisation from Different Groups of Countries and Products, 2015 (Per cent)

From Full Liberalisation of:	Agriculture and food	Textiles and clothing	Other manufactures	All Goods
Panel A: Distribution of Effects on *Global* Welfare				
Percentage due to:				
Developed[a] country policies	46	6	3	55
Developing countries' policies	17	8	20	45
All countries' policies	**63**	**14**	**23**	**100**
Panel B: Distribution of Effects on *Developing Countries'* Welfare				
Percentage due to:				
Developed[a] country policies	30	17	3	50
Developing countries' policies	33	10	7	50
All countries' policies	**63**	**27**	**10**	**100**

Note:

[a] Developed countries include the transition economies of Eastern Europe and the former Soviet Union.

Source: Anderson, Martin and van der Mensbrugghe (2005a, Table 12.6).

TABLE 5

Distribution of Global Welfare Impacts of Fully Removing Agricultural Tariffs and Subsidies, 2001 (Per cent)

Agricultural Liberalisation Component:	Beneficiary Region:		
	High-income[a] Countries	Developing Countries	World
High-income[a] countries' liberalisation of:			
Import market access	66	27	93
Export subsidies	5	−3	2
Domestic support	4	1	5
All measures	*75*	*25*	*100*

Note:

[a] High-income countries include the newly industrialised East Asian customs territories of Hong Kong, Korea, Singapore and Taiwan as well as Europe's transition economies that joined the EU in April 2004.

Source: Summarised from Hertel and Keeney (2005, Table 2.7).

(compare columns 1 and 2 of Table 5). Disciplining those domestic subsidies and phasing out export subsidies is nonetheless very important, so as to prevent re-instrumentation of assistance from tariffs to domestic subsidies and to bring agriculture into line with non-farm trade in terms of not using export subsidies.

In developing countries the poor would gain most from multilateral trade reform. Full global merchandise trade liberalisation would raise real factor returns for the poorest households most. This is implied in Table 6, where for developing countries the biggest factor price rise is for farm land, followed by

TABLE 6

Impacts of Full Global Merchandise Trade Liberalisation on Real Factor Prices, 2015[a]

(Per cent change relative to the baseline in 2015)

	Unskilled Wages	Skilled Wages	Capital	Land- owner Rent	CPI
Australia and New Zealand	3.1	1.1	−0.3	17.2	1.2
EU25 plus EFTA	0.0	1.3	0.7	−51.0	−1.3
United States	0.1	0.3	0.0	−9.2	−0.4
Canada	0.7	0.7	0.4	26.9	−0.9
Japan	1.3	2.2	1.1	−67.2	−0.1
Korea and Taiwan	6.5	7.1	3.8	−45.0	−0.7
Hong Kong and Singapore	3.2	1.6	0.3	4.4	1.1
Argentina	2.9	0.5	−0.7	21.3	0.3
Bangladesh	1.8	1.7	−0.2	1.8	−7.2
Brazil	2.7	1.4	1.6	32.4	2.2
China	2.2	2.2	2.8	−0.9	−0.4
India	2.8	4.6	1.8	−2.6	−6.0
Indonesia	3.3	1.5	0.9	1.0	0.5
Thailand	13.2	6.7	4.2	11.4	−0.6
Vietnam	25.3	17.6	11.0	6.8	−2.3
Russia	2.0	2.8	3.5	−2.2	−3.3
Mexico	2.0	1.6	0.5	0.6	−1.4
South Africa	2.8	2.5	1.8	5.7	−1.6
Turkey	1.3	3.4	1.1	−8.1	−0.3
Rest of South Asia	3.7	3.2	0.1	0.1	−2.7
Rest of East Asia	5.8	4.2	5.2	−0.9	−1.6
Rest of Latin America & Carib.	5.7	1.4	−0.4	17.8	−1.2
Rest of E. Europe & C. Asia	2.3	4.2	2.1	−0.3	−2.6
Middle East & North Africa	4.1	4.1	2.6	2.4	−3.1
Other Southern Africa	6.0	1.6	0.0	4.6	0.4
Rest of Sub-Saharan Africa	8.2	6.5	2.2	5.2	−5.0
Rest of the World	4.4	2.7	1.1	6.3	−1.4

Source: Anderson, Martin and van der Mensbrugghe (2005a, Table 12.10).

unskilled labour. Since farmers and other low-skilled workers constitute the vast majority of the poor in developing countries, such reform would reduce both inequity and poverty.

Large cuts in domestic support commitments are needed to erase binding overhang. In turning from the potential gains from full liberalisation to what might be achievable under a Doha partial reform package, the devil is going to be in the details. For example, commitments on domestic support for farmers are so much higher than actual support levels at present, that the 20 per cent cut in the total bound AMS promised in the July Framework Agreement as an early instalment will require no actual support reductions for any WTO member. Indeed a cut as huge as 75 per cent for those with most domestic support is needed to get some action, and even then it would only require cuts in 2001 levels of domestic support for four WTO actors: the US (by 28 per cent), the EU (by 18 per cent), Norway (by 16 per cent) and Australia by ten per cent – and the EU and Australia have already introduced reforms of that order since 2001, so may need to do no further cutting under even that formula.

Large cuts in bound rates are needed also to erase binding overhang in agricultural tariffs. Table 2 shows there is substantial binding overhang in agricultural tariffs: the average bound rate in developed countries is almost twice as high as the average applied rate, and in developing countries the ratio is even greater. Thus large reductions in bound rates are needed before it is possible to bring about *any* improvements in market access. To bring the global average actual agricultural tariff down by one-third, bound rates would have to be reduced for developed countries by at least 45 per cent, and up to 75 per cent for the highest tariffs, under a tiered formula.

A complex tiered formula may be little better than a proportional tariff cut. It turns out that, because of the large binding overhang, a tiered formula for cutting agricultural tariffs would generate not much more global welfare – and no more welfare for developing countries as a group – than a proportional cut of the same average size (columns 1 and 2 of Tables 7, 8 and 9). This suggests there may be little value in arguing over the finer details of a complex tiered formula just for the sake of reducing tariff escalation. Instead, a simple tariff cap of, say, 100 or even 200 per cent could achieve essentially the same outcome.

Even large cuts in bound tariffs do little if 'Sensitive Products' are allowed, except if a cap applies. If members succumb to the political temptation to put limits on tariff cuts for the most sensitive farm products, much of the prospective gain from Doha could evaporate. Even if only two per cent of HS6 agricultural tariff lines in developed countries are classified as sensitive (and four per cent in developing countries, to incorporate also their 'Special Products' request), and are thereby subject to just a 15 per cent tariff cut (as a substitute for the TRQ expansion mentioned in the Framework Agreement), the welfare gains from global agricultural reform would shrink by three-quarters. However, if at the same time any product with a bound tariff in excess of 200 per cent had to reduce it to that cap rate, the welfare gain would shrink by 'only' one-third (columns 3 and 4 of Tables 7, 8 and 9).

TRQ expansion could provide additional market access. Only a small number of farm products are subject to tariff rate quotas, but they protect over half of all developed countries' production and 44 per cent of their agricultural imports (de Gorter and Kliauga, 2005). Bringing down those products' (out-of-quota) MFN bound tariff could be supplemented by lowering their in-quota tariff or expanding the size of the quota. While this may increase the aggregate rent attached to those quotas and hence resistance to eventually removing them, the extent of binding overhang is such that quota expansion may be the only way to get increased market access for TRQ products in the Doha Round – especially if they are among the ones designated as 'sensitive' and hence subject to lesser cuts in their bound tariffs.

TABLE 7

Welfare Effects of Possible Doha Reform Scenarios, 2015

(Per cent difference from baseline, and Equivalent Variation in income in 2001 $ billion)

	Agricultural Subsidy Cuts[a] Plus:					
	Tiered Agricultural Tariff Cuts[b]	Propn'l Agricultural Tariff Cuts[b]	Scenario 2 Plus 2 Per Cent SSP	Scenario 3 Plus 200 Per Cent Cap	Scenario 1 Plus 50 Per Cent NAMA Cut for HICs[c]	Scenario 1 Plus 50 Per Cent NAMA Cut for HICs + DCs[d]
	Scenario 1	Scenario 2	Scenario 3	Scenario 4	Scenario 5	Scenario 6
High-income[e] countries	0.20	0.18	0.05	0.13	0.25	0.30
Middle-income countries	0.10	0.10	0.00	0.01	0.15	0.21
of which: *China*	*-0.02*	*-0.01*	*-0.05*	*-0.04*	*0.07*	*0.06*
Low-income countries	0.05	0.04	0.01	0.00	0.18	0.30
Total world	**0.18**	**0.16**	**0.04**	**0.10**	**0.23**	**0.28**
(and in $ billion)	*74.5*	*66.3*	*17.9*	*44.3*	*96.1*	*119.3*

Notes:

[a] Elimination of agricultural export subsidies and cuts in actual domestic support as of 2001 of 28 per cent in the US, 18 per cent in the EU, and 16 per cent in Norway.

[b] In Scenarios 1 and 2 the applied global average tariff on agricultural products is cut by roughly one-third, with larger cuts in developed countries, smaller in developing countries, and zero in least developed countries. In Scenario 1 there are three tiers for developed countries and four for developing countries, following Harbinson (WTO, 2003) but ten percentage points higher.

[c] Non-agricultural market access (NAMA) is expanded by a 50 per cent tariff cut for developed countries, 33 per cent for developing countries, and zero in least developed countries.

[d] Developing and least developed countries cut all agricultural and non-agricultural tariffs as much as developed countries.

[e] High-income countries (HICs) include the newly industrialised East Asian customs territories of Hong Kong, Korea, Singapore and Taiwan as well as Europe's transition economies that joined the EU in April 2004.

Source: Anderson, Martin and van der Mensbrugghe (2005a, Table 12.14).

TABLE 8
Dollar Change in Real Income in Alternative Doha Scenarios, 2015
(Change in real income in 2015 in 2001 $ billion compared to baseline scenario)

	Scen. 1	Scen. 2	Scen. 3	Scen. 4	Scen. 5	Scen. 6
Australia and New Zealand	2.0	2.2	1.2	1.2	2.4	2.8
EU25 plus EFTA	29.5	28.2	10.7	10.9	31.4	35.7
United States	3.0	3.4	2.5	2.1	4.9	6.6
Canada	1.4	1.2	0.4	0.4	0.9	1.0
Japan	18.9	15.1	1.4	12.9	23.7	25.4
Korea and Taiwan	10.9	7.3	1.7	15.9	15.0	22.6
Hong Kong and Singapore	−0.1	−0.1	−0.2	−0.2	1.5	2.2
Argentina	1.3	1.4	1.1	1.0	1.3	1.6
Bangladesh	0.0	0.0	0.0	0.0	−0.1	−0.1
Brazil	3.3	3.2	1.1	1.1	3.6	3.9
China	−0.5	−0.4	−1.4	−1.1	1.7	1.6
India	0.2	0.1	0.2	0.2	2.2	3.5
Indonesia	0.1	0.2	0.2	0.0	1.0	1.2
Thailand	0.9	1.0	0.8	0.8	2.0	2.7
Vietnam	−0.1	−0.1	−0.1	−0.1	−0.5	−0.6
Russia	−0.3	−0.1	−0.7	−0.7	0.8	1.5
Mexico	−0.2	−0.2	−0.3	−0.3	−0.9	−0.2
South Africa	0.1	0.1	0.2	0.3	0.4	0.7
Turkey	0.6	0.5	0.1	0.0	0.7	1.4
Rest of South Asia	0.2	0.2	0.1	0.2	0.3	0.7
Rest of East Asia	0.1	0.1	0.1	1.0	0.3	0.6
Rest of Latin America & the Carib.	3.7	3.7	0.5	0.4	3.9	4.0
Rest of E. Europe and Central Asia	−0.2	−0.2	−0.2	−0.2	−0.6	−0.7
Middle East and North Africa	−0.8	−0.9	−1.2	−1.2	−0.6	0.1
Other Southern Africa	0.1	0.1	0.0	0.0	0.1	0.2
Rest of Sub-Saharan Africa	0.0	0.0	−0.3	−0.3	−0.1	0.3
Rest of the World	0.4	0.3	0.0	0.0	0.6	0.6
High-income countries	**65.6**	**57.2**	**17.8**	**43.2**	**79.9**	**96.4**
Developing countries	**9.0**	**9.1**	**0.1**	**1.1**	**16.1**	**22.9**
Middle-income countries	8.0	8.3	0.0	1.0	12.5	17.1
Low-income countries	1.0	0.8	0.2	0.0	3.6	5.9
East Asia and Pacific	0.5	0.9	−0.4	0.6	4.5	5.5
South Asia	0.4	0.3	0.3	0.4	2.5	4.2
Eastern Europe and Central Asia	0.1	0.2	−0.9	−0.9	0.8	2.1
Middle East and North Africa	−0.8	−0.9	−1.2	−1.2	−0.6	0.1
Sub-Saharan Africa	0.3	0.3	−0.2	−0.1	0.4	1.2
Latin America & the Caribbean	8.1	8.0	2.5	2.1	7.9	9.2
World total	**74.5**	**66.3**	**17.9**	**44.3**	**96.1**	**119.3**

Source: Anderson, Martin and van der Mensbrugghe (2005a, Table 12.14).

TABLE 9
Percentage Change in Real Income in Alternative Doha Scenarios, 2015
(Change in real income in 2015 in per cent compared to baseline scenario)

	Scen. 1	Scen. 2	Scen. 3	Scen. 4	Scen. 5	Scen. 6
Australia and New Zealand	0.35	0.38	0.22	0.20	0.42	0.48
EU25 plus EFTA	0.29	0.28	0.11	0.11	0.31	0.36
United States	0.02	0.02	0.02	0.01	0.03	0.05
Canada	0.15	0.13	0.05	0.05	0.10	0.11
Japan	0.38	0.30	0.03	0.26	0.48	0.51
Korea and Taiwan	0.86	0.58	0.14	1.26	1.19	1.79
Hong Kong and Singapore	−0.02	−0.02	−0.04	−0.04	0.35	0.52
Argentina	0.32	0.34	0.27	0.26	0.34	0.39
Bangladesh	−0.06	−0.06	−0.03	−0.04	−0.10	−0.09
Brazil	0.50	0.49	0.17	0.17	0.55	0.59
China	−0.02	−0.01	−0.05	−0.04	0.07	0.06
India	0.02	0.02	0.03	0.02	0.25	0.40
Indonesia	0.05	0.08	0.09	0.01	0.37	0.44
Thailand	0.43	0.49	0.38	0.38	0.99	1.33
Vietnam	−0.20	−0.22	−0.11	−0.16	−0.83	−0.97
Russia	−0.06	−0.03	−0.15	−0.15	0.16	0.31
Mexico	−0.02	−0.02	−0.04	−0.04	−0.11	−0.02
South Africa	0.06	0.09	0.11	0.17	0.25	0.49
Turkey	0.25	0.22	0.02	0.02	0.26	0.55
Rest of South Asia	0.13	0.11	0.06	0.14	0.17	0.39
Rest of East Asia	0.02	0.05	0.04	0.36	0.09	0.22
Rest of Latin America & the Carib.	0.44	0.43	0.06	0.04	0.46	0.47
Rest of E. Europe and Central Asia	−0.06	−0.06	−0.09	−0.08	−0.22	−0.26
Middle East and North Africa	−0.07	−0.07	−0.10	−0.10	−0.05	0.01
Other Southern Africa	0.21	0.19	−0.03	−0.05	0.19	0.26
Rest of Sub-Saharan Africa	0.02	0.01	−0.14	−0.14	−0.02	0.13
Rest of the World	0.19	0.14	0.00	0.02	0.26	0.28
High-income countries	**0.20**	**0.18**	**0.05**	**0.13**	**0.25**	**0.30**
Developing countries	**0.09**	**0.09**	**0.00**	**0.01**	**0.16**	**0.22**
Middle-income countries	0.10	0.10	0.00	0.01	0.15	0.21
Low-income countries	0.05	0.04	0.01	0.00	0.18	0.30
East Asia and Pacific	0.01	0.03	−0.01	0.02	0.13	0.16
South Asia	0.03	0.02	0.03	0.03	0.21	0.36
Eastern Europe and Central Asia	0.01	0.02	−0.09	−0.09	0.08	0.21
Middle East and North Africa	−0.07	−0.07	−0.10	−0.10	−0.05	0.01
Sub-Saharan Africa	0.06	0.06	−0.04	−0.02	0.10	0.27
Latin America & the Caribbean	0.29	0.29	0.09	0.08	0.29	0.33
World total	**0.18**	**0.16**	**0.04**	**0.10**	**0.23**	**0.28**

Source: Anderson, Martin and van der Mensbrugghe (2005a, Table 12.14).

High binding overhang means most developing countries would have to make few cuts. Given the high binding overhang of developing countries, even with their high tariffs – and even if tiered formulae are used to cut highest bindings most – relatively few of them would have to cut their actual tariffs and subsidies at all (Jean, Laborde and Martin, 2005). That is even truer if 'Special Products' are subjected to smaller cuts and developing countries exercise their right – as laid out in the July Framework Agreement – to undertake lesser cuts (zero in the case of LDCs) than developed countries. Politically this makes it easier for developing and least developed countries to offer big cuts on bound rates – but it also means the benefits to them are smaller than if they had a smaller binding overhang.

Cotton subsidy cuts would help cotton-exporting developing countries. The removal of cotton subsidies (which have raised producer prices by well over 50 per cent in the US and EU – see Sumner, 2005) would raise the export price of cotton (although not equally across all exporters because of product differentiation). If those subsidies were removed as part of freeing all merchandise trade, that price rise is estimated to be eight per cent for Brazil but less for Sub-Saharan Africa on average. However, cotton exports from Sub-Saharan Africa would be a huge 75 per cent larger, and the share of all developing countries in global exports would be 85 per cent instead of 56 per cent in 2015, vindicating those countries' efforts to ensure cotton subsidies receive specific attention in the Doha negotiations.

Expanding non-agricultural market access would add substantially to the gains from agricultural reform. Adding a 50 per cent cut to non-agricultural tariffs by developed countries (and 33 per cent by developing countries and zero by LDCs) to the tiered formula cut to agricultural tariffs would double the gain from Doha for developing countries (compare Scenarios 1 and 5 in Tables 7, 8 and 9). That would bring the global gain to $96 billion from Doha merchandise liberalisation, which is a sizeable one-third of the potential welfare gain from full liberalisation of $287 billion. Adding services reform would of course boost that welfare gain even more.

Adding non-agricultural tariff reform to agricultural reform helps to balance the exchange of 'concessions'. The agricultural reforms would boost the annual value of world trade in 2015 by less than one-quarter of what would happen if non-agricultural tariffs were also reduced. The latter's inclusion would also help to balance the exchange of 'concessions' in terms of increases in bilateral trade values: in that case developing countries' exports to high-income countries would then be $62 billion, which is close to the $55 billion increase in high-income countries' exports to developing countries. With only agricultural reform, the latter's bilateral trade growth would be little more than half the former's (Table 10).

Most developing countries gain, and the rest could if they reform more. Even though much of the DC gains from that comprehensive Doha scenario go to numerous large developing countries, notably Brazil, Argentina and Other Latin America plus India, Thailand and South Africa, the rest of Sub-Saharan Africa gains

TABLE 10

Effects on Bilateral Merchandise Trade Flows of Adding Non-agricultural Tariff Cuts to
Agricultural Reform under Doha, 2015
(2001 $ billion increase over the baseline in 2015)

Exports from:	Exports to:			
	Propn'l Agric. Reform Only[a]		Agric. Plus Non-agric. Reform[b]	
	High-income[c] Countries	Developing Countries	High-income[c] Countries	Developing Countries
High-income[c] countries	20	11	80	55
Developing countries	18	5	62	16
Total world	**38**	**16**	**142**	**71**

Notes:
[a] Scenario 2 in Table 7.
[b] Scenario 5 in Table 7.
[c] High-income countries include the newly industrialised East Asian customs territories of Hong Kong, Korea, Singapore and Taiwan as well as Europe's transition economies that joined the EU in April 2004.

Source: Anderson, Martin and van der Mensbrugghe (2005a, Table 12.16).

too. This is particularly so when developing countries participate as full partners in the negotiations. An important part of this result comes from the increases in market access – on a non-discriminatory basis – by other developing countries.

Preference erosion may be less of an issue than commonly assumed. Some least developed countries in Sub-Saharan Africa and elsewhere appear to be slight losers in our Doha simulations when developed countries cut their tariffs and those LDCs choose not to reform at all themselves.[7] These simulations overstate the benefits of tariff preferences for LDCs, however, since they ignore the trade-dampening effect of complex rules of origin and the grabbing of much of the rents by developed-country importers. Even if they would lose after correcting for those realities, it remains true that preference-receiving countries could always be compensated for preference erosion via increased aid at relatively very small cost to current preference providers – and in the process other developing countries currently hurt by LCD preferences would enjoy greater access to the markets of reforming developed countries.

Farm output and employment would grow in developing countries under Doha. Despite a few low-income countries losing slightly under our Doha scenarios when they choose to reform little themselves, in all the developing countries and regions shown the levels of output and employment on farms expand. It is only in the most protected developed countries of Western Europe, Northeast Asia and the US that these levels would fall – and even there it is only by small

[7] As warned by Panagariya (2004) among others, some low-income countries' terms of trade could deteriorate either because they would lose tariff preferences on their exports or because they are net food importers and so would face higher prices for their imports of temperate foods.

TABLE 11
Effects of a Comprehensive Doha Reform on Agricultural Output and Employment Growth,
by Region, 2005 to 2015
(Annual average growth rate, per cent)

	Output		Employment	
	Baseline	Scenario 5[a]	Baseline	Scenario 5[a]
Australia and New Zealand	3.5	4.3	0.4	1.0
Canada	3.5	4.0	0.2	0.6
United States	2.2	1.9	-0.8	-1.4
EU25 plus EFTA	1.0	-0.3	-1.8	-2.8
Japan	0.5	-1.4	-2.7	-4.1
Korea and Taiwan	2.2	1.5	-1.3	-2.1
Argentina	2.9	3.5	0.9	1.5
Bangladesh	4.2	4.2	1.1	1.2
Brazil	3.3	4.4	1.1	2.2
China	4.3	4.3	0.8	0.8
India	4.3	4.4	1.0	1.0
Indonesia	3.0	3.0	-0.7	-0.6
Thailand	-0.1	0.4	-4.6	-4.3
Vietnam	5.8	5.9	3.9	4.0
Russia	1.5	1.4	-2.3	-2.4
Mexico	3.9	4.0	2.0	2.3
South Africa	2.5	2.6	0.0	0.1
Turkey	3.0	3.0	-0.5	-0.5
Rest of South Asia	4.8	4.9	2.0	2.1
Rest of East Asia	3.7	3.8	0.2	0.3
Rest of Latin America & Carib.	4.4	5.3	1.9	2.6
Rest of E. Europe & C. Asia	3.3	3.3	0.0	0.0
Middle East & North Africa	4.0	4.0	1.5	1.5
Other Southern Africa	5.3	5.4	3.0	3.0
Rest of Sub-Saharan Africa	4.6	4.8	2.2	2.3
Rest of the World	5.0	5.5	2.4	2.7

Note:
[a] Scenario 5 in Table 7.

Source: Anderson, Martin and van der Mensbrugghe (2005a, Table 12.17).

amounts, contrary to the predictions of scaremongers who claim agriculture would be decimated in reforming countries (Table 11). Even if there was a move to completely free merchandise trade, the developed countries' share of the world's primary agricultural GDP by 2015 would be only slightly lower at 25 instead of 30 per cent (but their share of global agricultural exports would be diminished considerably more: from 53 to 38 per cent).

Poverty could be reduced under Doha. Under the full merchandise trade liberalisation scenario, extreme poverty in developing countries (those earning less than $1/day) would drop by 32 million in 2015 relative to the baseline level of 622 million, a reduction of five per cent. The majority of the poor by 2015 are projected to be in Sub-Saharan Africa (SSA), and there the reduction would be

TABLE 12

Changes in Poverty (those earning <$1/day) in Alternative Doha Scenarios Compared with Full Liberalisation, 2015

	Base-line Share	Full Liberalisation Share	Shares under Doha Alternatives		
			Doha Scenario 1	Doha Scenario 5	Doha Scenario 6
2015 Headcount (Per cent)					
East Asia & Pacific	0.9	0.8	0.9	0.9	0.9
Latin America & Carib.	6.9	6.6	6.9	6.9	6.8
South Asia	12.8	12.5	12.8	12.7	12.6
Sub-Saharan Africa	38.4	36.0	38.4	38.3	38.1
All developing countries	**10.2**	**9.7**	**10.2**	**10.2**	**10.1**
2015 Headcount	*2015 Level*	*Decrease from Baseline in Millions*	*Decrease from Baseline in Millions*		
East Asia & Pacific	19	2.2	0.1	0.3	0.5
Latin America & Carib.	43	2.1	0.3	0.4	0.5
South Asia	216	5.6	0.2	1.4	3.0
Sub-Saharan Africa	340	21.1	−0.1	0.5	2.2
All developing countries	**622**	**31.9**	**0.5**	**2.5**	**6.3**

Source: Authors' World Bank LINKAGE model simulations as reported in Anderson, Martin and van der Mensbrugghe (2005b, Table 17.7).

six per cent.[8] Under the Doha scenarios reported in Table 12, the poverty impacts are far more modest. The number of poor living on $1/day or less would fall by 2.5 million in the case of the core Doha Scenario 5 (of which 0.5 million are in SSA) and by 6.3 million in the case of Doha Scenario 6 (of which 2.2 million are in SSA). This corresponds to the relatively modest ambitions of the merchandise trade reforms as captured in these Doha scenarios. If only agriculture was reformed (Doha Scenario 1) there would be much less poverty alleviation globally and none at all in SSA. This shows the importance for poverty of including manufactured products in the Doha negotiations.

---

[8] The approach here has been to take the change in the average per capita consumption of the poor, apply an estimated income-to-poverty elasticity, and assess the impacts on the poverty headcount index. We have done this by calculating the change in the real wage of unskilled workers, deflating it by a food/clothing consumer price index which is more relevant for the poor than the total price index. That real wage grows, over all developing countries, by 3.6 per cent, or more than four times greater than the overall average income increase. We are assuming that the change in unskilled wages is fully passed through to households. Also, while the model closure has the loss in tariff revenues replaced by a change in direct household taxation, the poverty calculation assumes – realistically for many developing countries – that these tax increases only affect skilled workers and high-income households. While these simple calculations are not a substitute for more-detailed individual country case study analysis using detailed household surveys as in, for example, Hertel and Winters (2005), they are able to give a broad region-wide indication of the poverty impact.

Developing countries could trade off Special and Differential Treatment for more market access. If developing countries were to tone down their call for Special and Differential Treatment (see Josling, 2005), in terms of wanting smaller cuts and longer phase-in periods, reciprocity means they could expect bigger tariff and subsidy cuts from developed countries. Similarly, if they were to forego their call for lesser cuts for 'Special Products', they could demand that developed countries forego their call for some 'Sensitive Products' to be subject to smaller tariff cuts. A comparison of Scenarios 5 and 6 in Tables 7, 8 and 9 shows that the economic payoffs for low-income countries even if high-income countries do not reciprocate with larger offers is considerable. Moreover, by embracing those options to reform more in the context of the Doha Round would make it harder for high-income countries to resist the call to respond with larger reforms themselves.

4. KEY POLICY IMPLICATIONS

Among the numerous policy implications that can be drawn from the above findings, the following are worth highlighting.

Prospective gains are too large to not find the needed political will to make Doha a success. With gains of the order of $300 billion per year at stake from implementing the July Framework Agreement (even if no reforms are forthcoming in services and if the counterfactual would be the status quo rather than protectionist backsliding), the political will needs to be found to bring the Round to a success-ful conclusion, and the sooner the better. Multilateral cuts in MFN bindings are helpful also because they can lock in previous unilateral trade liberalisations that otherwise would remain unbound and hence be vulnerable to backsliding; and they can be used as an opportunity to multilateralise previously agreed preferen-tial trade agreements and thereby reduce the risk of trade diversion from those bilateral or regional arrangements (as stressed in Sutherland et al., 2004).

Since developed countries would gain most, and have the most capacity and influence, they need to show leadership at the WTO. The large developed coun-tries cannot generate a successful agreement on their own, but nor can the Doha Round succeed without a major push by those key traders. Their capacity to assist poorer economies could hardly manifest itself more clearly than in encourag-ing global economic integration via trade reform, and in particular in opening developed-country markets to the items of greatest importance to poorer countries, namely farm (and textile) products. The more that is done, the more developing countries will be encouraged to reciprocate by opening their own markets more – accelerating South-South trade in addition to South-North trade.

Outlawing agricultural export subsidies is the obvious first step. That will bring agriculture into line with the basic GATT rule against such measures, and in the process help to limit the extent to which governments encourage agricultural production by other means (since it would raise the cost of surplus disposal). China has already committed not to use them, and other developing countries too can find more efficient ways of stabilising their domestic food markets than by dumping surpluses abroad.

Even more importantly, agricultural tariff and domestic support bindings must be cut hugely to remove binding overhang and provide some genuine market opening. Getting rid of the binding overhang that resulted from the Uruguay Round, particularly with 'dirty tariffication', must be a priority.[9] The highest-subsidising countries, namely the EU, the US and Norway, need to reduce their domestic support not just for the sake of their own economies but also to encourage developing countries to reciprocate by opening their markets as a *quid pro quo*. But more than that is needed if market access is to expand. If a choice had to be made, reducing MFN bound tariffs in general would be preferable to raising tariff rate quotas, because the latter help only those lucky enough to obtain quotas and crowd out non-quota holders. (Being against the non-discrimination spirit of the GATT, they deserve the same fate as textile quotas which were abolished at the end of 2004.) Exempting even just a few Sensitive and Special Products is undesirable as it would reduce hugely the gains from reform and would tend to divert resources into, instead of away from, enterprises in which countries have their least comparative advantage. If it turns out to be politically impossible not to designate some Sensitive and Special Products, it would be crucial to impose a cap such that any product with a bound tariff in excess of, say, 100 per cent had to reduce it to that cap rate.

Expanding non-agricultural market access at the same time as reforming agriculture is essential. A balanced exchange of concession is impossible without adding other sectors, and it needs to be more than just textiles and clothing (which also benefit developing countries disproportionately) even though they are the other highly distorted sector. With other merchandise included, the trade expansion would be four times greater for both rich and poor countries – and poverty in low-income countries would be reduced considerably more.

South-South 'concessions' also are needed, especially for developing countries, which means reconsidering the opportunity for developing countries to liberalise less. Since developing countries are trading so much more with each other now, they are the major beneficiaries of reforms within their own regions. Upper middle-income countries might consider giving least developed countries duty-free access to their markets (mirroring the recent initiatives of developed countries), but better than such discriminatory action would be MFN tariff reductions by them. Even least developed countries should consider reducing their tariff binding overhang at least, since doing that in the context of Doha gives

---

[9] As Francois and Martin (2004) have shown, any binding cut is useful for the long run even if it brings no immediate cut in applied rates.

them more scope to demand 'concessions' (or compensation for preference erosion or other contributors to terms of trade deterioration) from richer countries – and yet would not require them to cut their own *applied* tariffs very much.

5. CONCLUSIONS

The good news in this paper is that there is a great deal to be gained from liberalising merchandise – and especially agricultural – trade under Doha, with a disproportionately high share of that potential gain available for developing countries (relative to their share of the global economy). Moreover, it is the poorest people in developing countries that appear to be most likely to gain from global trade liberalisation, namely farmers and unskilled labourers in developing countries. To realise that potential gain, it is in agriculture that by far the greatest cuts in bound tariffs and subsidies are required. However, the political sensitivity of farm support programmes, coupled with the complexities of the measures introduced in the Uruguay Round Agreement on Agriculture and of the modalities set out in the Doha Framework Agreement of July 2004, ensure the devil will be in the details of the final Doha agreement. It is for that reason that *ex ante* empirical analysis of the sort provided in the study summarised above is a prerequisite for countries engaged in the Doha Round of negotiations.

What emerges from our analysis is that developing countries would not *have* to reform very much under Doha, because of the large gaps between their tariff bindings and applied rates. That is even truer if they exercise their right (as laid out in the July Framework Agreement) to undertake lesser tariff cuts than developed countries. In that case, they gain little in terms of improved efficiency of national resource use. Yet, as Panagariya (2004) and others have warned, for a non-trivial number of low-income countries their terms of trade could deteriorate, as shown in Table 3. For some that is because they would lose tariff preferences on their exports. For others it is because they are net food importers and so would face higher prices for their imports of temperate foods. To realise more of their potential gains from trade, developing and least developed countries would need to forego some of the Special and Differential Treatment they have previously demanded, and perhaps also commit to additional unilateral trade (and complementary domestic) reforms, and to invest more in trade facilitation. High-income countries could encourage them to do so by being willing to open up their own markets more to developing-country exports,[10] and by providing more targeted aid.

---

[10] Limao and Olarreago (2005) suggest preference erosion could be addressed by replacing the current margin of preference with an equivalent import subsidy for products from preference-receiving countries, thereby retaining the preference status quo while taking away this reason not to undertake most-favoured-nation tariff cuts.

To that end, a new proposal has been put forward to reward developing-country commitments to greater trade reform with an expansion of trade-facilitating aid, to be provided by a major expansion of the current Integrated Framework which is operated by a consortium of international agencies for least developed countries (Hoekman, 2004 and 2005). This may well provide an attractive path for developing countries seeking to trade their way out of poverty, not least because it would help to offset the tendency for an expanded aid flow to cause a real exchange rate appreciation (see Commission for Africa, 2005, pp. 296–97). As well, it is potentially a far more efficient way for developed countries to assist people in low-income countries than the current systems of tariff preferences.

In conclusion, the July Framework Agreement does not guarantee major gains from the Doha Development Agenda. On the one hand, even if an agreement is ultimately reached, it may be very modest. How modest depends on, among other things, the nature of the agricultural tariff-cutting formula, the size of the cuts, the extent to which exceptions for Sensitive and Special Products are allowed, whether a tariff cap is introduced, and the extent to which Special and Differential Treatment is invoked by developing countries in terms of their market access commitments. But what is equally clear, on the other hand, is that major gains are possible if only the political will to reform protectionist policies – especially in agriculture – can be mustered.

REFERENCES

Aksoy, M. A. and J. C. Beghin (eds.) (2004), *Global Agricultural Trade and Developing Countries* (Washington DC: World Bank).

Anania, G., M. Bowman, C. Carter and A. McCalla (eds.) (2004), *Agricultural Policy Reform and the WTO: Where Are We Heading?* (London: Edward Elgar).

Anderson, K. and T. E. Josling (eds.) (2005), *The WTO and Agriculture* (London: Edward Elgar).

Anderson, K. and W. Martin (eds.) (2005), *Agricultural Trade Reform and the Doha Development Agenda* (New York: Palgrave Macmillan, forthcoming).

Anderson, K., W. Martin and D. van der Mensbrugghe (2005a), 'Market and Welfare Implications of Doha Reform Scenarios', Ch. 12 in K. Anderson and W. Martin (eds.), *Agricultural Trade Reform and the Doha Development Agenda* (New York: Palgrave Macmillan, forthcoming).

Anderson, K., W. Martin and D. van der Mensbrugghe (2005b), 'Global Impact of the Doha Scenarios on Poverty', Ch. 17 in T. W. Hertel and L. A. Winters (eds.), *Putting Development Back Into the Doha Agenda: Poverty Impacts of a WTO Agreement* (New York: Palgrave Macmillan, forthcoming).

Anderson, K., Y. Hayami and others (1986), *The Political Economy of Agricultural Protection: East Asia in International Perspective* (Boston, London and Sydney: Allen & Unwin).

Bouët, A., L. Fontagné and S. Jean (2005), 'Is Erosion of Preferences a Serious Concern?', Ch. 6 in K. Anderson and W. Martin (eds.), *Agricultural Trade Reform and the Doha Development Agenda,* (New York: Palgrave Macmillan, forthcoming).

Commission for Africa (2005), *Our Common Interest* (London: UK Department for International Development, March).

Dollar, D. and A. Kraay (2004), 'Trade, Growth and Poverty', *Economic Journal,* **114** (February), F22-49.

FAO (2004), *The State of Food and Agriculture 2003–04* (Rome: UN Food and Agriculture Organisation).

Finger, J. M. and P. Schuler (2001), 'Implementation of Uruguay Round Commitments: The Development Challenge', Ch. 7 in B. Hoekman and W. Martin (eds.), *Developing Countries and the WTO: A Pro-Active Agenda* (Oxford: Blackwell).

Finger, J. M. and L. A. Winters (2002), 'Reciprocity in the WTO', Ch. 7 in B. Hoekman, A. Matoo and P. English (eds.), *Development, Trade and the WTO: A Handbook* (Washington DC: World Bank).

Francois, J. F. and W. Martin (2004), 'Commercial Policy, Bindings and Market Access', *European Economic Review*, **48**, 3, 665–79.

Goldin, I. and O. Knudsen (eds.) (1990), *Agricultural Trade Liberalization: Implications for Developing Countries* (Paris: OECD).

de Gorter, H. and E. Kliauga (2005), 'Consequences of TRQ Expansions and In-quota Tariff Reductions', Ch. 5 in K. Anderson and W. Martin (eds.), *Agricultural Trade Reform and the Doha Development Agenda* (New York: Palgrave Macmillan, forthcoming).

Hart, C. E. and J. C. Beghin (2005), 'Rethinking Domestic Support Disciplines', Ch. 8 in K. Anderson and W. Martin (eds.), *Agricultural Trade Reform and the Doha Development Agenda*, (New York: Palgrave Macmillan, forthcoming).

Hathaway, D. and M. Ingco (1996), 'Agricultural Liberalization and the Uruguay Round', Ch. 2 in W. Martin and L. A. Winters (eds.), *The Uruguay Round and the Developing Countries* (Cambridge and New York: Cambridge University Press).

Hertel, T. W. and R. Keeney (2005), 'What's at Stake: The Relative Importance of Import Barriers, Export Subsidies and Domestic Support', Ch. 2 in K. Anderson and W. Martin (eds.), *Agricultural Trade Reform and the Doha Development Agenda* (New York: Palgrave Macmillan, forthcoming).

Hertel, T. W. and L. A. Winters (eds.) (2005), *Putting Development Back Into the Doha Agenda: Poverty Impacts of a WTO Agreement* (New York: Palgrave Macmillan, forthcoming).

Hoekman, B. (2004), 'Operationalizing the Concept of Policy Space in the WTO: Beyond Special and Differential Treatment', Paper presented to the 3rd Annual Conference on Preparing the Doha Development Round, European University Institute (2–3 July).

Hoekman, B. (2005), 'Making the WTO More Supportive of Development', *Finance and Development*, March, 14–18.

Hoekman, B., F. Ng and M. Olarreaga (2004), 'Agricultural Tariffs versus Subsidies: What's More Important for Developing Countries?', *World Bank Economic Review*, **18**, 2, 175–204.

Hoekman, B. and P. Messerlin (2005), 'Removing the Exception of Agricultural Export Subsidies', Ch. 7 in K. Anderson and W. Martin (eds.), *Agricultural Trade Reform and the Doha Development Agenda*, (New York: Palgrave Macmillan, forthcoming).

Ingco, M. D. and J. D. Nash (eds.) (2004), *Agriculture and the WTO: Creating a Trading System for Development* (Washington DC: World Bank; and New York: Oxford University Press).

Ingco, M. D. and L. A. Winters (eds.) (2004), *Agriculture and the New Trade Agenda: Creating a Global Trading Environment for Development* (Cambridge and New York: Cambridge University Press).

Jank, M. S. (ed.) (2004), *Agricultural Trade Liberalization: Policies and Implications for Latin America* (Washington DC: Inter-American Development Bank).

Jean, S., D. Laborde and W. Martin (2005), 'Consequences of Alternative Formulas for Agricultural Tariff Cuts', Ch. 4 in K. Anderson and W. Martin (eds.), *Agricultural Trade Reform and the Doha Development Agenda* (New York: Palgrave Macmillan, forthcoming).

Jensen, H. G. and H. Zobbe (2005), 'Consequences of Reducing AMS Limits', Ch. 8 in K. Anderson and W. Martin (eds.), *Agricultural Trade Reform and the Doha Development Agenda*, (New York: Palgrave Macmillan, forthcoming).

Josling, T. (2005), 'Consequences of Special and Differential Treatment for Developing Countries', Ch. 3 in K. Anderson and W. Martin (eds.), *Agricultural Trade Reform and the Doha Development Agenda* (New York: Palgrave Macmillan, forthcoming).

Josling, T. E., S. Tangermann and T. K. Warley (1996), *Agriculture in the GATT* (London: Macmillan; and New York: St. Martin's Press).

Legg, W. (2003), 'Agricultural Subsidies: Measurement and Use in Policy Evaluation', *Journal of Agricultural Economics*, **54**, 2, 175–200.

Limao, N. and M. Olarreaga (2005), 'Trade Preferences to Small Developing Countries and the Welfare Costs of Lost Multilateral Liberalization', Policy Research Working Paper No. 3565 (World Bank, Washington DC, March).

Lindert, P. (1991), 'Historical Patterns of Agricultural Protection', in P. Timmer (ed.), *Agriculture and the State* (Ithaca, NY: Cornell University Press).

Martin, W. and L. A. Winters (eds.) (1996), *The Uruguay Round and the Developing Countries* (Cambridge and New York: Cambridge University Press).

Orden, D. and E. Diaz-Bonilla (2005), 'Holograms and Ghosts: New and Old Ideas for Reforming Agricultural Policies', Ch. 11 in K. Anderson and W. Martin (eds.), *Agricultural Trade Reform and the Doha Development Agenda*, (New York: Palgrave Macmillan, forthcoming).

Panagariya, A. (2004), 'Subsidies and Trade Barriers: Alternative Perspective 10.2', in B. Lomborg (ed.), *Global Crises, Global Solutions* (Cambridge and New York: Cambridge University Press), 592–601.

Sumner, D. A. (2005), 'Reducing Cotton Subsidies: The DDA Cotton Initiative', Ch. 10 in K. Anderson and W. Martin (eds.), *Agricultural Trade Reform and the Doha Development Agenda* (New York: Palgrave Macmillan, forthcoming).

Sutherland, P. et al. (2004), *The Future of the WTO*, Report by the Consultative Board (Geneva: World Trade Organisation).

Tyers, R. and K. Anderson (1992), *Disarray in World Food Markets: A Quantitative Assessment* (Cambridge and New York: Cambridge University Press).

van der Mensbrugghe, D. (2004), 'LINKAGE Technical Reference Document: Version 6.0' (Mimeo, The World Bank, Washington DC, accessible at http://siteresources.worldbank.org/ INTPROSPECTS/Resources/334934-1100792545130/LinkageTechNote.pdf).

Winters, L. A. (2004), 'Trade Liberalization and Economic Performance: An Overview', *Economic Journal*, **114** (February), F4–21.

Winters, L. A., N. McCulloch and A. McKay (2004), 'Trade Liberalization and Poverty: The Empirical Evidence', *Journal of Economic Literature*, **62**, 1, 72–115.

World Bank (1986), *World Development Report 1986* (New York: Oxford University Press).

WTO (2003), 'Negotiations on Agriculture: First Draft of Modalities for the Further Commitments', TN/AG/W/1/Rev.1 (Geneva: World Trade Organisation, 19 March, The Harbinson Draft).

WTO (2004), 'Doha Work Programme: Decision Adopted by the General Council on 1 August 2004', WT/L/579 (Geneva: World Trade Organisation, The July Framework Agreement).

7

Multilateral Agricultural Trade Liberalisation: The Contrasting Fortunes of Developing Countries in the Doha Round

Antoine Bouët, Jean-Christophe Bureau, Yvan Decreux and Sébastien Jean

1. INTRODUCTION

𝕿HE agricultural sector has been one of the most contentious issues in the multilateral trade negotiations that have been taking place since 1999. Discussions on agriculture have delayed the conclusion of the so-called 'Doha Round' of negotiations under the auspices of the World Trade Organisation (WTO), launched by the 2001 Ministerial Declaration. After 13 major meetings, some 45 proposals and submissions from 127 countries, members failed to agree on numerical targets, formulas and other 'modalities' on the agricultural sector

The authors are grateful to one anonymous referee for comments and helpful criticism. They thank Alan Matthews, John Beghin, Tom Hertel, Tim Josling, Alex Gohin and Stephen Tokarick for valuable comments on earlier versions. The database has benefited from numerous contributions during its development, including contributions from UNCTAD, from many members of the GTAP consortium, researchers from Purdue University, from the Economic Research Service of the US Department of Agriculture, from the FOI in Copenhagen and the OECD Secretariat in Paris. The list would be too long to quote them all. The usual disclaimer applies.

before the scheduled deadlines. It was only in July 2004 that an agreement was found on some general principles. However, crucial technical aspects, such as the exact degree of tariff reduction (bands and thresholds) and the level of cuts in distorting farm support have been left to future negotiation.

During these long-drawn-out negotiations, developing countries (hereafter DCs) have emerged as a significant political force. They built a united front to oppose an agreement during the 2003 Ministerial Cancún meeting. Since then, they have vehemently criticised the farm policies and agricultural tariffs in developed countries. During the year 2004, DCs have extracted some concessions from developed countries, namely the (conditional) ending of European Union (EU) export subsidies, and the promise that significant cuts will take place for highly protective tariffs. They also secured agreement that issues of particular interest for them, like cotton, would be examined.

Several assessments of the effect of an agricultural agreement in the Doha Round have been published during the last years. Most simulations with Applied General Equilibrium (AGE) models have concluded that developing countries would reap large benefits from agricultural trade liberalisation. The World Bank, in particular, makes a strong case for the large gains that developing countries would draw from an agreement on agriculture. However, we believe that there are several reasons why many AGE simulations have been excessively optimistic in this area, and that general conclusions might have been drawn on the basis of models that rely on insufficiently detailed data. In this article, we assess the impact of the Doha agreement, with a particular focus on three aspects that are, in our opinion, the weak points of most existing models: (i) a precise measurement of protection, including trade preferences, regional agreements, and the gap between applied and bound protection, at a disaggregated product level; (ii) a precise accounting of the complex effects of the various types of domestic support; (iii) a distinction between the various groups of DCs.

We first explain why we believe that many assessments of multilateral negotiations using AGE models have led to questionable conclusions regarding the effect of an agricultural agreement on DCs. We then describe the main features of our model. We focus on the differences with other models, on experiment design, and on the baseline assumptions. We describe the data, in particular our original treatment of tariff protection. In a second part of the article, we present the results of our simulations of the August 2004 agreement, using figures from the last draft compromise available for issues still under negotiation. We then provide some explanations for the results and undertake some sensitivity analysis. Introducing better protection data, accounting for quota rents, distinguishing the multiple forms of agricultural support, and using a careful measurement of the actual impact of posted liberalisation lead to conclusions that differ from the ones often reached by AGE modellers, regarding the impact of agricultural trade liberalisation on DCs.

2. AGE MODELS AND WTO NEGOTIATIONS

AGE models were extensively used to assess the impact of trade negotiations during the Uruguay Round, with a particular effort by researchers working in international organisations, like the Organisation for Economic Co-operation and Development (hereafter OECD). The consequences of the Round for developing countries were given particular attention (Goldin and Knudsen, 1990; and Martin and Winters, 1996). The Global Trade Analysis Project (GTAP) made possible a dramatic expansion of AGE-based approaches (Hertel, 1997). For several years, AGE models have been at the core of the economic assessments of the Doha Round negotiations (see Beghin, Roland-Host and van der Mensbrugghe, 2002; Diao, Somwaru and Roe, 2001; Francois, van Meijl and van Tongeren, 2003; and Frandsen et al., 2003, for example).

Obviously, not all models lead to similar results regarding the effect of a WTO agreement. However, most simulations conducted with AGE models suggest that DCs will be major gainers under a Doha agreement (see Hertel, Hoekman and Martin, 2003; and Goldin, Knudsen and van der Mensbrugghe, 2003, for example). According to some simulations, DCs would reap two-thirds of the US$500 billion gains generated by ambitious trade liberalisation in the agricultural sector (The World Bank, 2004). We believe that several limitations of the models used mean these conclusions must be questioned.

a. Acknowledging DCs Diversity

First, general conclusions about DCs as a whole could be misleading, and the impact of the Doha Round on these countries is likely to be uneven. With the ending of export subsidies and a decrease in tariffs and production-enhancing subsidies, world agricultural prices are likely to go up. Higher prices and better access to agricultural markets in developed countries should benefit DCs, whose comparative advantages often lie in agriculture. However, not all DCs are net exporters of agricultural products. Not all net food-importing countries have the capacity to increase significantly their production, should unfair competition and subsidies be eliminated in OECD countries. In such cases, trade liberalisation will mainly increase the food import bill. A multilateral agreement on agriculture will also have contrasted effects because some DCs export products subject to a high level of distorting support or to tariff peaks in OECD countries or in India and China (sugar, beef, cotton, groundnuts). Other DCs export products whose markets are much less distorted (coffee, cocoa, fish) and will gain less.

b. Erosion of Preferences and Trade Diversion

The preferences granted either under preferential regimes linked to economic development criteria (e.g. the General System of Preferences or GSP, or the specific regimes offered to Least Developed Countries – LDCs – by most OECD countries) or on a geographical basis (e.g. the EU Lomé/Cotonou agreements, the US Africa Growth Opportunity Act, the Caribbean Basin Economic Recovery Act) are of considerable importance for some countries (see OECD, 2005). This is particularly the case for some small and highly specialised economies, which have developed specific agricultural sectors under a preferential access to the EU or US market. The ending of these preferences, or even the erosion of the preferential margins which would follow a multilateral decrease in tariffs, may have a significant negative impact. Some DCs might lose some markets to the benefit of developed countries such as Australia or New Zealand, or other DCs such as Brazil. To our knowledge, however, no AGE assessment of multilateral liberalisation has so far fully accounted for preferential regimes (the recent work on Africa by Achterbosch et al., 2004, is an exception). Due to the difficulty of gathering the relevant information, only a few agreements are generally accounted for.

c. Posted vs. Actual Liberalisation

Many AGE models rely on crude assumptions on the level of protection and domestic support. It is often ignored that many countries apply tariffs that are only a fraction of their bound tariffs (often one-third of the level of bound tariffs in DCs, see Gibson et al., 2001). As multilateral tariff reductions are made on the basis of bound tariffs, the actual impact of a tariff cut will often be overestimated.[1] Reductions in farm support are negotiated on the basis of a maximum Aggregate Measure of Support (AMS), an indicator that combines estimates of the production-distorting support paid by taxpayers and consumers. In the EU, for example, the actual AMS as notified to the WTO is only a fraction of the ceiling on which countries negotiate reductions, and the recent EU policy reforms will soon reduce the actual AMS to a very small figure. That is, cuts in distorting support decided during the Doha Round will result in only a small change in the actual level of EU support. Again, ignoring the gap between the figures used in the negotiation and the actual figures can lead to misleading results.[2]

In the present article, we attempt to improve on existing models by addressing these issues. The model that we use shares some general features of other AGE models (e.g. some recent versions of the GTAP model including imperfect competition, or the LINKAGE model, see Hertel, 1997; or van der Mensbrugghe,

[1] Another source of overstatement of actual liberalisation is the overstatement of initial protection, when not yet implemented commitments (such as those under the URAA for DCs, or those under the accession package for newly-acceded WTO members) are not taken into account, as is usually the case.

[2] Note that, in addition, modellers do not always make allowance for blue box exemptions and *de minimis* payments when modelling cuts in support.

2002, respectively). It contains some specific aspects, such as product differentiation and increasing returns to scale in some sectors, endogenous land supply in some countries and a dual labour market in developing countries. Agricultural policies (including output quotas, market price support measures and expenditure ceilings) are explicitly modelled, and consistency is ensured between intervention prices, export subsidies and tariffs. However, the major improvements are in the area of data on protection, a precise representation of the various forms of farm support, and scenarios that account for the existing gap between negotiated trade liberalisation and actual changes.

3. MODEL AND DATA

a. Main Characteristics of the Model

The model used in this article is a multi-sector, multi-region general equilibrium model. While sharing basic features with the MIRAGE model (described in Bchir et al., 2002), it has been developed specifically to assess the consequences of agricultural trade liberalisation. The model distinguishes 30 sectors (including 23 agricultural and food sectors) and 11 country groups. In particular, large agricultural exporters (developing members of the Cairns Group) and sub-Saharan Africa are distinguished. All agricultural sectors are perfectly competitive, but industrial (including food) sectors and services are not. Imperfect competition is represented with an oligopolistic framework à la Cournot. It accounts for horizontal product differentiation linked to varieties, but also to geographical origin (nested Armington-Dixit-Stiglitz utility function). Some degree of vertical product differentiation is introduced in industrial sectors, by distinguishing two quality ranges, according to the country of origin of the product. (This is not the case, however, for agricultural commodities.)

Although MIRAGE is a dynamic and sequential model, here we present only static comparative simulations. The impact of some of our contributions (e.g. applied tariffs, detailed farm policy instruments, actual reductions, etc.) should appear more clearly than with a dynamic version which would have taken us further away from a *ceteris paribus* comparison with other studies. Capital stock is assumed to be perfectly mobile across sectors and we ignore foreign direct investment. In terms of macroeconomic closure, investment is savings-driven, and the current balance is assumed to be exogenous. In the simulations presented here, we also ignore the possible impact of trade policy on economy-wide capital stock (through income or the rate of return to capital in the dynamic version of the model). Land supply behaves as an isoelastic function of the real return to land (van der Mensbrugghe, 2002). Regions are accordingly classified either as land-constrained or not, and different values of supply elasticities are assumed.[3] Land mobility across the agricultural sector is assumed to be imperfect.

All developing countries are assumed to have dual economies, with an urban market that is distinct from a 'traditional' market in rural areas (Lewis, 1954; and Harris and Todaro, 1970). The modern sector (industry and services) pays an efficiency wage to unskilled workers, above their marginal productivity. It is thus faced with a totally elastic supply of unskilled labour. The primary sector (i.e., agriculture), in contrast, pays a competitive wage. The supply of unskilled labour available for the primary sector is set as a residual, once the 'modern' sector has set its unskilled labour employment level. The specification provides a simple way to account for a hidden unemployment in developing countries, and to depart from the standard assumption of balanced labour markets used in AGE models, in spite of its obvious inappropriateness in the DCs case. In all countries, labour is imperfectly mobile between agricultural activities and other sectors, and substitution is represented by a Constant Elasticity of Transformation function.

b. Some Original Contributions to the Modelling of Agricultural Trade Liberalisation

While the general architecture of the model remains relatively standard, compared to recent efforts in AGE modelling (with the exception of the dual labour market assumption), we introduce some major improvements in the data and the treatment of agricultural policies. As in many other models, we use the GTAP database for accounting matrices, trade costs and non-farm policies (Dimaranan and MacDougall, 2002). However, our protection data and data on farm support rely on original work. Here, tariff protection relies on applied tariffs. A special database was developed in collaboration with the International Trade Commission (ITC), the MAcMap dataset. The exact methodology is described in Bouët et al. (2004). MAcMap provides *ad valorem* tariffs, and estimates of the *ad valorem* equivalents of specific tariffs and tariff quotas (based on the in- or out-of-quota tariff, depending on which one is binding). Tariff quota rents are also computed, for those quotas that are filled, and are assumed to be kept by exporters. Protection is measured at a bilateral level: for each product, for each of the 163 reporting countries, an *ad valorem* equivalent of all these protective instruments is calculated for each of 208 partners. All preferential agreements, including

---

[3] The values of the elasticities are similar to those used in the LINKAGE model, i.e. 0.25 for land-constrained countries and 1 for other countries. We thank Dominique van der Mensbrugghe for providing us with information and advice on this point. The transformation elasticity of land mobility across sectors is set to 0.5.

those of the EU, are taken into account. This information was put together at the six-digit level of the Harmonised System (HS) of classification (hereafter HS6), i.e. for 5,111 goods. The aggregation procedure uses weights based on the exports of each partner country to a reference group of countries which the importer belongs to, in order to avoid the well-known endogeneity bias that affects import-weighted average tariffs. The bilateral matrices at the HS6 level make it possible to account for country-specific aggregate tariffs, and for country-specific aggregate tariff reductions. A change in the EU vector of bound tariffs, for example, will have a different impact on different countries because not all products are eligible for the same preferences. In addition, a given multilateral reduction in a bound tariff will result in a different change in the applied tariff across countries, because, for each product, the margin between bound and applied tariffs differs.

Another contribution is the data for agriculture in OECD countries. Here we build on existing work on the modelling of agricultural policy (Frandsen, Gerfeldt and Jensen, 2003; and Burfisher, Robinson and Thierfelder, 2002) and we developed a precise representation of EU, US, Canadian and Japanese farm support. Information on farm policies at a very detailed level is used so as to take into account the actual effect of each payment. Subsidies are introduced as price wedges, either on output, on variable inputs, on land or on capital. Market price support is explicitly modelled, through the combination of tariffs and of export subsidies. The WTO ceilings cap the corresponding export subsidies, and reaching the ceiling entails an endogenous adjustment of the market price that can be supported. Production quotas are also explicitly modelled, and originate rents. Some of the (semi-decoupled) EU direct payments are treated as subsidies to the animal capital. Some others are treated as subsidies to land. The fully decoupled ones are treated as a return to self-employed labour and have therefore an indirect effect on production, by pulling some of the primary factor into the sector, reflecting that no payment is fully decoupled in agriculture. Set-aside is taken into account in the US and the EU, and modelled as a negative shock on the productivity of land (Bach, Frandsen and Jensen, 2000). The original information mainly comes from the OECD for the calculation of producer support estimates (additional data for non-standard commodities were provided by the OECD Secretariat and national sources). The effect of the EU enlargement, of a full implementation of the Agenda 2000 reform in the EU including the June 2003 Mid Term Review reforms, and of the 2002 US Farm Security and Rural Investment (FSRI) Act in the US, are taken into account.

Whereas data about domestic support are introduced in the baseline as a shock from the original GTAP database, tariffs are introduced with the standard MIRAGE procedure described in Bchir et al. (2002). This procedure is intended to alter the remaining data as little as possible, through a change in all final demand components.

c. Experiment Design

We established both a baseline and a trade liberalisation scenario that is used to shock the baseline equilibrium. While it is intended to represent a mid-term reference point which the changes brought about by a Doha agreement can be compared to, the baseline is a somewhat fictitious situation. It corresponds to the situation as it was in 2001 (the last year for which the required data were available), but assuming that the EU enlargement has taken place and that the EU and US recent changes in farm policies are fully implemented. This avoids using forecast data originating from other models, while making it possible to account for the recent changes in agricultural policies. Such changes are important since, in the EU, they introduce some budget caps that restrict market intervention and therefore on price support. In brief, the baseline equilibrium is obtained as a result of pre-experiment simulation where the raw data (MAcMap_HS6 for protection including the EU Everything But Arms initiative and the US Africa Growth Opportunity Act; GTAP version 5.3 for other data), is shocked by assuming that the 2003 US farm policy and the 2006 EU farm policy are in place; the Uruguay Round Agreement on Agriculture commitments are fully implemented by DCs; newly acceded WTO members (among which China) enter the WTO and implements the corresponding commitments made in terms of bound protection; and the Multi-fibre Arrangement is phased out. This baseline is the reference point to which our scenario of agricultural trade liberalisation will be compared.

WTO countries agreed on liberalising agricultural trade in August 2004 (WTO, 2004). However, the agreement leaves many technical issues to further negotiations. The only precise commitment is the ending of export subsidies on a date that is not specified. In the area of market access, there is a commitment to using a tiered formula, with deeper cuts in higher tariffs and 'flexibilities' for sensitive products. However, the number of bands, the thresholds for defining the bands and the tariff reduction in each band remain under negotiation. In the domestic support area, an element of harmonisation will in principle be introduced, meaning that higher levels of permitted trade-distorting support policies will be subject to deeper cuts. Thus, there is little precise information on what will be the actual technical modalities, and at this point a scenario must be elaborated. The last proposal in the Doha Round containing precise commitments is the draft compromise of March 2003 (WTO, 2003). It failed to attract a consensus. Later proposals such as the one discussed in the 2003 Cancún ministerial meeting may take better into account the evolution in negotiating positions but contain no precise quantification. In addition, if one analyses the various country proposals submitted between 2001 and 2003, the technical provisions included in WTO (2003) appear close to the centre of gravity of country proposals regarding domestic support, tariff bands and tariff reductions. In our scenario, we therefore use the March 2003 proposal to fill the grey areas that have been left by the

August 2004 Decision on technical aspects, such as cuts in tariffs and reduction in the AMS ceiling. The tariff bands and reductions that are used in the scenario range from a 40 per cent cut for small tariffs (those less than 15 per cent *ad valorem*) to a 60 per cent cut in high tariffs (those larger than 90 per cent; see WTO, 2003). We assumed that the reduction in tariffs will be less constraining for developing countries, along the lines of the March 2003 proposal, and consistent with the principle of Special and Differential Treatment (SDT) outlined in the August 2004 declaration. Our scenario also includes the end of export subsidies and a cut of 55 per cent in the various elements of support linked to output and inputs.[4]

d. Initial Protection Patterns

In the baseline, the 30 matrices of 11×11 average tariffs are constructed on the basis of applied tariffs, i.e. taking into account the gap that may exist between bound and actual most favoured nation tariffs, tariff quotas, free trade areas and preferential regimes. Average tariffs for an aggregate of all sectors are presented in Table 1. The figures refer to the average tariff imposed by the importer (column) to each supplier (row). The last row indicates the average agricultural protection by importing zone and the last column the average tariff faced by the supplier's aggregate exports.

Since trade between countries within each region considered in this aggregation is not explicitly modelled, tariffs on intra-regional trade are assumed to be zero. This assumption is likely to reduce somewhat the assessed impact of liberalisation, since the benefits reaped from lowering the corresponding distortions are not taken into account here. The corresponding bias is difficult to gauge. Noteworthily, however, most regions considered include countries linked by Regional Trade Agreements, so that intra-regional tariffs are low in most cases.

Table 1 shows that the agricultural sector is very protected in some countries, even when preferential regimes are taken into account. For example, the average tariff on agricultural goods imposed by EFTA countries is 47.7 per cent, the one imposed by the EU is 16.7 per cent. Note that the EU figure is smaller than the one that is found in most studies (e.g. Gibson et al., 2001) and the present GTAP database. The reason is that the EU grants significant preferences to sub-Saharan Africa, EFTA and Mediterranean countries. These preferences result in a much lower average EU tariff applied to sub-Saharan exports (6.7 per cent) than to the

---

[4] Here, we considered that 'distorting' support included support coupled to production, as measured by the AMS and blue box payments. We also included payments notified by the US under the '*de minimis* clause' (this clause states that some payments do not have to be counted against the AMS if they amount to a small fraction of the value of production, but in recent years it was used by the US which would have otherwise exceeded the AMS ceiling).

TABLE 1
Bilateral Tariff, All Agricultural Products Aggregate (Per cent)

	EU25	USA	Asia Developed	EFTA	Cairns Developed	Mediterranean	Sub-Saharan Africa	Cairns Developing	China	South Asia	RoW	Average
EU25		5.8	22.2	52.0	15.7	35.1	30.2	16.1	25.5	52.8	26.2	18.1
USA	16.2		28.9	57.9	5.1	23.3	18.9	13.2	27.4	45.4	12.7	18.8
Asia Developed	12.5	3.7		17.9	6.2	32.2	31.4	17.3	25.8	51.6	24.8	16.0
EFTA	7.9	3.9	11.6		10.6	21.4	22.9	19.1	30.5	43.0	21.3	10.7
Cairns Developed	25.9	3.4	24.9	79.8		37.4	14.7	11.8	16.9	42.6	18.7	21.2
Mediterranean	7.3	4.0	14.1	25.7	3.7		30.2	20.3	23.6	34.9	22.9	12.7
Sub-Saharan Africa	6.7	3.0	12.0	8.9	0.7	18.0		26.1	14.7	35.0	17.8	10.2
Cairns Developing	18.3	3.8	24.0	34.7	5.9	28.9	27.9		29.3	65.0	23.0	20.8
China	13.5	5.1	21.7	36.7	8.7	36.2	26.0	19.6		46.5	29.2	16.3
South Asia	14.4	1.8	33.7	21.9	1.8	37.4	24.4	17.4	14.5		20.0	16.7
Rest of the World	15.1	2.1	17.4	25.8	2.6	32.5	25.1	19.7	22.9	45.6		15.1
Average	16.7	4.7	22.5	47.7	10.8	30.8	26.3	16.0	25.1	52.6	21.1	

Source: MAcMap_HS6 and authors' calculation. Year 2001. Ad valorem equivalents.

exports originating from the developed members of the Cairns Group (25.9 per cent). US preferences, including the North American Free Trade Agreement, and non-reciprocal preferences (the GSP) are also taken into account. Figures in Table 1 show that there are some significant preferential margins, which would be eroded by a multilateral reduction in bound tariffs.

Sub-Saharan Africa faces the lowest level of protection against its agro-food exports (10.2 per cent). Agricultural exports from the developed members of the Cairns Group, for instance, are subject to a much higher average tariff (21.2 per cent). The differences between these two figures reflect both the existence of preferences granted to African countries, and the composition of exports: Cairns Group countries indeed export products that face high tariffs in OECD countries (such as beef, sugar or dairy), while sub-Saharan Africa exports large amounts of coffee, cocoa and flowers, that face lower tariffs.

Broadly speaking, protection is often considerable in the sugar, meat, cereal and dairy sectors. The highest duties are the ones imposed on rice by the group of Asian developed countries. It is noteworthy that there is sometimes a significant degree of protection of the processing sector: trade in fibres is nearly free, while trade on processed cotton and apparels faces high tariffs in many countries.

e. The Doha Agreement Scenario: Effects on Protection

In our scenario, the cuts for the different tariff bands described in WTO (2003) are applied to the bound tariffs. But in the changes applied to our baseline matrices of tariffs, the new level of bound tariffs only becomes the applied tariff if the new bound level is lower than the initial applied tariff. The procedure is applied to all bilateral tariffs at the HS6 level. The new vectors of tariffs obtained are then aggregated in the model classification. The *ad valorem* equivalent of bound duties at the HS6 level was constructed, using each country's consolidated tariff schedule, in a way consistent with that used for measuring applied protection in MAcMap. This computation of resulting applied tariff cuts thus contrasts with existing studies by making it possible to take into account the gap between bound and applied tariffs at a detailed level, while also allowing the harmonising effect of the formula to be accurately reflected. In addition, out-of-quota tariff cuts are reflected in lowered TRQ rents.

Table 2 shows the resulting changes in applied tariffs (change in percentage points) imposed by each group on imports of agricultural and food products from each partner group. The last line indicates the change in average protection in each group of importing countries. The last column shows the changes in market access faced by each group of exporting countries. For example, our Doha agreement scenario leads to a reduction of 2.9 percentage points in applied agricultural tariffs of EFTA, of 7.1 points in the EU25, and of 0.8 points in the US. While initial tariffs were also high, SDT and the fact that there was a very large degree

TABLE 2

Impact of the Tariff-cut Scenario on Market Access for Agricultural Products

	EU25	USA	Asia Developed	EFTA	Cairns Developed	Mediterranean	Sub-Saharan Africa	Cairns Developing	China	South Asia	RoW	Average
EU25		-1.0	-6.2	-3.3	-2.3	-4.2	-0.4	-1.2	-10.4	-1.8	-1.0	-3.1
USA	-6.0		-6.5	-2.7	-1.1	-2.9	-0.2	-0.9	-10.4	-5.9	-0.4	-4.3
Asia Developed	-4.6	-0.8		-2.9	-1.1	-2.5	-0.2	-0.6	-9.2	-0.3	-1.1	-3.0
EFTA	-2.5	-0.5	-1.4		-1.1	-2.7	-0.1	-0.5	-10.0	-0.2	-1.2	-1.9
Cairns Developed	-12.1	-0.2	-6.7	-2.7		-3.8	-0.5	-1.0	-6.7	-4.7	-0.4	-6.4
Mediterranean	-2.9	-0.8	-3.5	-2.2	-0.9		-0.2	-1.0	-9.1	-1.8	-1.0	-2.6
Sub-Saharan Africa	-3.3	-0.1	-4.1	-0.7	-0.1	-1.1		-0.3	-5.1	-0.4	-1.1	-2.2
Cairns Developing	-8.0	-0.7	-5.4	-1.9	-1.4	-2.6	-0.2		-10.1	-1.8	-0.6	-4.6
China	-4.5	-1.5	-5.9	-2.5	-2.7	-4.4	-0.7	-0.8		-7.3	-0.8	-3.6
South Asia	-7.0	-0.3	-9.7	-4.2	-0.2	-4.9	-0.3	-1.0	-3.8		-0.5	-3.9
Rest of the World	-6.6	-0.2	-5.0	-2.5	-0.5	-3.4	-0.7	-1.0	-8.5	-2.3		-4.2
Average	-7.1	-0.8	-5.9	-2.9	-1.8	-3.3	-0.3	-1.0	-9.4	-2.7	-0.7	

Note:
In percentage points (i.e. the figures correspond to $x - y$ if a tariff of x per cent is reduced and results in a y per cent tariff).

Source: MAcMap_HS6 and authors' calculation. Year 2001.

of so-called 'binding overhang' (i.e. bound tariffs were higher than applied tariffs) result in limited changes for DCs. In Table 2, the last column shows that sub-Saharan countries is one of the regions that benefits least from the opening of markets, both because of its export structure (cocoa and coffee face low tariffs) and because of the preferential regimes. The average tariff faced by sub-Saharan agricultural exports only decreases by 2.2 percentage points. By contrast, the cut amounts to 4.6 percentage points for developing members of the Cairns Group. This suggests that, among DCs, multilateral liberalisation opens markets for Argentina, and Brazil exports more than for Mediterranean and African countries. Moreover, Table 2 shows that the greatest beneficiaries, from a mercantilist point of view, are developed countries. The developed members of the Cairns Group face an average tariff that decreases by 6.4 percentage points. The tariff cuts for EU and US exports also exceed the cuts for DCs, in percentage points. Despite a very high initial protection, applying the March 2003 formula does not entail a large openness of EFTA due to a binding overhang phenomenon.

Table 3 shows changes in the average tariff protection faced by each country group's exports by sector, in percentage points. A tiered formula cut in import duties would result in large market access improvements in rice (Developed Asia) and sugar (EU, Developed Asia).

4. SIMULATION RESULTS

The simulation consists of a shock to the baseline using our Doha agreement scenario, i.e. the changes in tariffs described in the previous section, as well as the suppression of export subsidies and the cut in trade-distorting domestic support. The model ensures consistency between various policies. In some cases, this requires making endogenous changes in policy variables. For example, the suppression of export subsidies and the cut in tariffs make some EU intervention price levels unsustainable (leading to unrealistic levels of inventories and exceeding the EU agricultural budget constraint agreed upon in 2003). In such a case of unbalanced domestic markets, the intervention price, which normally acts as a floor price for the producer in the model, is assumed to be adjusted by EU authorities, and becomes an endogenous variable. In the case of tariff rate quotas, the rent associated with the gap between the in- and out-of-quota tariffs is positive only if the quota is filled by calculated imports.

The combination of changes to the three pillars, domestic support, border protection and export competition, leads to a consistent scenario. In the following tables, the figures correspond to an assessment of the effects of the three pillars independently, and the last column the combination of the three, i.e. the changes brought by a Doha agreement to a mid-term reference situation represented by our baseline.

TABLE 3

Impact of the Tariff-cut Scenario on Market Access by Sector

	EU25	USA	Asia Developed	EFTA	Cairns Developed	Mediterranean	Sub-Saharan Africa	Cairns Developing	China	South Asia	RoW	Agriculture and Food
Paddy rice	-30.5	-1.8	-81.3	0.0	0.0	-0.1	0.0	-0.1	0.0	-23.0	-0.2	-17.6
Processed rice	-82.2	-1.3	-66.5	0.0	0.0	-0.1	0.0	-0.1	0.0	-21.0	-0.2	-18.9
Coarse grains	-4.2	-0.4	-25.7	0.0	0.0	-0.7	0.0	-1.1	-7.5	-14.1	-0.6	-5.3
Wheat	-0.2	-1.0	-0.4	0.0	0.0	-1.2	0.0	-0.3	0.0	-28.5	-0.6	-1.2
Sugar	-76.9	0.0	-64.1	-26.6	-0.9	0.0	-0.3	-3.0	-0.1	0.0	-0.2	-20.6
Oilseeds	0.0	-1.3	-1.9	0.0	0.0	0.0	0.0	0.0	-36.1	0.0	-0.2	-4.6
Live animals	-17.6	0.0	-6.7	0.0	0.0	-6.5	0.0	-0.2	-2.0	0.0	-0.1	-6.3
Animal products	-1.8	-0.1	-3.4	-0.2	-1.1	-0.5	-0.1	-0.3	-3.1	0.0	-1.2	-1.5
Meat	-29.0	-0.1	-11.0	-0.3	-0.1	-25.0	-0.3	-2.0	-10.9	0.0	-0.2	-11.8
Meat products	-7.7	-1.6	-15.3	-6.1	-9.6	-17.0	-0.4	-2.6	-5.9	0.0	-0.2	-6.7
Dairy products	-18.3	-0.6	-4.7	-8.1	-1.6	-4.6	-0.6	0.0	-16.3	0.0	-1.3	-4.7
Fibres	0.0	0.0	0.0	0.0	0.0	-0.4	-0.2	-0.2	0.0	0.0	-0.1	-0.1
Fruits & vegetables	-7.6	-1.2	-5.4	-1.0	-0.5	-8.9	-2.0	-1.8	-8.0	0.0	-0.5	-4.2
Other crops	-0.8	-0.3	-0.7	-1.4	-0.4	-1.5	-0.4	-0.4	-9.0	0.0	-2.1	-1.1
Fats	-1.8	-1.4	-1.5	-3.8	-0.4	-0.5	0.0	0.0	-6.1	0.0	-0.2	-1.5
Beverages & tobacco	-6.2	-0.2	-4.0	-3.6	-2.8	-5.2	-0.2	-3.2	-24.7	0.0	-3.4	-4.1
Food	-2.8	-1.0	-2.4	-2.2	-1.4	-2.6	-0.5	-0.6	-6.3	0.0	-0.1	-2.0
Total agro-food	-7.1	-0.8	-5.9	-2.9	-1.8	-3.3	-0.3	-1.0	-9.4	-2.7	-0.7	

Note:

In percentage points (i.e. the figures correspond to $x - y$ if a tariff of x per cent is reduced and results in a y per cent tariff).

Source: MAcMap_HS6 and authors' calculation. Year 2001.

a. World Prices

The first expected impact of a multilateral liberalisation is an increase in world prices. *Ceteris paribus*, removing protection should decrease export surpluses or increase import demand in protective countries and therefore push world prices up. So do cuts in production support and the removal of export subsidies. Indeed, Table 4 shows that world agricultural prices will increase. In the case of rice, cotton and to a lesser extent oilseeds and cereals, the main source of the increase is the removal of domestic support. In the case of sugar, it is the ending of (EU) export subsidies. In the fruits and vegetable as well as in the beverage sector, the main source is the decrease in tariffs. Overall, the increase in world price is significant in the fibres sector (cotton), and significant in the rice and oilseed sectors. In other cases, the increase in world prices is limited.[5]

TABLE 4
Impact of the Doha Agreement Scenario on World Prices (Import prices)

Sector	Initial Share in World Imports	Domestic Support	Export Subsidies	Tariffs	Doha Agreement, 3 Pillars
Paddy rice	0.6	8.2	0.1	1.3	9.4
Processed rice	1.2	0.6	0.0	0.3	1.0
Coarse grains	3.6	2.6	0.1	0.5	3.1
Wheat	3.9	1.4	0.1	0.9	2.3
Sugar	2.7	0.2	5.6	−1.5	2.8
Oilseeds	5.7	9.1	0.0	0.5	9.7
Live animals	1.2	0.9	0.1	0.7	1.6
Animal products	3.4	0.6	0.0	0.1	0.8
Meat	4.0	0.6	0.1	0.5	1.2
Meat products	4.8	0.3	1.5	0.1	2.0
Dairy products	3.6	0.3	2.3	0.0	2.7
Fibres	3.6	25.6	0.0	0.2	26.0
Fruits & vegetables	8.3	0.1	0.2	0.5	0.8
Other crops	10.1	0.8	0.0	0.4	1.2
Fats	7.2	2.8	0.0	0.2	3.0
Beverages and tobacco	11.0	0.1	0.5	0.3	0.3
Processed food	25.0	0.3	0.6	0.4	0.9
Total agro-food	100.0	2.1	0.5	0.3	2.8

Notes:
World imports here refer to imports between the regions considered in the model. Imports between countries within the same region are not considered. 'World price' is the Fisher index of all import prices.

Source: Authors' simulations.

---

[5] The case of sugar, whose world prices show a slight decrease following a reduction in tariffs, reflects the way that we measured world prices, i.e. as import prices. Sugar is subject to a tariff quota in the EU TRQs: the decrease in out-of-quota tariffs lowers the rent, which is assumed to be kept by the exporting country and treated as an increase in import prices.

b. Quantities Traded

Table 5 suggests that, overall, the quantities of agricultural products traded internationally will grow by some six per cent. The main driving force is the decrease in tariffs. The suppression of export subsidies only has a limited effect. One reason is that EU export subsidies have already decreased dramatically since the late 1990s, and this was taken into account in the baseline. In some cases, such as the US (cotton) and the EU (sugar), the Doha agreement will result in a significant decrease in some exports after domestic or export subsidies are cut, but it is offset by an increase in the exports of some other products due to improved market access in third countries. This is not the case for EFTA countries. The decrease in tariffs results in a significant increase in exports of Cairns Group countries and China. Mediterranean countries' exports of agricultural products also increase in spite of the erosion of their (very limited) preferential access to the EU (note, however, that they experience a fall in exports of non-agricultural products such as garments). Sub-Saharan African countries experience a smaller increase in exports than most other developing countries. This results mainly from the erosion of preferences on the EU's market. As a general rule, exports of the poorest countries (sub-Saharan Africa and South Asia, which includes most LDCs, plus India) increase significantly less than the average exports of the rest of the world.

TABLE 5
Impacts of Doha Agreement Scenario on Agro-food Exports (Per cent change)

	Initial Level	Domestic Support	Export Subsidies	Tariffs	Doha Agreement, 3 Pillars
EU25	61,642	−1.9	−4.2	7.4	2.7
USA	69,969	−6.7	0.6	7.2	0.8
Asia Developed	5,716	0.6	1.2	10.7	11.8
EFTA	6,428	2.4	−6.6	2.7	−3.8
Cairns Developed	38,875	2.2	0.6	10.2	12.8
Mediterranean	8,304	2.0	−0.2	6.2	8.8
Cairns Developing	54,934	2.7	−0.1	7.9	10.4
China	11,947	2.0	0.0	11.0	13.2
RoW	35,074	2.1	−0.5	5.5	6.8
South Asia	7,513	3.1	−0.4	3.3	6.4
Sub-Saharan Africa	12,420	3.3	−1.2	2.7	4.7
World	312,822	−0.5	−0.9	7.4	6.1
Richest Countries	182,630	−2.6	−1.3	7.9	4.2
Developing Countries	110,260	2.4	−0.2	7.3	9.4
Poorest Countries	19,933	3.3	−0.9	2.9	5.4

Note:
Initial levels are expressed in millions of 1997 US dollars. The figures refer to f.o.b. values.

Source: Authors' simulations.

If we now focus on the effect of the Doha agreement on net trade, the increase in imports exceeds the increase in exports in the case of developed countries in Asia and Europe. The trade balance for agricultural products worsens in the case of Japan and Western Europe. The growth in imports also offsets the growth in exports in the case of China and South Asian countries. The trade balance of Cairns Group countries, especially that of the developed members, increases a lot (imports grow by three per cent and exports by 13 per cent).

c. Terms of Trade

Our Doha agreement agricultural scenario results in significant terms of trade variations. The Cairns Group developing countries' terms of trade improve. So do the terms of trade of sub-Saharan Africa. Among developing countries, the role of cotton appears significant in explaining changes in terms of trade. The cotton price is a major driving force of the improved terms of trade of sub-Saharan Africa, but also the deterioration of terms of trade in Mediterranean countries, which are large importers of cotton. This finding illustrates the importance of the cotton issue for DCs, and provides some justification for the specific negotiation on cotton, a commitment of WTO members in the July 2004 agreement.

d. Welfare

Table 6 shows the impact of a Doha agreement on agriculture in terms of welfare. Overall, the changes in welfare are small. Basically, the agreement on agriculture that was reached in July 2004 would lead to a mere 0.1 per cent increase in world welfare. The fact that the actual outcome of the negotiations on technical modalities might differ from our scenario is unlikely to change the magnitude of this result. On the opposite, the fact that some 'sensitive products', i.e. those where most of the existing distortions are concentrated, are likely to be excluded from the discipline, suggest that our small figure might even be optimistic.

Countries that reduce their own domestic distortions are the main gainers in the agreement. This is clearly the case for the US (provided that the domestic support is reduced by as much as included in our scenario). It is also the case of the EU, of developed Asia and EFTA if the agreement on tariff cuts is close to the one we included in our scenario, that is if these countries do not make a large use of the provisions for 'sensitive products' of the July 2004 Declaration. In all these cases, most gains are linked to an improved efficiency of resource allocation. The impact of ending export subsidies is quite small, again reflecting that the recent changes in the CAP have already led to a decrease in domestic price and a decrease in production. A second category of winners are those countries for which trade liberalisation result in significant export opportunities. This is particularly the case of developed countries of the Cairns Group, but the

TABLE 6
Impacts on Welfare (Per cent change)

	Initial GDP (Billion 1997 USD)	Domestic Support	Export Subsidies	Tariffs	Doha Agreement, 3 Pillars
EU25	8,235	0.04	0.01	0.09	0.14
USA	7,952	0.05	0.00	0.00	0.05
Asia Developed	5,233	−0.05	0.00	0.11	0.05
EFTA	408	−0.04	0.08	0.03	0.11
Cairns Developed	1,092	−0.01	0.00	0.04	0.04
Mediterranean	454	−0.27	−0.07	0.16	−0.16
Cairns Developing	2,012	−0.02	0.00	0.02	0.00
China	876	−0.21	0.00	0.38	0.15
RoW	2,026	−0.07	−0.06	0.01	−0.10
South Asia	527	−0.01	0.00	0.19	0.17
Sub-Saharan Africa	207	0.01	−0.08	0.03	−0.03
World	29,023	0.02	0.00	0.06	0.08
Richest Countries	22,920	0.02	0.00	0.06	0.08
Developing Countries	5,368	−0.09	−0.03	0.08	−0.03
Poorest Countries	734	−0.01	−0.03	0.15	0.11

Source: Authors' simulations.

gains remain limited (welfare increases by 0.5 per cent). For developing countries of the Cairns Group, there is no change in welfare, overall. Note, however, that this reflects contrasting effects between the agricultural sector (which gains) and other sectors, and between producers and consumers: the latter are adversely affected by higher food prices.[6] A decomposition of welfare gains also shows that the decrease of rents earned from TRQs and the relative shift of resources away from the (modern) industrial sector balance the benefits reaped from improved terms of trade and increased arable land usage.

A Doha agreement results in welfare losses for several groups of developing countries. Mediterranean countries suffer from the higher price of cotton caused by the reduction in US and EU domestic subsidies which affects their garment industry and, as net food-importing countries, from the higher price of agricultural products. Because they already benefit from some (limited) preferential access to the EU market, the benefits they reap from the decrease in agricultural tariffs are not sufficient to offset the negative effects of higher world prices. Sub-Saharan African countries also experience a welfare loss as a consequence of a Doha agreement, in spite of a slight improvement in their terms of trade. This results from the combined effect of higher prices for food imports, and from

---

[6] Note that our group of 'developing members of the Cairns Group' includes not only efficient agricultural exporters such as Brazil and Argentina, but also many Asian countries such as Malaysia, Indonesia, Philippines, etc. Welfare effects are also contrasted between the different members of the group.

TABLE 7

Impacts on the Real Return to Land and Agricultural Labour (Per cent change)

	Land				Labour			
	Domestic Support	Export Subsidies	Tariffs	Doha Agreement, 3 Pillars	Domestic Support	Export Subsidies	Tariffs	Doha Agreement, 3 Pillars
EU25	−14.6	0.0	−0.4	−15.1	−0.5	0.0	−0.5	−1.1
USA	−0.4	0.0	0.2	−0.2	−2.2	0.0	0.6	−1.7
Asia Developed	0.5	0.0	−2.3	−1.8	0.3	0.0	−1.2	−0.8
EFTA	1.1	0.5	−0.5	1.1	0.3	−1.6	0.2	−1.5
Cairns Developed	−0.3	0.0	1.3	1.1	1.0	0.1	1.7	2.8
Mediterranean	0.7	0.0	0.0	0.8	0.0	−0.1	0.3	0.2
Cairns Developing	0.6	0.0	0.0	0.6	0.5	0.0	0.8	1.4
China	0.5	0.0	−0.3	0.3	−0.1	0.1	0.9	0.7
RoW	1.1	0.0	0.0	1.1	0.6	−0.2	0.7	1.1
South Asia	−0.1	0.0	0.0	−0.1	0.5	0.0	0.2	0.6
Sub-Saharan Africa	0.2	−0.1	0.0	0.2	1.1	−0.2	0.3	1.2

Source: Authors' simulations.

the extra competition faced by their exports due to preference erosion. The elimination of EU export subsidies is the major force driving welfare losses, but the decomposition of welfare changes shows that reduced TRQ rents contributes significantly to the welfare loss observed for sub-Saharan Africa. The actual effect of a future agreement may even be more negative than what is suggested by the figures in Table 6. It is uncertain whether future negotiations will lead to a cut in US cotton subsidies by 55 per cent as we assumed in this scenario, because of well-organised interest groups.

e. Impact on the Agricultural Sector

The global welfare effects hide contrasted effects between the farm sector and other sectors, especially in DCs. The effect on the farm sector can be seen through the changes in the returns to land and the changes in the return to agricultural labour. We focus here on the returns to workers that are specific to the agricultural sector.[7] Table 7 shows that trade liberalisation in the agricultural

---

[7] This excludes skilled workers, since this type of work is assumed to be perfectly mobile across sectors. The imperfect mobility (and therefore the sector specificity) thus only concerns unskilled workers, but they contribute almost 90 per cent of labour value added in the agricultural sector worldwide, and to more than 80 per cent in the EU in the model, which relies for this aspect on the GTAP database.

sector has very significant consequences, especially for EU farmers. Indeed, the cut in domestic support, which is assumed to remain uncompensated by lump-sum transfers or any other green-box type of subsidies in our scenario, has a very large effect on returns to land in the EU. The farm sector in developed Cairns Group countries benefits from the agreement. This is also true in most developing countries, but in smaller proportions. Indeed, returns to land in sub-Saharan Africa only increase by 0.2 per cent and returns to labour by 1.2 per cent. The figures are respectively 0.6 per cent and 1.4 per cent in the developing members of the Cairns Group.

5. COMMENTS AND SENSITIVITY ANALYSIS

A surprising result is the limited increase in trade and welfare resulting from a Doha agreement. Indeed, the gains in world welfare that we obtain are significantly smaller than those found by other authors. Another difference with most other studies is that we do not find that all countries gain from multilateral trade liberalisation in agriculture. Some DCs like sub-Saharan Africa experience some (slight) net losses, even though the farm sector enjoys some small benefits from trade liberalisation. Such differences with a large body of the literature demand explanations and some sensitivity analysis.

One explanation for the small welfare gains resulting from the agreement is that the agricultural and food sector only represents a small proportion of the gross domestic product in many economies, and here we simulated only the impact of the agricultural component of the Doha agreement. Other authors have focused on a larger agreement (e.g. Hertel, Hoekman and Martin, 2003; and Francois, van Meijl and van Tongeren, 2003). They obtain significant gains in the textiles sector, for example, or gains linked to specific (and somewhat ad hoc) assumptions on trade facilitation or positive externalities of trade liberalisation. Another explanation is that our scenario accounts only for the changes in tariffs and domestic support that result from actual changes in applied tariffs and policies. Because of data availability, most modellers apply the cuts in bound tariffs negotiated under the WTO as if they were made on applied tariffs. As a sensitivity analysis, we ran our tariff-cut scenario on the applied tariffs, rather than the bound tariffs. Under this alternative assumption, the subsequent increase in world agricultural exports is much higher (15.0 per cent to be compared to 6.1 per cent when the gap between applied and bound duties is taken into account) and the increase of agricultural exports of the Cairns developing countries is also larger than in Table 5 (+21.5 per cent, that is to say a US$11.2 billion augmentation, while our result gives US$5.7 billion).

The negative outcome found for sub-Saharan and Mediterranean countries as a result of implementing the Doha Agenda is among the striking features of the results. As mentioned above, a likely explanation for this finding is the erosion of the tariff preferences these countries enjoyed on their export market. In order to check for this explanation, we carried out an additional simulation of the Doha Agenda, where trade preferences are not taken into account in the baseline.[8] This simulation also highlights what difference covering exhaustively trade preferences makes on the assessed impact of multilateral liberalisation. On average, the difference with the standard assessment is not large. However, agrofood exports of sub-Saharan African and Mediterranean countries increase substantially more under this scenario (+7.0 per cent vs. +4.7 per cent for sub-Saharan Africa when preferences are accounted for, and 13.4 per cent vs. 8.8 per cent for Mediterranean countries). More importantly, the impact on welfare is significantly improved for these two regions. In particular, the loss previously found for sub-Saharan African countries is changed for a slight gain (+0.06 per cent) when preferences are not accounted for. This confirms that the erosion of preferences significantly harms sub-Saharan African and Mediterranean countries as a result of multilateral liberalisation, in spite of the fairly limited liberalisation actually delivered by the Harbinson proposal, as emphasised above.

A puzzling result is the small welfare changes for the Cairns Group countries, even though these countries experience a significant increase in exports. Indeed, given the figures in Table 6, it is surprising that the developed members of the Cairns Group fight so hard for agricultural liberalisation, which would barely bring them an increase in welfare corresponding to a few months of GDP growth. It is even more surprising that the Doha agreement results in no welfare gain for the developing countries of the Cairns Group, since countries such as Brazil and Argentina are assumed to reap large benefits from agricultural trade liberalisation. Because some of the results might be dependent on the model specification, the following sections provide some sensitivity analysis.

First, the Armington specification may underestimate the increase in imports of Cairns Group products by the EU, following a decrease in EU domestic support. It is well known that the Armington assumption is questionable for agricultural products (Alston et al., 1990), even though it remains used by most modellers because of its parsimony in parameters. Agricultural goods are often relatively homogeneous and the Armington assumption tends to overestimate the degree of differentiation of goods according to their origin. Recent econometric estimates suggest that elasticities could be larger than the ones we used in the model (see Erkel-Rousse and Mirza, 2002). In order to assess the sensitivity of the results

---

[8] This is done by substituting, in the benchmark data, MFN duties to applied duties. However, five exceptions are made, to account for large agreements: the EU, NAFTA, ANZCERTA, the EU-EFTA Agreement and SACU are still taken into account. This ensures that the coverage of preferential regimes under this alternative simulation is exactly the same as in GTAP version 5.3 database, which so far has been the workhorse for assessing the impact of multilateral liberalisation.

to the assumptions on the substitution between domestic products and imports, we modified the model's elasticities of substitution in the agricultural sector.[9] Doubling the value of the elasticities affects trade and welfare. World agro-food exports increase by almost 11 per cent (rather than six per cent in our results), with the same uneven distribution amongst zones: developed countries exports of the Cairns Group increase considerably (+20.2 per cent), while the increase in exports of sub-Saharan Africa after trade liberalisation is a modest 6.2 per cent. Welfare increases are larger in economies where government intervention in agriculture generates large distortions (EU, developed Asia). The welfare change in sub-Saharan Africa is still negative (−0.04 per cent instead of −0.03 per cent).

Some unwanted consequences of our assumption of imperfect competition *à la* Dixit-Stiglitz and increasing returns to scale in industrial sectors have been documented (Francois and Roland-Holst, 1998). Francois, van Meijl and van Tongeren (2003) explain that they ran into a problem that also affects our results. When large agricultural producers expand their farm output, they draw resources from their industrial sectors, which contract. The presence of economies of scale in these sectors, and the 'love of variety' effect linked to the Dixit-Stiglitz specification, implies the predicted contraction of these sectors leads to negative welfare effects. This could contribute to the low welfare gains in the developing members of the Cairns Group, which were expected to draw larger gains from the Doha Round in our results. In order to assess how important this effect is, we ran the same simulation assuming perfect competition in all sectors. That is, the economies of scale and love of variety effects are eliminated. The changes in welfare and in other macroeconomic variables are indeed slightly affected by this assumption: for example, welfare in Cairns developing countries now increase by 0.04 per cent while it increased by 0.01 per cent under the imperfect competition assumption. The welfare gains are also larger for the developed members of the Cairns Group (0.08 per cent instead of 0.04 per cent), and the small welfare loss for sub-Saharan Africa (−0.01 per cent) disappears under the perfect competition assumption. The changes are nevertheless very limited for these three groups of countries. The welfare changes in other countries remain practically the same under this alternative assumption.

Unlike most AGE models (with the exception of the LINKAGE model, the source of inspiration for our specification) we introduced some flexibility in land supply in some large countries, with a low population density. While we believe that an exogenous land assumption understates supply response, this assumption

---

[9] The source of the substitution elasticities is the GTAP database. Elasticities of substitution between domestic and imported goods range between 2 and 3.8, averaging 2.3, in agricultural sectors. Elasticities between imports of different origin are roughly twice this level. Note, however, that when applied to small levels of imports, larger elasticities still lead to a small increase in trade flows.

is important since it dampens world price effects. We ran a simulation under the assumption of exogenous land. The endogenous land assumption does not affect significantly the results, even if world prices increase by 2.5 per cent (rather than 2.8 per cent in our simulations). The impact is very minor on the world price of goods exported by DCs, and on DC welfare changes.

Another potential explanation for the difference in results with other studies is the dual labour market assumption for DCs. We ran the simulation relaxing this assumption. Under the dual market assumption, an expansion of the agricultural sector means that some resources are drawn into a less productive sector. Under the single market assumption, the welfare losses for Mediterranean and sub-Saharan African countries are smaller. The welfare gains for the developing members of the Cairns Group are larger, but remain very limited (+0.3 per cent). However, the differences remain very small compared to our basic simulation, a few per cent of a percentage point in the computed changes. That is, none of the specific modelling assumptions described in this section affects significantly our findings.

6. CONCLUSION

We used an AGE model to assess the effects of an agreement on agriculture in the Doha Round of negotiations. Because the July 2004 framework agreement did not lead to a decision on the precise modalities of the cuts in tariffs and domestic support, we assumed that further negotiations will lead to modalities that we could approximate with the provisions included in the WTO draft compromise proposal of March 2003.

Our work includes significant innovations. Our data on applied protection rely on original work which assesses the protection arising from *ad valorem* tariffs, specific tariffs and tariff rate quotas at a highly disaggregated level (HS6 classification), taking into account all preferential agreements. *Ad-valorem*-equivalent bound duties, the ones subject to liberalisation, are also estimated at the HS6 level. Domestic support in the EU and the US are represented through a variety of instruments, also using original and very detailed data on the various policy tools. The effect of the FSRI and the 2003 reform of the CAP are included, assuming full implementation in an enlarged EU. In establishing scenarios for simulation, we accounted for the fact that commitments on bound tariffs and AMS ceilings show only a remote connection with the changes in actual tariffs and policies, given the 'binding overhang' that characterises the tariff structure in many countries, and the gap between actual support and AMS ceilings. The tariff cuts are applied on some 5,000 different tariffs at the six-digit level before the new variables are aggregated consistently with our 30-sector and 11-country group model.

The results show very significant differences with most of the findings of other similar AGE models. Because the data that were developed for this project will be made available to a large public as part of the future version of the GTAP database (GTAP6), more refined assessments of the effect of the Doha negotiations by the large community of users of these data will be made possible. Our estimates of the impact of a Doha agreement on agriculture suggest much lower welfare gains than most other studies. In addition, we find that a large number of developing countries would actually experience a loss in welfare, a result that is seldom observed with AGE models. Cairns Group countries would expand their agricultural output and exports. However, in terms of welfare, the main winners are developed countries that reduce their own distorting support. Negative consequences are nevertheless significant for the farm sector in the EU. They are more limited for developed Asia and the US.

Our results suggest that the erosion of existing preferences will be an important problem, especially for sub-Saharan Africa. African countries which benefit from preferential access to the EU and the US will face competition from Cairns Group countries. Overall, sub-Saharan countries will experience a decrease in welfare, even under our optimistic assumption that US and EU cotton and tobacco subsidies will be reduced by a large amount. Overall, there will be a limited increase in world prices for agricultural products. However, this limited increase will negatively affect some net food importers and some cotton importers such as Mediterranean countries. Like sub-Saharan African countries, they will not gain on other grounds, because of the erosion of preferential margins and diminished rents on their quota-constrained exports to the EU.

A sensitivity analysis shows that these results are hardly affected by the various assumptions that make our model specific, compared to other AGE models (dual labour market, endogenous land supply, monopolistic competition, etc.). That is, the differences between our conclusions and those of most AGE modellers mainly come from the use of better data, namely on preferential tariffs, and more careful design of the actual effect of the posted reductions in tariff and farm support. In particular, our results suggest that better data would modify significantly the conclusions that are often drawn about the benefits of trade liberalisation for developing countries. General conclusions that developing countries will reap most of the benefits from trade liberalisation in agriculture do not seem to hold when one takes properly into account applied tariffs, the erosion of preferences, and trade diversion. Clearly, the effects on developing countries will be contrasted, and some groups of countries such as sub-Saharan Africa are more likely to suffer than to benefit from a multilateral trade liberalisation.

Corrective measures are needed for possible losers, but the present Special and Differentiated Treatment (SDT) provisions under the WTO cannot be considered as an adequate response. Eligibility to the SDT relies on self-declaration of countries, and the one-size-fits-all status of 'developing' country does not account for the considerable differences between DCs (Korea and Haiti are examples). In addition, the SDT (under its present form) merely allow developing countries to opt out of liberalisation measures. Opting out is not an adequate response to the erosion of preferences for, say, African or Caribbean countries.

In order to make the results of a Doha Round more consistent with Pareto-improvement principles, more differentiation between developing countries should be allowed. In that sense, our findings are at odds with the idea that preferences should be as little discriminating as possible, an idea which is widely shared amongst economists (see IPC), and which is also at the core of the evolution of multilateral trade rules (e.g. the 'Enabling clause' for the GSP, the need to be granted a waiver for other non-reciprocal regimes).

The specific treatment mentioned for LDCs in the July 2004 Decision is consistent with extra differentiation across developing countries, but not all potential losers are LDCs. The 2004 decision of the WTO Appellate body on the EU drug-fighting-related provisions of the GSP leaves a door open for further differentiation, under well-defined conditions. This might be a way to amend the SDT in a way that would reflect the growing heterogeneity of the developing countries. Clearly, introducing more differentiation between countries raises difficult issues. The risk exists that eligibility would be subject to questionable political conditions (already an issue in some US non-reciprocal preferential schemes), or that discrimination reflects arbitrary historical ties (an issue in EU preferences). More objective criteria would be preferable, and preferential treatments should be GSP-consistent rather than based on geography. Some elements of differentiation are already introduced in the EU and US GSP, in particular the EU system of graduation, which involves development indicators. While more assessment of the potential unwanted effects would be needed, there might be a source of inspiration for revised modalities of the SDT, in spite of the likely opposition from the most advanced DCs.

REFERENCES

Achterbosch, T. J., H. Ben Hamouda, P. N. Osakwe and van F. W. Tongeren (2004), 'Trade Liberalisation under the Doha Development Agenda, Options and Consequences for Africa', Working Paper (Agricultural Economics Research Institute, The Hague: LEI).

Alston, J., C. Carter, R. Green and D. Pick (1990), 'Whither Armington Trade Models?', *American Journal of Agricultural Economics*, **72**, 2, 455–67.

Bach, C. F., S. E. Frandsen and H. G. Jensen (2000), 'Agricultural and Economy-wide Effects of European Enlargement: Modelling the Common Agricultural Policy', *Journal of Agricultural Economics*, **51**, 2, 162–80.

Bchir, M. H., Y. Decreux, J. L. Guérin and S. Jean (2002), 'MIRAGE, A CGE Model for Trade Policy Analysis', CEPII Working Paper 2002-17 (Paris: Centre d'Etudes Prospectives et d'Informations Internationales).

Beghin, J. C., D. Roland-Holst and D. van der Mensbrugghe (2002), 'Global Agricultural Trade and the Doha Round: What are the Implications for North and South?', Working Paper 02-WP 308 (CARD, Iowa State University).

Bouët, A., Y. Decreux, L. Fontagné, S. Jean and D. Laborde (2004), 'A Consistent, Ad-valorem Equivalent Measure of Applied Protection Across the World: The MAcMap-HS6 Database', Working Paper 2004-21 (Paris: Centre d'Etudes Prospectives et d'Informations Internationales).

Burfisher, M., S. Robinson and K. Thierfelder (2002), 'The Global Impacts of Farm Policy Reforms in OECD Countries', *American Journal of Agricultural Economics*, **82**, 3, 768–74.

Diao, X., A. Somwaru and T. Roe (2001), 'A Global Analysis of Agricultural Trade Reform in WTO Member Countries', Economic Development Centre Paper (University of Minnesota).

Dimaranan, B. V. and R. A. McDougall (2002), *Global Trade Assistance and Production: The GTAP5 Data Base* (Centre for Global Trade Analysis, Purdue University).

Erkel-Rousse, H. and D. Mirza (2002), 'Import Price Elasticities: Reconsidering the Evidence', *Canadian Journal of Economics*, **35**, 282–306.

Francois, F. J. and D. W. Roland-Holst (1998), 'Scale Economies and Imperfect Competition', Ch. 11 in J. F. Francois and K. A. Reinert (eds.), *Applied Methods for Trade Policy Analysis* (Cambridge: Cambridge University Press) 331–63.

Francois, J., H. van Meijl and F. van Tongeren (2003), 'Economic Implication of Trade Liberalisation under the Doha Round', CEPII Working Paper 2003-20 (Paris: Centre d'Etudes Prospectives et d'Informations Internationales).

Frandsen, S. E., B. Gerfeldt and H. G. Jensen (2003), 'The Impacts of Redesigning European Agricultural Support', *Review of Urban and Regional Development Studies*, **15**, 2, 106–31.

Frandsen, S. E., H. G. Jensen, K. M. Lind, P. P. Meelgard and W. Yu (2003), 'Note on the Harbinson Draft on Modalities in WTO Agriculture Negotiations', mimeo (Agricultural Policy Research Division, Danish Research Institute of Food Economics).

Gibson, P., J. Wainio, D. Whitley and M. Bohman (2001), 'Profiles of Tariffs in Global Agricultural Markets', Agricultural Economic Report 796 (Washington DC: Economic Research Service, US Department of Agriculture).

Goldin, I. and O. Knudsen (eds.) (1990), *Trade Liberalisation: Implications for Developing Countries* (Paris: Organisation for Economic Co-operation and Development).

Goldin, I., O. Knudsen and D. van der Mensbrugghe (2003), 'For Whom the Bell Tolls: Incomplete Trade Liberalisation and Developing Countries', Presented at the Trade Consortium (University of Calabria, University of California joint meeting, Capri, June).

Harris, J. and M. P. Todaro (1970), 'Migration, Unemployment and Development: A Two-sector Analysis', *American Economic Review*, **60**, 1, 126–42.

Hertel, T. (ed.) (1997), *Global Trade Analysis. Modelling and Applications* (Cambridge: Cambridge University Press).

Hertel, T., B. M. Hoekman and W. Martin (2003), 'Agricultural Negotiations in the Context of a Broader Round: A Developing Country Perspective', Ch. 6, in P. L. Kennedy and W. W. Koo (eds.), *Agricultural Trade Policies in the New Millennium* (New York: Haworth Press, Inc.).

IPC (2003), 'Revisiting Special Preferences for Developing Countries', *IPC Brief* (International Food & Trade Policy Council).

Lewis, W. A. (1954), 'Economic Development with Unlimited Supplies of Labour', *Manchester School of Economics and Social Studies*, **22**, 2, 139–91.

Martin, W. and L. A. Winters (eds.) (1996), *The Uruguay Round and the Developing Countries* (Cambridge: Cambridge University Press).

OECD (2005), *Preferential Trading Arrangements in the Agriculture and Food Markets. The Case of the European Union and the United States* (Paris: Organisation for Economic Co-operation and Development).

The World Bank (2004), *Global Economic Prospects 2004. Realizing the Development Promise of the Doha Agenda* (Washington DC: The World Bank).

Van der Mensbrugghe, D. (2002), 'LINKAGE Technical Reference Document, Version 5.3' (Washington DC: The World Bank).

WTO (2003), 'Negotiations on Agriculture. First Draft on Modalities for the Further Commitments', TN/AG/W/1/Rev.1/, Committee on Agriculture (Special session, 18 March, Geneva: World Trade Organisation).

WTO (2004), 'Doha Work Programme: Draft General Council Decision of 31 July 2004', WT/GC/W/535 and corrigendum (General Council, Geneva: World Trade Organisation).

8

Over-optimism and the IMF

Graham Bird

1. INTRODUCTION

𝕬 N important part of the literature on the International Monetary Fund (IMF) involves evaluative studies which set out to assess the impact of the stabilisation and adjustment programmes that have been negotiated by governments with the Fund. How successful have these programmes been? Unsurprisingly perhaps, answering this question raises fundamental methodological issues. Before and after comparisons implicitly assume that other things have remained as they were, so that observed changes can be attributed to Fund-backed programmes. Comparisons between what was targeted and what was achieved implicitly assume that the targets were reasonable. Attempts to compare what happened with what would have happened in the absence of a Fund programme encounter the problem of the counterfactual, and there appears to be no scientifically satisfactory way of dealing with this problem even though researchers have made valiant attempts to overcome it as best they can.[1]

While the results that emerge from these studies have been nuanced, some influential observers and analysts of the Fund have claimed that IMF programmes, and the conditionality they embody, do not work. They sometimes go on to suggest that, in its conventional *ex post* form, IMF conditionality should be abandoned and should be replaced by *ex ante* conditionality (IFIAC, 2000). The Fund has responded by claiming that, where programmes fail, it is often because of a lack of commitment by the government concerned. Failure reflects poor implementation. To try and remedy this, recent reform has focused on 'streamlining' conditionality

---

[1] For a review of this literature, see Haque and Khan (1998). Some of the more influential contributions include Killick et al. (1994), Goldstein and Montiel (1986), Edwards (1989), Khan (1990), Conway (1994) and Killick, Malik and Manuel (1992). Recent papers include Przeworski and Vreeland (2002), Barro and Lee (2001), Evrensel (2002) and Hutchison and Noy (2003). A theme of this recent research has been the effect of IMF programmes on economic growth. While the consensus seems to be that the short-run effect will be negative, this result depends on the precise specification of the estimating models, on the time frame chosen and on the countries studied.

to reduce the number and range of conditions stipulated in agreements and on increasing the degree of national ownership of programmes by encouraging broader participation in the discussions that culminate in an agreement (IMF, 2001).

An interesting, but generally overlooked, dimension of the discussion of IMF programmes is the negative bias involved in interpreting their impact. Where targets are not achieved, programmes are presented as 'failing'. But if performance falls short of the targets set, might this be because the targets are in fact set unrealistically high? In this context, programmes could simultaneously achieve a great deal and yet still be perceived as having failed. The problem might be one of over-optimism on the part of those negotiating the programme rather than a lack of achievement.

This paper offers an examination of IMF programmes adopting this alternative approach. The organisation of the paper is as follows. Section 2 explores the factors that may lead to over-optimism. Clearly, from time to time, forecasts may go wrong, but random errors should imply that under-prediction will be as frequent as over-prediction. Here we focus on why there may be a systematic bias towards over-optimism. We do not do this by presenting a critical analysis of IMF forecasting techniques, but rather by exploring whether political economy factors will encourage an optimistic slant to be placed on predictions. Furthermore, we consider whether these factors will lead to universal over-optimism or whether they are more likely to induce it in some areas of economic performance than in others. Indeed, are there reasons to anticipate that over-optimism may occur in terms of some elements of programmes, alongside under-optimism (pessimism) in other elements?

Without presenting a formal model or test, Section 3 goes on to collate some of the available empirical evidence relating to over-optimism. This draws heavily on research undertaken by the Independent Evaluation Office of the IMF (IEO) in the context of its reports on other issues, but it also makes use of current research within the Fund's own Research Department and elsewhere. The evidence is found to be consistent with the claim that the Fund exhibits over-optimism in some areas.

Section 4 then examines the consequences of this for the design and effectiveness of IMF programmes. What is the impact of over-optimism on implementation and the longer-term effects on reputation and credibility both from the point of view of the IMF and the governments concerned? Suggesting that realism is preferable to optimism, Section 5 suggests a number of reforms that could bring about such a shift in institutional aspirations and operations. Section 6 offers a few concluding remarks that reposition the discussion in this paper into the broader debate about IMF programmes and reform.

2. MOTIVATIONS FOR OVER-OPTIMISM

IMF programmes emerge from negotiations between staff from the IMF and representatives of the governments seeking financial assistance. An agreement incorporates predictions about the performance of key economic variables and lays down conditions in terms of specific policy variables. The former will influence the latter (and vice versa), and the Fund takes these inter-relationships into account within the context of a financial programming framework. For example, assumptions about the rate of economic growth carry with them implications for the amount of tax revenue generated, and this will in turn influence the extent to which discretionary fiscal policy needs to be adjusted. It will also have implications for the growth of money demand and this will affect targets relating to credit creation.

Once a programme has been agreed between Fund staff and the government, it then has to be approved by the Fund's Executive Board. In addition to this, it has to be approved implicitly by the country upon whose behalf the government has negotiated it. Otherwise, compliance will be adversely affected.[2]

What motivations lie behind the staff of the IMF who are involved in this process, once the Fund has been approached by a government for a loan? It may be assumed that they will want to 'get to yes'. They want to reach an agreement with the government that is then endorsed by the Executive Board. After all, its Articles of Agreement delineate a role where the IMF assists countries in balance of payments need, and this will not be achieved if programmes are not agreed. Moreover, the staff involved will not further their careers by failing to negotiate agreements. There will be both a personal and an institutional desire to get an agreement.

In order to do so, the Fund staff have to ensure that the negotiated programme is acceptable both to the government concerned and to the IMF Executive Board. The government, it may be assumed, will want the loan to be as large as possible. It will also want to minimise the domestic political costs of accepting and implementing the related conditionality. In short, the government will want to maximise the benefits and minimise the costs of the programme. This will give it the best chance of 'selling' it nationally and retaining its own political integrity. Having taken the decision to turn to the IMF, governments will not want to be rejected.

But from the viewpoint of both the IMF's staff and the government, there will be constraints on their desire to reach agreement. The IMF will be anxious not to undermine its financial reputation. It will therefore not be prepared to say yes at any cost. An approved programme must be internally consistent and coherent. However, the effects of individual programmes on institutional reputation may be somewhat intangible and difficult to take into account. There may also be an inconsistency between personal and institutional ambitions with staff adopting a short-term view. Furthermore, the Fund will also be constrained in terms of the amount it can lend, and this will influence the details of programmes.

---

[2] For an analysis of compliance in the context of IMF programmes, see Bird (2002 and 2003).

Governments will not endorse programmes that they believe will merely secure their political demise. If they believe that, with the best deal they can reach, the costs still outweigh the benefits, they will not sign the agreement.

While both the IMF and the government will enter into negotiations with the objective of reaching an agreement – although not at any cost – they will tend to be looking for different things from it. The IMF is a financial institution. Its primary concern will be to strengthen a country's balance of payments in the relatively near term. It will, however, want to achieve this while minimising adverse effects on other aspects of economic performance, in particular economic growth, in order to be consistent with its Articles of Agreement.[3] Governments will have a rather different agenda. Their primary long-term aim, it may be assumed, is to raise national living standards. To achieve this, they will be keen to maximise the rate of economic growth. The balance of payments will be perceived by them as a short-term constraint on achieving this long-run objective. In circumstances where the IMF has become involved, the balance of payments constraint has become binding and governments are seeking to relax it. What is an objective for the Fund is a constraint for governments. Governments will therefore enter into negotiations with the Fund to overcome balance of payments problems and re-establish economic growth as soon as possible.

What about the Fund's Executive Board? Where does this fit into the story? For the Board, defending the Fund's reputation will be a significant factor. But the Board will also have a bias towards saying 'yes'. After all, it is making decisions about whether to assist members of the institution. Even members of the Board opposed to a particular programme are more likely to abstain rather than vote against it. And yet the Board will need to satisfy itself that programmes make economic sense and have a good chance of being implemented. The staff of the Fund who are helping to design them will be aware of this.[4]

With the motivations discussed above, it may be anticipated that there will be a tendency towards optimism built into the design of IMF programmes. A key

---

[3] The Articles of Agreement spell out the purposes of the IMF. Article 1 (ii) explains that the Fund's role is 'to facilitate the expansion and balanced growth of international trade and to contribute thereby to the promotion and maintenance of high levels of employment and real income and to the development of the productive resources of all members as primary objectives of economic policy'. Article 1 (v) says that it is 'to give confidence to members by making the general resources of the Fund temporarily available to them under adequate safeguards, thus providing them with the opportunity to correct maladjustments in their balance of payments without resorting to measures destructive of national or international prosperity'. Article 1 (vi) stresses that the Fund should try 'to shorten the duration and lessen the degree of disequilibrium in the international balance of payments of members'.

[4] By saying 'no', the Board may feel that governments will be forced to adopt measures that more strongly compress domestic aggregate demand. These may have overspill effects on other member countries. Thus a bias towards saying 'yes' may reflect the desire to contain crises. Over-optimism about economic performance under a programme may be a way of justifying this underlying desire.

element relates to economic growth. Why is this central? By being optimistic about the prospects for economic growth, there will be related optimism about tax revenue. Programmes will then require less adjustment in terms of discretionary tax policy and government expenditure in order to achieve specific fiscal targets and, therefore, related monetary targets as well. Tax rates will not need to be increased so much, nor government expenditure cut so much.

Indeed, assuming a relatively high rate of economic growth, it may also be assumed that the demand for money will grow relatively strongly, implying greater latitude for money supply growth. By requiring smaller changes in fiscal policy, and by making optimistic assumptions about economic growth, programmes may be presented as involving relatively modest political costs. This then increases the perceived probability that they will be implemented. It also, of course, raises the probability that governments will agree to them and that the Executive Board will endorse them. If the anticipated economic growth is unforthcoming, the implication is that the improvement in the current account of the balance of payments will probably be greater than expected, and, as noted above, securing an improvement in the balance of payments is the Fund's top priority. In short, it seems to serve the interests of all parties to be optimistic about economic growth.

Over-optimism may not be limited to economic growth. There may be similar over-optimism with respect to export growth and capital inflows from abroad. What lies behind this? Starting off from a given balance of payments situation, programmes involve a combination of adjustment and financing. Adjustment with growth will be more attractive politically since it involves smaller sacrifices in terms of current living standards. Essentially, export capacity is created by increasing domestic production rather than by reducing domestic consumption. At the same time, increased export demand and supply may be associated with exchange rate depreciation. Indeed, over-optimism with respect to economic growth is likely to go hand in hand with over-optimism about export growth, since this implies that the economic growth will avoid a balance of payments constraint and be sustainable.

Sacrifices in current consumption may also be avoided by borrowing from abroad. As this increases, so the immediate need for adjustment via reducing domestic aggregate demand falls, as does the need for financing from the IMF. There will therefore be an incentive for the IMF to be optimistic about capital inflows since this justifies a more limited level of IMF financing, and makes viable programmes that embody relatively modest amounts of domestic adjustment. Moreover, capital inflows may be endogenous to IMF programmes. Those that are optimistic about future economic growth and export performance are likely to prove more attractive to foreign investors. There will be an important element of self-fulfilling prophecy here since, to the extent that it exists, the external financing constraint on economic growth may be relaxed by the enhanced prospects for economic growth. It will again be in the interests of IMF staff, governments and the Fund's Executive Board to be positive and optimistic about the future inflow of foreign capital. Optimism with respect to economic growth, export growth and capital inflows is therefore positively correlated.[5]

But what allows the IMF and governments to exhibit optimism? Why is it not corrected over time? There is only limited scientific consensus over the causes of economic growth, and forecasting it is notoriously imprecise. Much the same could be said about the behavioural response to changes in exchange rates, the determinants of private sector saving and investment, and the reactions of capital markets to IMF programmes. To be optimistic about economic growth and these other variables does not require forecasters to be unprofessional. With a slower than projected rate of economic growth, the costs of implementing programmes will rise above the level that was anticipated by governments at the outset, and this will reduce the rate of implementation. But will a poor record of implementation not then sensitise governments and the Fund to over-optimism? Will they not learn from past mistakes and scale down future growth projections?

There are reasons to expect that over-optimism will not be corrected through time. From a government's perspective, reducing the projected growth rate almost certainly implies increasing the targeted degree of fiscal adjustment. Moreover, there may be little domestic political cost associated with failing to implement programmes as originally agreed – there may even be a domestic political benefit to be had.[6] And, in any case, programmes may be modified or waivers may be granted.[7] Ultimately the government could effectively cancel the arrangement and negotiate a new one. If growth over-optimism enables governments to get what they perceive as a better deal from the IMF, why would they want to be anything other than as optimistic about growth as they are allowed to be, especially when this does not prejudice subsequent arrangements?

Apart from the incentives to perpetuate over-optimism, there will be somewhat limited institutional learning on the side of governments. For many countries, borrowing from the IMF is a reasonably infrequent occurrence and it is unlikely that there will be great continuity in terms of the government personnel negotiating programmes. The mobility of personnel may also be a factor that reduces 'learning' on the part of the IMF staff involved in designing country-specific

---

[5] The whole set of relationships will involve significant endogeneity. Projected economic growth will help attract capital. Capital inflows may facilitate economic growth and export expansion which then attract further capital inflows.

[6] Governments may present themselves domestically as standing up to the IMF and defending national sovereignty over the design of economic policy. They may indeed never have been committed to the original programme and have agreed to it merely to secure the initial level of financial assistance.

[7] The IEO (2002) reports that waivers are granted relating to 25 per cent or more of structural performance criteria. The percentage for quantitative performance criteria is very much lower at about two per cent for countries drawing GRA resources from the Fund.

programmes. The composition of 'missions' may vary from one to the next. But, in any event, the ongoing incentive will again be to reach an agreement rather than to ensure that it is fully implemented. The poor implementation of past or current agreements will not therefore effectively police over-optimism with respect to future ones. Furthermore, institutionally, IMF arrangements under current consideration are more likely to be judged against their contemporary counterparts than against their historical ancestors. In this way, growth over-optimism is more likely to perpetuate itself rather than constrain itself.

One might imagine that it would be the Executive Board, mindful of the Fund's reputation that would eventually be the constraining force on over-optimism. The problem here is one of time inconsistency. Erosion of reputation is likely to be gradual and intangible. There will therefore be an incentive to apply a high discount rate to it. The reputational costs of over-optimism will therefore seem low in present-value terms. Juxtaposed against these, there may be strong short-term political pressures to agree to loans. Powerful advanced countries may attempt to reward 'friends' and influence 'foes' by endorsing IMF loans. Institutional arrangements that encourage a consensual approach by the Board may facilitate and perpetuate this. It is not difficult to imagine a model where one powerful advanced country 'buys off' opposition on the Board to a programme in a country that it wants to support for largely political reasons by making future commitments not to oppose programmes in countries that other advanced countries may favour. Growth over-optimism may provide apparent economic justification. If this is the case, it cannot be assumed that over-optimism will be self-correcting. Indeed, it is more likely to be self-perpetuating.

What about countries that fall into arrears in terms of their obligations to the Fund? Both the Fund's staff and the Executive Board may be expected to be concerned about arrears since not only will they weaken the Fund's financial position but they will also mean that those countries in arrears will be excluded from access to further IMF resources. Such concern may to some extent police over-optimism in terms of loans to countries that do not have outstanding obligations, but it may encourage it in the case of countries with such obligations. There may be an element of defensive lending with new loans being used as a way of allowing indebted countries to fulfil their existing commitments. The desire to prevent countries from falling into arrears may motivate over-optimism in terms of new programmes in countries with existing obligations. The desire to maintain comparability between programmes may then mean that over-optimism spreads to programmes with countries that do not have outstanding obligations to the Fund.

What emerges from the above discussion? We see that governments as well as the IMF's staff and Executive Board will be predisposed towards excessive optimism in IMF programmes, particularly with respect to economic growth, export growth and capital inflows. The reasons for over-optimism are largely 'political' and institutional. The economic uncertainties surrounding the causes of economic growth, behavioural responses to policy changes and the modalities through which the catalytic effect of IMF programmes may work, permit these factors to exert an influence. By being optimistic about economic growth, export growth and capital inflows, programmes may be presented in a way that makes them appear more viable. The adjustment costs seem lower and the probability that the programmes will be implemented therefore seems higher. Of course, should neither economic growth nor capital inflows be forthcoming at the rate projected, actual costs will turn out to be higher than anticipated, and therefore the chances of the programmes actually being implemented will be lower. However, a low *ex post* rate of implementation is unlikely to correct future over-optimism since the implied loss of institutional reputation associated with it is likely to be less significant than the contemporary reasons for its continuance. Moreover, governments may encounter low political costs from poor implementation. Political economy factors therefore point to serial over-optimism in IMF programmes with respect to economic growth, export growth and capital flows.[8] Is this what we find when we examine the empirical evidence?

3. EVIDENCE ON OVER-OPTIMISM

Traditionally, studies that have attempted to evaluate the effects of IMF programmes have focused on final macroeconomic outcomes or policy variables. They have generally avoided examining the accuracy of projections and whether targets have been hit, since this methodology raises the question of whether the targets themselves are attainable. Failure to hit targets could after all indicate either poor performance or poor target selection. However, in this paper, our focus is precisely on the accuracy of projecting and the selection of targets, so the wisdom surrounding their specification is of central importance. Insights into this could no doubt be provided by a retrospective examination of IMF forecasts and the underlying models upon which they are based. Is there some in-built bias? We do not follow this route, although we allude to work that does. Instead, a moment's reflection suggests that a good target will be one that is both challenging and feasible. If targets are always hit, this provides *prima facie* evidence that they are insufficiently challenging. There is under-ambition or a pessimism bias. If, on the other hand, targets are never hit, and indeed missed by a significant amount, this provides equivalent evidence of over-optimism. Between these two

---

[8] There may also be a tendency for bureaucracies (as agents) to be over-ambitious about what they can achieve in order to try and show themselves in a positive light (to their principals), and therefore secure their future. Easterly (2002), for example, stresses this argument when discussing the ambitions of aid agencies as compared to their actual achievements – as he sees them.

TABLE 1

Optimism of Real GDP and Export Projections in ESAF Programmes[1]

	Prolonged Users		'Temporary' Users	
	Mean	Median	Mean	Median
Merchandise export growth				
Out-turn	7.4	5.8	17.2	13.6
Projected	10.5	9.9	12.5	12.5
Real GDP growth				
Out-turn	3.5	3.7	4.2	5.4
Projected	4.1	4.0	5.0	4.7

Note:

[1] Average annual growth in per cent for years T to $T+4$, where T is the year in which the programme started.

Source: IMF Policy Development and Review Department and IEO Calculations.

extremes – where targets are sometimes hit and sometimes missed – there has to be some degree of subjective judgement. But evidence of a reasonably systematic and significant failure to achieve targets would provide support for a bias towards over-optimism. It would suggest that targets have become excessively challenging to the extent of becoming generally unfeasible.[9]

There are a number of recent studies upon which we can draw to provide evidence on this issue. These comprise both econometric and case study research. To begin with, the first three reports published by the Independent Evaluation Office (IEO) of the IMF are a very useful source of material (IEO, 2002, 2003a and 2003b). Table 1, taken from the IEO's report on the prolonged use of IMF resources, provides a comparison between programme projections and outcomes in ESAF (Enhanced Structural Adjustment Facility) programmes. It suggests that projections for exports were 'greatly over-optimistic' for prolonged users, but not for temporary users – although in neither case was the bias statistically significant, given the large variability in both projections and out-turns. Projections for real GDP growth were generally over-optimistic for both groups of users, with the errors tending to rise in the later years of multi-year programmes.

In the case of arrangements using general resources (GRA), which typically involve a shorter time frame, an analysis undertaken by the IEO, based on a database assembled by Musso and Phillips (2001), is summarised in Table 2. This suggests that growth projections were over-optimistic for both temporary and prolonged users, with the discrepancy between projected and actual out-turns being greater in the former group.

---

[9] It may be underlined here that, within the financial programming framework used by the Fund, targets which relate to intermediate policy variables such as the fiscal balance, monetary growth and the exchange rate will be linked to projections relating to economic growth, exogenous export growth, investment and savings rates.

TABLE 2
Accuracy of Short-term Projections for Users of General Resources[1]

	Prolonged Users		'Temporary' Users	
	Mean	Median	Mean	Median
Real GDP growth				
Out-turn	1.7	3.9	−0.9	0.2
Projected	2.4	3.4	0.2	−1.0
Difference[1]	−0.7	0.0	−1.1	−0.4

Note:
[1] The median of the differences is not necessarily equal to the difference of the respective medians.

Source: Database assembled by Musso and Phillips (2001) and IEO Calculations.

TABLE 3
Realism of Programme Projections: Average Projections Less Outcomes[1] – Case Studies
(All figures are percentage points a year)

	Pakistan	Philippines[2]	Senegal	Morocco[3]
Real GDP growth	1.4	2.1	1.7	1.2
Export growth (in US dollar terms)	5.7	2.5	2.8	0.9
Fiscal balance (in per cent of GDP)	1.9	1.6	1.9	1.8
Government revenue (in per cent of GDP)	1.3	1.1[4]	–	–
National saving (in per cent of GDP)	2.3	0.5[5]	2.8	−0.8

Notes:
[1] Average of all initial projections for programmes since 1983, for the year in which the programme started and the two succeeding years.
[2] Growth and ratios expressed in relation to GNP, rather than GDP.
[3] For Morocco, except for export growth, projections are for the year in which the programme started and the immediately succeeding year, due to the limited time horizon of projections in programme documents.
[4] National government tax revenue as a per cent of GDP.
[5] The apparent rise in the saving rate in the late 1990s and early 2000s may be over-stated as a result of statistical weaknesses.

Source: IMF staff reports.

Further information presented by the IEO based on case studies provides additional evidence in support of over-optimism. This is summarised in Table 3. Although the data do not allow a fine distinction to be made between over-optimism and weak implementation, the IEO claims that:

the more extensive discussion in the country studies suggests that . . . both the authorities and staff recognised that programs were often built on very optimistic projections (IEO, 2002, p. 53).

Later in their report, the IEO points out that its survey of mission chiefs suggests that 'internal incentives create a tendency to over-promise'. Thus:

About 45 per cent of mission chiefs surveyed by the IEO reported that the need to show balance of payments viability by the end of the medium term projection period had led to *ex ante* over-optimistic projections or over-ambitious program objectives 'frequently' or 'always', with another 28 per cent reporting the same phenomenon 'sometimes'. In contrast, only about one quarter reported this practice occurring 'never' or only 'occasionally' (IEO, 2002, p. 65).

In its third report, dealing with fiscal adjustment in IMF programmes, the IEO (2003b) again claims that its analysis of actual and projected economic growth across a large sample of programmes suggests that, apart from in transition countries, programmes exhibited over-optimism; with this being particularly significant in programmes that started from a more adverse situation. The IEO points out that:

> Growth slowdowns between the first and second year of the program occurred twice as often as they were projected, with programs tending to under-predict significantly more situations of adverse output developments than under-predict situations of favourable output developments. Negative growth for the second year of the program was projected in only 1.3 per cent of cases, but in reality happened ten times more frequently (IEO, 2003b, p. 6).

The IEO also presents evidence of over-optimism in terms of investment rates in 60 per cent of 83 stand-by and extended arrangements examined. In about one-quarter of these cases, investment rates were five percentage points of GDP or more below projections. Furthermore, in terms of fiscal targets, the IEO finds that only about one-half of the programmed improvement in overall and primary fiscal balances was achieved, with almost all the fiscal adjustment occurring in the first year of programmes. Over-optimism about fiscal adjustment is clearly linked to over-optimism with respect to economic growth, with the IEO finding that, whereas slower than anticipated economic growth seems to be associated with revenue shortfalls, it is not associated with lower levels of expenditure. Fiscal over-optimism with respect to revenue was particularly pronounced in the programmes that targeted 'large' fiscal adjustment of more than three percentage points of GDP over two years. A brief summary of fiscal performance running from one year before to one year after IMF programmes is presented in Table 4.

In its second report dealing with the Fund's involvement in capital account crises in Indonesia, Korea and Brazil, the IEO points out that:

> contrary to the expectation that IMF support would certify the effectiveness of an adjustment program and help achieve smooth adjustment, many of the IMF supported programs initially failed to achieve a turnaround in market sentiment (IEO, 2003a).

In a similar vein, Ghosh et al. (2002) examine the effects of eight IMF programmes in crisis-hit countries during the 1990s, covering Mexico, Thailand, Korea, Indonesia, Brazil, Turkey and Argentina. The authors point out that:

> It is striking that in every instance in our sample, the outcome (for private capital flows) was worse than projected. Even in cases where the magnitude of the error was small, such as Argentina (1995), the program does not appear to have had a strong catalytic effect (Ghosh et al., 2002, p. 14).

TABLE 4
Changes in Fiscal Balances from $(T - 1)$ to $(T + 1)$[1]
(All figures are in per cent of GDP)

	All Arrangements	ESAF/ PRGF	SBA/EFF	
			Transition Countries	Non-transition Countries
Envisaged				
Government balance	1.7	1.6	1.1	2.0
Primary balance[2]	1.4	1.0	0.4	2.0
Government revenues	0.4	0.4	−1.7	1.3
Government expenditures	−1.2	−1.2	−2.8	−0.7
Actual				
Government balance	0.8	1.0	1.8	0.2
Primary balance[2]	0.7	0.6	0.3	1.0
Government revenues	0.2	0.1	−1.4	0.9
Government expenditures	−0.7	−1.0	−3.2	0.6
Count	133	60	21	52

Notes:
[1] Figures subject to rounding errors.
[2] Based on a sample of 115 arrangements.

Source: MONA and WEO databases.

If, in general, actual economic growth is slower than projected, private sector investment is lower than projected and capital inflows are smaller than projected, it might be expected to follow that the current account of the balance of payments would be found to improve by more than is projected, although in theory this could be offset by shortfalls in fiscal adjustment. There is some empirical support for the excess performance of the actual current account as compared with projections. Based on a sample of 115 programmes during the 1990s, the IEO finds that, whereas a deficit of 0.3 per cent of GDP is envisaged in the year following a programme, a surplus of 0.3 per cent is actually achieved. This finding is, to some extent, confirmed by other research; but only to *some* extent.

In a study related to the IEO's investigations, Atoian et al. (2003) examine the accuracy of IMF projections relating to the ratio of fiscal surplus to GDP and the current account of the balance of payments surplus to GDP across 175 programmes during 1993–2001, and over a number of time horizons. In summary, they conclude that 'projections differ substantially from those actually achieved' (p. 3). Fiscal adjustment seems to fall further short of projections over longer time horizons, whereas in terms of the current account, the improvement is more marked than was projected in the short term but less marked than projected over a longer time horizon. Interestingly, the authors explore various potential reasons for the divergence of actual from projected values and find that it may be explained by incomplete information concerning initial conditions, differences in

TABLE 5
Objectives in IMF Programmes: Programme vs. Actual

	Programme				Difference (programme/ minus actual)		
	t − 3	t − 2	t − 1	Actual	t − 3	t − 2	t − 1
Real GDP growth (in per cent)							
All programme-years	5.2	4.6	3.5	1.8	3.4	2.8	1.7
PRGFs	5.7	5.3	4.7	3.3	2.4	2.0	1.4
SBAs	4.5	3.8	2.0	0.3	4.2	3.5	1.7
o/w large access	4.1	2.9	1.3	1.1	3.0	1.8	0.2
CPI inflation (per cent, end-of-period)							
All programme-years	5.0	6.0	8.0	10.3	−5.3	−4.3	−2.3
PRGFs	4.3	5.0	7.0	8.4	−4.1	−3.4	−1.4
SBAs	6.0	7.0	9.1	13.2	−7.2	−6.2	−4.1
o/w large access	6.0	6.3	6.6	8.9	−2.9	−2.6	−2.3
Current account balance (per cent of GDP)							
All programme-years	−8.6	−9.1	−9.4	−9.4	0.8	0.3	0.0
PRGFs	−11.4	−12.4	−13.2	−13.9	2.5	1.5	0.7
SBAs	−4.1	−4.7	−4.6	−4.5	0.4	−0.2	−0.1
o/w large access	−2.1	−1.3	−1.3	−1.0	−1.1	−0.3	−0.3

Notes:
The table reports means by group except for inflation for which medians are reported due to outliers. All observations are used for each sample. The same general pattern is preserved if sample size is kept constant across columns. The last three columns report the difference between the programme columns and the actual columns.

Source: Baqir et al. (2004).

the 'model' underlying IMF projections as compared with that suggested by the data on out-turns, differences between the reforms assumed within the projections and those actually implemented, and random errors in the actual data.

In other research conducted within the Fund, Baqir et al. (2004) also discover evidence of over-optimism. They examine 94 programmes over the period 1989 to 2002 comparing the objectives in terms of both economic performance and policy variables over the three years prior to the programme with the actual out-turns. Their findings are summarised in Table 5. Typically, out-turns fell short of targets in the areas of economic growth and inflation, but were broadly in line with current account balance of payments objectives. As far as policy variables are concerned they also find evidence of over-ambition. The study offers an additional degree of disaggregation by exploring differences between programme types.

Baqir et al. (2004) discover that over-ambition is least marked in the case of high-profile stand-by arrangements. How can this be explained? The authors of the study suggest that the closer scrutiny that high-profile programmes receive may encourage greater realism. They also suggest that a greater awareness of the domestic political constraints on adjustment may be factored into these programmes. In terms of our earlier analysis other explanations may also be available. In the case of high-profile programmes, perceived failure in achieving targets may be assessed as having a larger negative impact on both the IMF's and the government's reputation. Moreover, the crisis conditions under which governments turn to the Fund may make it less necessary to talk up the growth prospects of programmes, first because the government can demonstrate the need for IMF involvement, and second because the Executive Board of the Fund needs less persuasion to participate given the systemic economic and political import-ance of high-profile countries. Finally, it may also be that since high-profile countries are defined by Baqir et al. to include those that receive relatively large amounts of IMF finance, this allows the related programmes to call for less adjustment. The degree of adjustment contained in programmes will be dictated by the amount of finance supplied. With more finance, less optimism is required in terms of economic growth, export growth and other capital flows in order to make programmes appear viable. Less short-term emphasis will need to be placed on reducing fiscal deficits.

While the research reported above is in some respects limited, it all seems to point in a similar direction. Moreover, the findings reported by the IEO are based on both large sample econometric investigation and a wide range of case studies. Overall, therefore, there is strong empirical evidence of a tendency for IMF programmes to fall short of both the policy targets established and the envisaged macroeconomic outcomes. Although disaggregation shows a measure of diver-sity, there remains a systematic tendency to fall short of projections and targets. According to our definition, IMF programmes exhibit serial over-optimism. Does this matter? Is it a problem?

4. IS OVER-OPTIMISM A PROBLEM?

As discussed in Section 2, and up until recently, over-optimism in IMF pro-grammes has not been widely perceived to be a problem. Indeed, it has fulfilled certain positive political economy functions and, to a point, has enabled the 'system' to work. The question is exactly 'to what point'? In the world of *realpolitik*, over-optimism may have kept IMF money moving. It has enabled the IMF to justify making loans and has enabled governments to survive the domes-tic political consequences of involving the Fund in the design of macroeconomic policy. It may spur countries on to make greater efforts to reform. But it remains of concern that targets are systematically missed. Ultimately, what is the point in having them if they are merely something of a cosmetic exercise?

Serial over-optimism involves five associated problems. First, there are the transactions costs associated with negotiating detailed conditionality that is then not implemented or does not deliver what is intended. Secondly, it means that when performance in terms of policy reform and macroeconomic outcomes is not forthcoming, this will have to be dealt with in other ways such as by modifying programmes, granting waivers or negotiating replacement programmes. These are likely to be inferior alternatives to delineating a realistic programme at the outset. The process of granting modifications and waivers lacks transparency and carries with it significant uncertainties which make macroeconomic management that much more difficult. Thirdly, serial over-optimism will gradually undermine the Fund's reputation, at a time when the institution is keen to strengthen its signalling role. Over-optimism is indeed inconsistent with an effective signalling function – unless the degree of over-optimism is predictable, which it is not. If the Fund wishes to improve its catalytic effect on private capital flows, it is hardly likely to achieve this if the policies and outcomes it predicts do not materialise. What value then for the Fund's good housekeeping seal of approval? Fourthly, if economic growth, current account improvement and capital inflows are over-predicted, it follows that the amount of adjustment and the amount of IMF lending needed will be under-predicted. This will have important conse-quences for the politics of adjustment and for policies relating to the financing capacity of the Fund. Thus, quota increases may be rejected as an indirect conse-quence of over-optimism relating to IMF programmes. Fifth and finally, over-optimism will create a psychology of institutional failure. Psychologically, it may be better to set realistic targets and achieve them than to set overly optimistic targets and miss them.

Two questions lead on from this. What can be done to overcome the bias towards over-optimism? And, given that over-optimism is there for a reason, how likely is it that the bias will be addressed? We turn to the first of these questions in the next section, and examine the second in the concluding remarks that follow.

5. POLICIES FOR DEALING WITH OVER-OPTIMISM

There are a number of potential policy responses to IMF over-optimism. First, having identified areas where there is a systematic bias, such as in predicting economic growth and fiscal adjustment, predictions and targets could be scaled back. The trick here would be to find the appropriate degree of scaling back. If taken too far, the discipline and signalling roles of IMF programmes could be weakened. In this regard, a reasonably full retrospective evaluation of why targets have been missed would be needed in order to feed into future programme design. Such an evaluation would have country-specific elements, but could also help to identify more general areas of over-optimism. Thus it is increasingly recognised that 'institutions' have an important bearing on growth, but that it takes a long time to change them. Historically, programmes may have been over-optimistic with regard to the speed at which such changes may be brought about, and this expectation could be modified downwards.[10]

Secondly, a greater understanding of the political economy of policy implementation would enable the Fund to form a more realistic view about the chances of programme success. Research is beginning to identify the factors that influence implementation and more formal analysis of these in the context of IMF programmes should constrain over-optimism.[11] This could pan out in various ways. If targets were not to be changed, there would at least be a reduction in the perceived probability that they would be met. But, more helpfully, greater recognition of the problems associated with implementation could lead to targets being adjusted to more realistic levels. The perceived success of IMF programmes could then be increased without there necessarily being any improvement in actual performance. However, it is not impossible that actual performance could improve if governments believed that the adjustment targets were more realistic and attainable. There could be a positive impact on ownership and therefore on outcomes.

Thirdly, since the current policy of using modifications, waivers and replacement programmes to deal with situations where targets are not met lacks transparency and, as a consequence, creates uncertainty which disrupts signalling, a clearer policy that delineates the circumstances in which they would be permitted, alongside more realistic targets, might help overcome these shortcomings.

Fourthly, existing methods of introducing flexibility into IMF programmes could be taken one stage further, by contemplating alternative scenarios at the outset of programmes rather than by modifying them as time goes by. Essentially, the sensitivity of programmes to various factors would be considered *ex ante*. What are the things that threaten the success of programmes and to which are they vulnerable? Rather than having one central prediction for economic growth or export growth, there could be a 'fan' of possible outcomes with approximate probabilities attached to them. Targets would be set according to the most probable outcomes, but there would be contingent conditionality which would be dependent on alternative events. For example, where economic growth turned out to be less strong than anticipated, there would already be contingent plans with respect to fiscal policy. In effect, the design of programmes and their targets would attempt to endogenise external shocks. A disadvantage of this approach might be that it would appear to increase the time and effort needed when programmes are being initially negotiated. However, this would not necessarily be the case. If governments (and indeed the Fund) believed that they had alternative plans for dealing with different states of the world, they might be less

---

[10] The IEO reports referred to earlier again provide compelling evidence that the time taken to implement institutional changes has been underestimated in the past.

[11] For a discussion of how this might be achieved, see Bird (2003) and Bird and Willett (2004).

concerned about the 'central forecast' embedded in the IMF programme. There would be an 'insurance policy' to deal with the vulnerabilities surrounding the initial programme. The advantage of this approach would be to reduce un-certainty about future economic policy and about IMF support. This would in turn strengthen the Fund's signalling role and would remove (or at least reduce) the stigma of failure. Rather than failing to implement 'Plan A', countries would instead be switching to and then successfully implementing 'Plan B'.[12]

6. CONCLUDING REMARKS

There is a large and long-standing literature on IMF conditionality and the effects of IMF programmes. Concern that they do not work well in terms of influencing policy variables and macroeconomic outcomes has led to suggestions that *ex ante* conditionality should be abandoned (IFIAC, 2000). It has also led the IMF to pursue a policy of 'streamlining' conditionality in such a way as to focus on a narrower range of variables and to encourage greater 'ownership' of programmes. Indeed, ownership is prescribed as a key to improving the extent to which programmes negotiated with the IMF are then implemented by governments.

It is against this background that this paper examines whether IMF programmes are perceived to fail because the targets and predictions they embody are over-optimistic. There are reasons to believe that the Fund's staff involved in design-ing programmes, the governments that commit to implementing them and the Fund's Executive Board that approves them, will be inclined to exploit the scope for over-optimism that the lack of scientific consensus about the underlying eco-nomics allows them. There are strong political economy motivations for over-optimism. Empirical evidence, limited as it is, endorses the *a priori* presumption that over-optimism will exist. Moreover, up until now, political and institutional factors have resulted in the bias towards optimism being perpetuated rather than corrected.

Yet, over-optimism, or a lack of realism, has its downside. Target setting becomes discredited if targets are systematically missed, and this will gradually adversely affect the reputation of those engaged in setting the targets. Not least, setting targets will fail to transmit the signals that they are intended to transmit if they lack credibility. Increasing attention is therefore being paid to the way in which targets are set within the context of IMF programmes. The degree of

---

[12] Time would, of course, also be saved later in the 'life' of a programme as modifications and waivers would be less likely to be needed. Programme reviews might also become somewhat more straightforward. On top of this, the 'mortality rate' of programmes might be expected to fall as a consequence, making replacement programmes less necessary.

under-achievement has reached a threshold where it has become an important policy issue. Moreover, the Fund's Independent Evaluation Office has begun to highlight the issue and to correct the information asymmetries that previously allowed it to occur.

This paper examines various ways in which realism could replace over-optimism. The basic policy shift advocated is to move away from dealing with over-optimism in IMF programmes by means of *ex post* modifications, waivers and programme replacement, and towards a contingent approach to conditionality. An important benefit from such a shift would be to alter the psychology of failure. At present, the Fund suffers from the paradox of over-optimism. By assuming things will turn out better than they actually do, the Fund creates the impression that it is failing when, in fact, its achievements may be significantly positive. Frustration is the difference between aspirations and achievement, and much of the current frustration with IMF programmes and conditionality may be associated with unrealistically optimistic aspirations rather than serious under-achievement.

REFERENCES

Atoian, R., P. Conway, M. Selowsky and T. Tsikata (2003), 'Macroeconomic Adjustment in IMF Supported Programs: Projections and Reality', Paper presented at a conference on the Role of the IMF and World Bank in the Global Economy (Yale University, 25–27 April).

Baqir, R., R. Ramcharan and R. Sahay (2004), 'IMF Program Design and Growth: Is Optimism Deliberate? Is It Defensible?', Paper presented at the Jacques Polak Annual Research Conference IMF (Washington DC, IMF).

Barro, R. J. and J. W. Lee (2001), 'IMF Programs: Who Is Chosen and What Are the Effects?', Working Paper (Harvard University).

Bird, G. (2002), 'The Completion Rate of IMF Programmes: What We Know, Don't Know and Need to Know', *The World Economy*, 25, 6, 833–47.

Bird, G. (2003), 'The Implementation of IMF Programmes: A Conceptual Framework and Policy Agenda', Working Paper (Surrey Centre for International Economic Studies).

Bird, G. and T. Willett (2004), 'IMF Conditionality, Implementation and the New Political Economy of Ownership', *Comparative Economic Studies*, 46, 423–50.

Conway, P. (1994), 'IMF Lending Programs: Participation and Impact', *Journal of Development Economics*, 45, 2, 355–91.

Easterly, W. (2002), 'The Cartel of Good Intentions: The Problem of Bureaucracy in Foreign Aid', *Journal of Policy Reform*, 5, 4, 223–50.

Edwards, S. (1989), 'The International Monetary Fund and the Developing Countries: A Critical Evaluation', *Carnegie-Rochester Conference Series on Public Policy*, 31, 7–68.

Evrensel, A. Y. (2002), 'Effectiveness of IMF-supported Stabilization Programs in Developing Countries', *Journal of International Money and Finance*, 21, 565–87.

Ghosh, A., T. Lane, M. Schultze-Gattas, A. Bulir, J. Hamann and A. Mourmouras (2002), 'IMF-supported Programs in Capital Account Crisis', IMF Occasional Paper No. 210 (Washington DC, IMF).

Goldstein, M. and P. Montiel (1986), 'Evaluating Fund Stabilization Programs with Multicountry Data: Some Methodological Pitfalls', *IMF Staff Papers*, 33, 2, 304–44.

Haque, N. U. and M. S. Khan (1998), 'Do IMF-supported Programs Work? A Survey of the Cross-country Empirical Evidence', IMF Working Paper No. 98/169 (Washington DC, IMF).

Hutchison, M. M. and I. Noy (2003), 'Macroeconomics Effects of IMF-sponsored Programs in Latin America: Output Costs, Program Recidivism and the Vicious Circle of Failed Stabilizations', *Journal of International Money and Finance*, **22**, 991–1014.

Independent Evaluation Office (2002), *Evaluation of Prolonged Use of IMF Resources* (Washington DC, IMF).

Independent Evaluation Office (2003a), *The IMF and Recent Capital Account Crises: Indonesia, Korea, Brazil* (Washington DC, IMF).

Independent Evaluation Office (2003b), *Fiscal Adjustment in IMF-supported Programs* (Washington DC, IMF).

International Financial Institution Advisory Commission (2000), *Report of the International Financial Institution Advisory Commission* (The Meltzer Report) (Washington DC, US Government Printing Office).

International Monetary Fund (2001), 'Conditionality in Fund-supported Programs: Overview' (mimeographed, Washington DC, IMF).

Khan, M. S. (1990), 'The Macroeconomics Effects of Fund-supported Adjustment Programs', *IMF Staff Papers*, **37**, 2, 1–23.

Killick, T., G. Bird, J. Sharpley and M. Sutton (1984), *The Quest for Economic Stabilisation: The IMF and the Third World* (London, Gower and Overseas Development Institute).

Killick, T., M. Malik and M. Manuel (1992), 'What Can We Know About the Effects of IMF Programmes?', *The World Economy*, **15**, 5, 575–97.

Musso, A. and S. Phillips (2001), 'Comparing Projections and Outcomes of IMF-supported Programs', IMF Working Paper No. c1/45 (Washington DC, IMF).

Przeworski, A. and J. R. Vreeland (2002), 'The Effects of IMF Programs on Economic Growth', *Journal of Development Economics*, **62**, 2, 385–421.

Index